Praise for *Deep Spirit*

"Fact or fiction? *Deep Spirit* is an ingenious and imaginative story about the evolution of consciousness, alien intelligence, and the transformative power of dreams. It explores ultimate questions about life and death, and takes you on a roller-coaster ride through the mysteries of science and spirituality. Whether scientist or mystic, a lover of quiet wisdom or action and suspense, Christian de Quincey's visionary tale will take you into realms beyond imagination. Fast-paced and easy to read, this is a book to take to the beach, to read on the train or plane, to curl up with in bed. Pick it up, and you won't put it down. Rich with images and characters that leap off the page, I can easily see *Deep Spirit* transformed into Spiritual Cinema. But don't wait for the movie—read the book first."

—Stephen Simon
Academy Award winning Producer/Director: *Somewhere in Time, What Dreams May Come,* and *Indigo*
Co-founder The Spiritual Cinema Circle

"Christian de Quincey breaks new ground: *Deep Spirit* is the first book to cross sophisticated mainstream adventure story with frontier science and new age wisdom—*Jurassic Park* meets *The Celestine Prophecy.* Few other books, fiction or nonfiction, have so successfully popularized a thoughtful blending of modern science, shamanic wisdom, mind-body philosophy, and mystical experience. One thing is certain: The conventional scientific view of consciousness is pitifully limited. De Quincey uses the power of story to reveal new ideas about the origins, destiny, and reach of the mind."

—Larry Dossey, MD
author *The Extraordinary Healing Power of Ordinary Things*

"Deep Spirit is far more than a story. It is a call for a higher consciousness, and ends with one of the most lucid descriptions of unity consciousness I have read for a long time. Christian de Quincey writes with an easy style; and his insights are both grounded in science and reflect the perennial philosophy of mystics from time immemorial."

—Peter Russell
author *From Science to God,* and *The Global Brain*

Deep Spirit
Cracking the Noetic Code

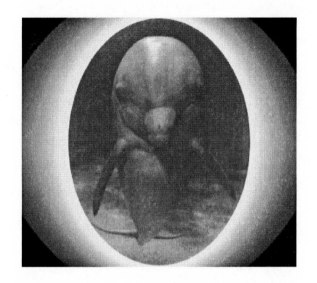

Cosmos. Consciousness. Contact.

Christian de Quincey

The Wisdom Academy Press

The Wisdom Academy Press

Half Moon Bay
California
www.thewisdomacademy.org

Library of Congress Cataloging-in-Publication Data
de Quincey, Christian.
   Deep Spirit: Cracking the Noetic Code / Christian de Quincey

Summary: "A narrative exploration of the evolution of consciousness, the future of humanity, and different ways of knowing."—Provided by publisher.

ISBN: 978-0-6152-1557-0
1. Consciousness. 2. Evolution. 3. Interspecies communication. 4. Alien intelligence. 5. SETI. 6. Science & spirit. I. Title.
First Edition

Cover image: "Cosmic Dewdrop," courtesy of Cory Ench, www.enchgallery.com.

For Reba and Oblio

your love and inspiration fill the spaces between my words

Author's Note

"If we really listen, we can hear a message from the birth of time."

This insight came to me one evening long ago, and in a flurry of creativity I began writing. Many years later, it became this story.

I saw the entire history of the universe as one long adventure between spirit and matter—a dance between unity and diversity. The secret to understanding this relationship lies all around us—written in the stars, in the oceans, in the flesh of the Earth itself.

Clearly, we live in a magnificent world, despite this era of deep divisions. Perhaps it has always been that way—although dilemmas show up differently at different times.

Today, the deepest split is between science and spirit. While most people believe that unseen forces influence our lives, mainstream science tells us otherwise. Fundamentally, it's a clash of beliefs. But it doesn't have to be that way.

I have spent a long career working to build bridges, and I've realized that the gulf between these two different views of the world is based on a profound misunderstanding. We all live in the one universe, and we can discover a deeper unity behind all differences—not just between science and spirituality, but also between thinking and feeling, dreams and reality, humanity and nature, between the feminine and masculine. But we need to look and listen with our hearts as well as our heads. We need both spiritual wisdom and scientific knowledge to decode the ancient echo from the birth of time.

I wanted to write a book that documents this adventure; something that works for both New Age visionaries and serious scientists—in fact, for anyone who likes a good story about the mystery and the meaning of life.

This is it.

Early in the twenty-first century the world was already on course for a major transformation—a revolutionary shift in consciousness. The visions and dreams of millions were about to become reality. The key: a worldwide quest for the "noetic code," a new way of knowing that builds on the ancient wisdom traditions of shamans, the perennial philosophy of mystics, and the profound insights of modern science. But the quest is threatened by a powerful force determined to keep the Great Dream down.

Prologue

If you are open, just one fleeting moment can change your life. Sometimes, it's an unexpected meeting. Sometimes it comes in a dream. And when it happens, you just *know*.

A few years ago, I spent two weeks interviewing a remarkable man about his extraordinary life. Dara Martin, a NASA explorer who went far beyond his science, now lives in a cabin on the edge of the Pacific. I went there to record his story.

His first words stopped me cold: *"Sometimes evolution gets it wrong. We've got one last chance to get it right."* It seems impossible. But a scientist with impeccable credentials was telling me that the human species might be an evolutionary error. What if he is right? What, if anything, can we do about it?

Then he startled me with a very personal question:

"What would happen if you not only changed your mind about who you are, your place in the universe, the meaning of life . . . about time, death, and immortality? What if, in changing your mind, you actually *lost your mind?* Would you think you were insane or would you know you were enlightened?"

He handed me a `sheaf of papers. "Here," he said, "it happened to me. This is a story about our future—our next evolutionary leap."

1

Lights in the Sky

No-one saw it coming. For a few brief moments, the early evening sky lit up bright as midday. On the bluffs overlooking San Francisco Bay, the only sound came from a gaggle of children laughing and playing in the tall grass on the Marin Headlands. Far below, the deep Pacific sparkled in the late summer light.

Suddenly, the children fell silent—a dark shadow loomed across the headland, and then, in an instant, everything blazed white. No longer running, they looked up, astonished. Out of nowhere, a brilliant ball of fire streaked through the sky then abruptly dipped and vanished into the ocean. The waves rose up to engulf it, and the air cracked with a thunder that shook the heavens. A shower of lights ripped through the upper atmosphere, and disappeared over the horizon. It was the greatest fireworks display they had ever seen—except this was not the fourth of July.

Some fifty miles south, in a dim auditorium at Stanford University, Professor Dara Martin lectured to an audience of colleagues and attentive students. A beam of light slanted down from the back of the room to a screen behind him, projecting Hubble images from deep space.

"Compliments of NASA, I bring the vast cosmos to your very own eyes." Sporting a couple of day's stubble, the professor scratched his chin absent-mindedly with his hand-held remote, and then clicked to a dramatic animation, complete with sound effects, depicting the birth of the universe.

"Fourteen billion years ago, it all started with a Big Bang. Today, all we hear is a faint echo."

He clicked to a new image.

"For centuries, scientists have been listening to the skies and have heard nothing but the constant rhythms of the stars spinning through space. Yes, the distant galaxies talk to us, but they speak only of chaotic fires, explosive hells of dead matter. Random noise, meaningless cosmic chatter."

Next image.

"Now I'm here to tell you that the famous echo from the birth of time may not be just random snow on your TV. I've discovered an anomaly. The Big Bang echo seems to contain some kind of *pattern*."

He enunciated this last sentence slowly, emphasizing the final word and, peering out through the dim light, eyed his audience carefully, watching for reactions. A murmur of disbelief rippled through the auditorium, as the air thickened with anticipation. He continued . . .

"We live in an unimaginably vast universe, with countless billions of galaxies, stars, and planets. There must be—there *is*—intelligent life out there. And perhaps it is already communicating with us."

A smart-ass student blurted out:

"Are you telling us you've found a hidden message in the Big Bang—put there by some lonely E.T.?"

The murmuring turned to snickering. The professor walked slowly and deliberately over to the wiseass, sat on the armrest of his chair, and whispered, loud enough for his neighbors to hear . . .

"Lonely? And when was the last time you had a good big bang, eh?"

The student's face turned an open-a-hole-and-bury-me-ten-feet-deep crimson, as the class roared with laughter. The professor patted him on the shoulder and gave him a friendly wink.

"A good scientist always keeps an open mind."

* * *

NASA scientist Dara Martin, a no-nonsense astrobiololgist, was married to his job—searching the heavens for signs of extraterrestrial life. A single-minded workaholic, his career distracted him from the pain of a recent divorce. At home later that evening, following a hectic few days lecturing and puzzling over some highly unusual data, he relaxed in front of the TV. He flipped through the channels, almost in a daze. "Typical Saturday fluff," he muttered to himself, and began shuffling through an assortment of photos and technical papers littering the floor. Then, a news flash caught his attention: *"Children see mysterious lights in the sky."*

He turned up the volume and leaned forward as a reporter shoved his microphone in front of a hippy-looking Earth Mother.

"Yeah, I saw it too . . . a divine spectacle. Nothing's an accident, y'know. Everything is part of a greater plan. You just need to know how to look—not with your eyes . . ."

The reporter pulled the microphone away, but the Earth Mother snatched it back, and intoned like an oracle, waving her index finger at the TV camera.

"We are not alone. They're everywhere. Scientists have overlooked the most important clue, right under their noses. Our culture is hypnotized by logic. We no longer pay attention to the wisdom of dreams. But our children are not so blind. Those kids saw something. Perhaps below the waves ancient messages lie waiting for us . . ."

* * *

Dara jumped into his SUV and headed north on 280, hell-bent for the Golden Gate Bridge, and across to the Marin Headlands. He struggled to fix his earpiece, as he talked excitedly on his cell phone to his NASA colleague and boss Graham Bechtel.

"Graham, you know for months I've been monitoring a strange point of light—possibly the most remote object ever discovered."

He swerved to avoid a rubber traffic cone bouncing over from another lane, clipped by an oncoming tourist bus.

"Yet the light from the quasar is far too bright for such a distant object. Really puzzling. It seems to be extremely far away, and yet very close at the same time."

He exited off the bridge.

"I've also detected bursts of radio waves arriving in unusual patterns. Quite peculiar. I'm going back to the lab later to check the data one more time."

He paused, as he listened to Bechtel on the other end.

"I'm now in Marin, on my way to the headlands to check out whatever it was those kids saw. Did you catch it on the news . . .?"

He paused again, then:

"Hey, I know it sounds weird . . . but I wonder if there's some connection between the strange lights they saw and the anomalous data I've been getting. What if those radio waves are caused by undetected meteors, or whatever those unidentified objects are?" Another pause. "What if they are signals?"

He slipped his phone into the dashboard holster and flipped on the speaker as the car spiraled up the coast road to the headlands.

"Dara, old chap, I'm beginning to get a little concerned. You seem to be noticing weird coincidences everywhere lately." Bechtel's British accent crackled through the static, his condescending tone irritated Martin. Not wishing to make an issue with his boss, he let the remark slide.

"Got to go, Graham. I've arrived. Call you later."

He pulled into a parking lot in an abandoned military lookout. A small crowd had gathered on the cliffs near where the children had witnessed the mysterious flying object. He approached the reporters and onlookers circled around the Earth Mother, who was still intoning, as she clutched two kids close to her. Bright camera lights beamed onto the trio, as a couple of helicopters hovered a few hundred yards out over the water. Spotlights from the choppers sliced through the dusk speckling the surface in ovals of white light. He stood aside and listened.

"Greater forces are at work in the cosmos than the powers of reason and the senses can detect," the Earth Mother addressed the crowd. "Streaming through us at every moment, they carry messages for the soul. If we had the ears to listen, the eyes to see, and the wisdom to understand, we might know . . ."

Dara muttered to himself, "Crazy New-Agers . . ." then walked to the cliff edge and stared out at the ocean. The air was still and hushed as the setting sun cast a carpet of red and gold on the quieted waves.

Bechtel's parting comment still irritated him. What if his boss was right, though? What about all those strange "coincidences" peppering his life recently? First, the mysterious quasar, so remote it should hardly be detectable yet was unaccountably bright; followed by even stranger radio signals from *somewhere* in space; then there was that curious email, and disturbing dream . . .

His cell phone rang. Bechtel.

"Huh? . . . They sure don't waste any time, do they? . . . Yes, of course, I'll get my report to the NASA brass before the eclipse. That's three weeks away. But why the rush? I'd like more time to see if there's any connection between the mystery balls of fire and the anomalous radio data. . . . Yes, Graham, I know it's a long shot. Just call it scientific instinct or something. Humor me . . . I'll get a draft to you next week."

Before heading back to Palo Alto, he introduced himself to the Earth Mother and left his NASA card.

"Please call me as soon as you can. Now is not a good time to talk. I need to get back to check on something. It may be related to what the kids saw. I'd like to talk to them before the details begin to fade. I think it could be important."

2
Intelligence Seeks Expression

Frontier research is a strange-attractor. Over the years, Dara Martin had grown used to messages from cranks and weirdoes, and he'd learned it was best not to get involved. Like the cryptic email he got yesterday, they usually came from nuts who'd been abducted by UFOs, had met the aliens in person and had the scars to prove it. Or from New Age channelers, with some mysterious psychic hotline to the stars, who'd been instructed by angels or aliens to share a science-shattering message that would save mankind.

In the early days, he had been foolhardy enough to humor some of these "leads," only to be invariably sorry afterwards. He quickly learned they were a distraction from his real work as a scientist scanning the heavens for signs of life.

His early dreams and musings had led Dara to a rare career: astrobiology. His job blended biology, the study of life, with astronomy, the study of planets and stars. As a young postgraduate student at Stanford University, he showed such exceptional brilliance and mastery of his field, they dubbed him the "new Einstein."

On the practical side, he developed an original and powerful technique for analyzing light and radio emissions from distant stars, opening up new horizons for exploration of deep space. His theoretical work extended the so-called anthropic principle—not only do we live in a universe that obviously supports the evolution of human beings; it is also a universe that produces very different forms of life. He called it the "*xenotropic* principle," and he convinced many colleagues that right back at the beginning, when our universe came swirling out of a cosmic mystery, the seeds of "alien" non-carbon life must have been already present—even at the Big Bang. He had worked out how a form of life based on photons could have evolved very early on in the universe, even before the first stars. His controversial insights revolutionized the field of xenobiology—the search for "alien life."

But then he shocked his colleagues with an even more outrageous idea. He published a paper, "L.I.F.E.—Light-Intelligence Finds Expression," updating the famous Drake Equation that spells out the chances of contacting life beyond Earth. He had speculated that highly advanced extraterrestrial civilizations might communicate using some kind of ESP, not just "nuts and bolts" technology. If true, it would dramatically increase the chances of contact. But, he quickly discovered, talk of extrasensory perception in the halls of science is academic suicide. Overnight, the rising star came crashing down to Earth.

The effect was sobering. Afraid of being totally dismissed as a starry-eyed novice, the young scientist retracted his "inspired" speculations. Silenced, he retreated back to the technology of telescopes and spectrum analyzers, and spent his days combing the skies for evidence of stars like our own capable of supporting the evolution of life, as we know it. With each passing year, the freedom of dreams and wild imagination that fired his youthful enthusiasm gave way more and more to the slow, studious gathering of scientific data.

By the time he joined a team of scientists and philosophers working on the search for extraterrestrial intelligence, an international project known as SETI, Dara had put aside all his youthful dreams. In their place, he had developed a passion for the clarity and precision of mature science.

He liked to call it "true brainwashing"—cleaning out the debris of superstition, leaving the mind clear to deal with what is really real. He dutifully sacrificed imagination and myth to the gods of rationalism. If you couldn't measure it, or organize it into neat logical categories, why waste your time? The way to search for intelligent life in the universe was through sophisticated technology, computers, radio telescopes, and satellites, and by rigorously analyzing the data sent back from space using the best-tested and most coherent scientific theories—not by pushing speculation beyond the frontiers of science.

And certainly not by responding to kooky email messages. He was sure he had grown beyond such temptations. But no. Once again he had fallen victim to the overtures of an anonymous UFO crank by answering yesterday's cryptic email. It bothered him. As he drove back down 280 toward Stanford, he wondered why he so often went against his better judgment?

It was like an addiction. Behind his deep faith in hard technology, bolstered by a mind trained to attack every problem with laser-sharp logic, lurked a gambler's instinct—he never completely ruled out the apparently outrageous. Some unexpected source of information just might provide the missing link, surprise him with a long-sought-for clue and point him in the right direction. Searching for life beyond our planet is a cosmic version of looking for a needle in a haystack. Searching for intelligent life is more like looking for the needle's shadow. Given the extreme odds against, his gambler's instinct had kept hope alive in the early days.

Even that instinct had been blunted a long time ago. He'd been burned too often by the weirdoes, and embarrassed too often by his colleagues and professors. But from time to time old habits resurface, and once again curiosity had gotten the better of him. Yesterday's mysterious email had simply said:

Intelligence seeks expression. This is a matter of grave importance. Click here if you are interested.

He had clicked on the highlighted blue "X" at the bottom of the message expecting to be connected to a page on the World Wide Web. Instead, a reply bounced back: "Response received. Thank you. Will be in touch." That was it.

The phrase "intelligence seeks expression" echoed in his head as he passed the rolling hills covering the two-mile-long high-energy accelerator at SLAC. Back at Stanford, he went straight to his computer to check if the mystery cyberkook had followed up. The usual list of messages from colleagues, plus inevitable junk ads, scrolled up on his screen, but nothing from The Kook.

Dara pushed the keyboard away, sat back, and closed his eyes. His temples throbbed, and his head felt heavy as though filled with wads of steel wool. Why, after so many false leads, had he responded to yet one more crank? Why should it be any different this time? The question was rhetorical. It didn't need an answer. Didn't even need to be asked. For as long as he could remember, the remotest possibility that *anything* might confirm the existence of life beyond Earth hooked him like a magician's spell. He clicked back to the original message.

Intelligence seeks expression. The words danced together like interlocking snakes, making nonsense connections, clouding his fuzzy, half-awake, consciousness. The phrase sounded urgent. He felt he was supposed to *do* something. But what?

Dara leaned back in his chair and absent-mindedly glanced around the room: a cluttered office, stacked with books and magazines, precariously piled and tilting, and an assortment of boxes bulging with electronic odds and ends, like the entrails of some disemboweled robot. Around the walls he had pinned a collection of Hubble space photos showcasing the universe in all its surreal magnificence—spiral galaxies and nebulae mimicking cosmic seahorses, brilliant bursts of supernovae, and multicolored clouds of interstellar gas giving birth to new stars. In the center of them all, his favorite: a large oval blue and purple photograph of the universe itself—an image of the background radiation left over from the Big Bang.

* * *

As a young boy, Dara's imagination roamed the galaxy picturing the strange forms of life that might live on distant planets. Almost anything was possible. But then in college he learned how all life on Earth is built up from complicated fragile rings of carbon-based molecules, like DNA and protein, and how that ruled out life forms in regions either too hot or too cold, or inhospitable in some other way. If the conditions on a planet were not just right, it would be impossible for life to ever get a foothold. *Unless some other type of sentience could evolve.*

Dara knew the chances of our galaxy containing millions of planets with some kind of bio-system were very good. It would be just a matter of time before the discovery of alien life would be confirmed—even if only some simple creature like primitive bacteria or the cosmic equivalent of yeast. Granted, it would be a long jump from single-cells, neither yet plant nor animal, to life that sparkled with intelligence. But that, too, Dara believed, would be just a matter of time. "They" had to be out there. We could not be alone. Those countless billions of galaxies, each teaming with its own countless billions of stars, which between them would likely have many millions of planets of just the right type—that all of this could nevertheless be deathly silent and barren was unthinkable.

On the other hand, given the vast, immensely vast, spaces separating the stars and the galaxies, it was equally unlikely that any of those other life forms, no matter how intelligent or technologically advanced, could—or would want to—travel the almost unimaginable interstellar distances between their homes and our tiny planet. Visits from ETs were the stuff of movies and overactive imaginations of kids, or the disturbed psyches of the mentally unstable. It just didn't make sense that they would come here. But that they were out there somewhere was a near certainty. The trick was to detect their cosmic signatures in the form of radio waves or some other technological sign, even if it was light-years away.

Intelligence seeks expression. It wouldn't go away. Each time the phrase got louder, pounding inside his head. Eyes half closed, he pushed against the desk and spun around in his chair. The room rushed about him in a blur. It was all he could do to liberate some of the pent-up energy in his tense muscles. He couldn't understand it, couldn't put it into words, but somehow the taut sinews in his arms, shoulders, and legs were responding to the cryptic message. His whole body tingled with suppressed meaning. As if the universe was trying to speak to him through messages in his own living flesh.

Outside, the rumble of distant thunder heralded thick dark clouds descending over the Bay Area. It didn't help his mood. Why this inexplicable sense of foreboding? Instinctively, he clicked one more time on the email. Something about that message left him feeling uneasy.

As he stared at the screen he knew it was already too late. He had broken his own golden rule, and there would be consequences. He shut down his computer, rearranged the papers on his desk in orderly piles, dropped them in his briefcase, and headed home. All night long, the message taunted him: "*Intelligence seeks expression.*" Expression for what? Through what?

He couldn't shake the feeling that the puzzling email was connected to the dream he'd had the night before. Like an after image, it still burned in his soul—vivid, disturbing. His dreams always came in fragments, but this was different. It was too structured, too *coherent* in a surreal kind of way, and hung together as if it carried a message—something important from his childhood, something calling out to him now as his work, his life, the universe itself, seemed about to explode.

3

Dream in a Blue Universe
(First Interlude)

Once upon a spacetime, Grumbalot found himself on the shore of a little rocky island in an unknown part of the world. In fact, it was so unknown, nobody was even sure if it was part of this world or some other—least of all, Grumbalot. He looked around to see what he could see, and as far as he could see, he was in the middle of a great underground lake in a vast cavern lit up by a million luminous stalactites, like stars on the ends of magnificent cosmic sparklers.

He pinched himself to see if he was still real. Everything was cast in a strange bluish light, even his skin had a blue tint, and that made him feel cold. A shiver ran up his spine as he realized he was afraid to be alone.

"Am I really a Grummel?" he wondered. "Grummels aren't blue all over like this. Maybe I'm not, maybe I never was." He doubted every thought that raced through his mind.

It is a scary feeling not to be sure of anything, especially of who you are. He had memories about all sorts of things he had done as a child in his homeland of Grummeldom, but try as he might he couldn't convince himself that his memories were any more real than anything else in his imagination. Maybe everything had been all a dream and he had just woken up. Or was he dreaming now and would wake up in the morning to find himself wrapped cozily in his comforter back home?

Confused, frightened, and tired, he wanted to find a way out, so he began wandering. It was a very strange place. Everything that grew on the island was blue, with occasional splotches of a kind of purple.

The leaves of the plants were huge, as big as tables, and they hung so low to the ground that as Grumbalot walked he found himself bouncing on a carpet of living color. From time to time he thought he heard a noise coming from underneath the leaves, a kind of high-pitched squeech, as if he had stepped on some tiny animal. More than once he stopped to investigate but could see nothing, just the blue leaves and the blue rocks.

As he walked on he came to a grove of stalagmites, rising up from the ground like spears of crystal. One stalagmite was particularly impressive. It must have been at least a hundred feet high, so high in fact that Grumbalot could barely make out its pointed top, way, way up above, almost touching the downward tip of a stalactite protruding from the ceiling of the great cavern.

While the stalactites gave off a luminescent blue glow, the stalagmites radiated a dim rust-colored light. The combined effect of the two colors was magical. Grumbalot stood for quite some time gazing at the scene, mesmerized by its otherworldly beauty. His attention focused on the gap between the huge towering stalagmite and huge stalactite reaching down like a giant finger of the gods.

For a split second, he thought he saw sparks of lightning flashing back and forth between the two points. As he stared at the gap, he forgot all about being lost. He noticed an unfamiliar sensation building up inside, as if he was being charged with some mysterious force. It wasn't like anything he had ever experienced before. At first, he thought he was feeling himself beginning to glow and then he realized that what was happening was much more like he was growing another layer of skin. He held his hands out in front of him and looked as closely as he could in the confused light. No, his skin seemed to be just as it ever was, except of course it was blue all over.

Then he did notice something. His skin wasn't changing or growing; but the blue light on his body seemed to form a shape all around him, like a shell. A hazy incandescent film hovered about two inches above his skin like a radiant sheath. When he looked down at himself he saw he was inside a bubble of light, a bubble that had the same contours as his body.

A moment later, the luminous bubble began to separate and drift away. It rose a few feet in the air to his right where it hovered for a while. The thin translucent film shimmered with multi-colored swirls, circular patterns pulsing in and out of each other in a rhythmic dance. As Grumbalot looked more closely he could see that the bubble shape had taken on a life of its own. It moved slowly away through the stalagmite grove, beckoning him. He hesitated, then, hypnotized by its beauty, he began to follow. He could make out a face, and was startled to see that its features looked very much like his own, except much more peaceful and graceful. Grumbalot was flabbergasted when he realized that the face on the luminous bubble was actually his. He was watching himself from a distance.

But there was something different about this other self. He couldn't grasp it at first, and then he knew what it was: His other self was him all right, but it was him as a girl.

"Come with me for a little way, Grumbalot, there's no need to be afraid," the bubble-girl spoke in a soft friendly voice. "I know you know who I am, for we have been I-together for a very long time."

4

Echoes from Space

Dara's dream haunted him night after night, each time unveiling another layer of the story. He woke groggy and disoriented, grateful this was Sunday, the one morning he could lie on in bed with a clear conscience. When the mist between dreaming and waking began to clear, he sat up, stretched his stocky frame, trying to release the dream—but it clung on insistently, lodged in his brainstem, nagging at him. Nothing specific was getting through; just a lingering awareness of something incomplete. None of it made sense. He poured himself a mug of strong, black coffee from the automatic maker beside the bed, and stumbled sleepily across the hallway to the den.

The computer screen glowed in the dim light. He left the curtains closed—even through the clouds, the late-morning sun would have been too much—and he slumped into the black leather chair at his desk.

Mechanically, he opened his email, and was both relieved and unnerved to see The Kook had contacted him again. This time, the message said more:

> If you are seriously interested in discovering other forms
> of intelligent life, leave your laboratory and get out into

the field. You're either on the bus, or off the bus. Otherwise just ignore this.

He couldn't ignore it. The moment he had clicked on the "X" in the original message he had allowed it to take root in him. And then a fleeting thought crossed his mind: Some other form of intelligence was seeking expression through *him*. He threw his arms around his middle, hugging his body in an involuntary protective gesture.

"Get a hold of yourself, man," he scolded. "You're a scientist. A damn good one."

Scientists don't usually put much credence in premonitions, he reminded himself. They are merely the mind's way of making sense from subtle sensory cues, but not enough to penetrate awareness. This was different. Something was beginning to filter through: a vague feeling, as much in his body as in his mind, that he'd better pay attention to unusual connections.

His dream. The mysterious email. The anomalies from space. Somehow, they all seemed to carry hidden meanings, like pieces of a puzzle. It was up to him to figure it out. But he was no psychoanalyst. Yes, dreams often colored his mood for the rest of the day—sometimes leaving him uneasy, sometimes contented, sometimes confused, sometimes horny—but they gave him nothing to grasp, nothing he could understand, nothing he could put to use in his waking hours. At best, they were the mind's way of sorting out the hodge-podge of information picked up by the brain throughout the day. Kind of like the way a computer can sort, organize, and backup megabytes of data—except dreams don't have logical connections.

As for the email: Why get sucked into some weirdo's fantasy? Dara knew he should be using his time and energy to focus on the anomaly in the three-degree background radiation.

He glanced at the digital clock on the wall above the computer just as it registered eleven-eleven. An hour at the gym on his way to the lab would help shake him loose from the strange events of the past couple of days. Besides, he could do with a good aerobic workout. Weeks without exercise, putting in far too much time at the office, had left the dead weight of his body hanging from his spine like a wet sack.

He scrambled through the closet for his tote bag, slung it over his shoulder, and headed out. The air was thick with the scent of eucalyptus and damp earth from the early morning rain. Overhead, dark gray clouds still shielded the sky from view. He felt cocooned in a silent, lonely world as he walked to his car. When he pulled the keys from his jacket, his wallet fell open to the ground into a small puddle. He picked it up and wiped it. Stuck behind the credit cards, its curled edge splattered with mud, an old photograph protruded. He pulled it out to clean it, and stood for a moment feeling a surge of old memories. The picture of Michelle, his ex-wife, reminded him of happier times. They were both younger, and smiling. Even now, he was attracted by her dimpled cheeks and her mischievous eyes glinting out from underneath her golden bangs. He looked fitter, in his prime.

Ever since high school, when he had been a champion athlete, Dara worked on keeping in top shape. Having turned forty, he had promised himself to stay as fit as a marathon runner. He always had strong legs, and regular training at the gym kept his upper body slim and firm. Until recently, he felt, and looked, more like a thirty-year-old. A few wisps of graying hair at his temples gave his angular face a distinguished look, especially contrasted with his California tan. Most of his life he had been injury free, but lately he noticed a stiffening in his knees and neck and a nagging pain deep inside the muscles of his right shoulder. When he looked in the mirror, he saw his head tilted to one side. The image amused him because he looked as if his right ear was cocked skyward, listening for a message from the heavens.

* * *

The lab was empty and, except for the constant background hum of computers, the place was silent. Dara spent a couple of hours going over his papers, checking equations, looking up tables in hefty tomes on astrophysics, and manipulating color graphics on his computer. This is where he felt most at home. Working with the reassuring certainties of mathematics.

Except that sometimes the certainties didn't quite work out.

A quasar is a "quasi-stellar object," so remote that it takes light many millions of years to travel across intergalactic space before reaching Earth. In fact, quasars are so distant none of their electromagnetic radiation reaches us in the form of visible light. We detect their presence only indirectly through periodic emissions of radio waves. By themselves, such waves are not particularly unusual—all stars naturally emit radio as a by-product of their internal nuclear reactions. Quasars are unusual because the intensity of their waves is typically much stronger than would be expected from a normal star.

Part of the job of scientists on the SETI project is to filter out naturally occurring radio waves and other background radiation to see if what remains has any significant pattern. If a pattern is found, bingo! We've got a dramatic clue that some intelligent being is sending meaningful signals. Whether or not the messages are intended for us is beside the point. Just to know they're out there communicating would be enough. From time to time, computer analyses reveal promising patterns, and the SETI folk get excited—maybe, finally, we've made contact. But these have always turned out to be false cues due to human error or to leakage from the detection equipment itself.

But what happened last week was different. While studying a remote quasar, Dara had noticed an unexpected pattern of blips in the cosmic background radiation. At first he assumed it was due to a technical malfunction, but when he double-checked the data the anomaly was still there. Something didn't add up.

And now, again, even with an additional week of data, his calculations confirmed the unexpected blips. He checked and crosschecked the printout, but the anomaly persisted. The signal wasn't coming from the quasar. It was even farther away. Much deeper back in time.

He pushed aside the clutter on his desk, and tapped vigorously on the keyboard, reworking the equations one more time. The computer bust into action, displaying an animated 3-D graphic of incoming signals. Columns of reds and purples shading into blues marched across his screen, as rapid Fourier transforms sifted their way through masses of data. The Doppler rate, the telltale marker of the signals' speed and distance, was both unbelievable and unmistakable. The famous "three-degree background radiation," the universal signature left over from the Big Bang, registered an impossible shift.

Dara reflexively inched closer to the monitor, head jutting forward like a bird of prey that has just sighted its quarry. His eyes bulged in astonishment as he rechecked the data. Detection location: the Gemini Mauna Kea observatory in Hawaii. The same result came in from the Arecibo Radio Observatory on Puerto Rico's north coast. . . . And from the giant radio telescope at Pune, India. . . . And from the Parkes observatory in Australia. . . . And, when he checked the data from the new gigantic Drake Square Kilometer Radio Telescope in South Africa, he could no longer doubt or believe his eyes. Simultaneously, he knew that what he was looking at was real, yet he also knew it couldn't be true. His mind flipped.

Trying to regain some degree of mental balance, he scrutinized the celestial coordinates: Instead of a specific spot in the heavens, the signals were coming in from multiple sources—from *everywhere.*

"The whole goddamn universe is talking to us," he shouted at the computer.

Tilting back in his chair, grinning like a madman and looking up at the ceiling, he corrected himself: "No, not just the universe . . . but the very moment of creation itself."

He danced around the room, alternately running to the window to look at the sky, and back to his computer to check out the data. He stopped, and stood motionless staring at the screen.

The patterns seemed to be organized in layers, as if there might be a code embedded in the background noise—as if the fourteen-billion-year-old echo from the Big Bang carried a message. But that was impossible, he reminded himself. He knew better than to get prematurely excited, he'd seen too many "codes" like this turn out to be nothing more than chance flukes. The universe was always sending out infuriating impostors—randomness impersonating intelligent order.

Nevertheless, nothing should ever be prematurely dismissed, either. Besides, the incoming signals were overwhelmingly consistent. Dara phoned Bechtel, but his boss was not at home. He sent the data via high-speed link, and left a breathless voice mail asking Bechtel to run tests Monday morning.

Driving home down University Avenue, past the tall palms standing like sentries on both sides of the long, straight road from the Stanford University campus, to the town of Palo Alto, Dara noticed the clouds had finally parted. Above the umbrellas of fronds, silhouetted against the evening sky, he saw the pinpoint lights of a handful of stars—the first he'd seen in as many days. By now, the last of the rains should have long since seeped into the earth. But it had been raining almost non-stop for weeks and through most of the summer. This had been the longest and wettest season on record. The sight of the stars lifted his heart a little, but dark-rimmed clouds, still heavy with the promise of more rain, threatened to close the gap and swallow the handle of the Big Dipper. He, too, felt something closing in on him. Something connected with the darkness and the sky. Something connected with the cryptic message on his computer, a message somehow calling forth unfinished business from childhood dreams.

He turned into his driveway, and as he crested the safety bump slowing the SUV to a stop, an image flashed through his mind: radio waves streaming into him from the remotest regions of space. The image came with a soundtrack: *Intelligence seeks expression.* It wouldn't let go, a background chorus to every rational thought. He voluntarily shivered in his seat, like a dog shaking off the rain, trying to rid himself of an unfamiliar and unwanted emotion. He felt it in his bones.

That night, he tossed in and out of sleep, burning with a fever that blurred the threshold between dreaming and being awake. And all night long, like a crazy, obsessive mantra, he kept repeating the words from the email: "Leave your laboratory and get out into the field . . . You're either on the bus, or off the bus . . . *on* the bus, or *off* the bus."

For an astrobiologist, "getting out into the field" could mean only one thing: Not just leaving the lab at NASA, but *leaving the planet.* He was a scientist, for chrissake, not an astronaut. Astronomers and cosmologists study the universe with telescopes and speculation; the methodology of an astrobiologist isn't all that different. Using data gathered from Earth-based and orbiting telescopes to inform and guide theory, a good astrobiologist like Dara could spend an entire, and fruitful, career without traveling much beyond the walls of his research lab. He didn't even have to visit the radio telescopes. All their data were downloaded into computers and shot at lightning speeds along fiber-optic cables right to the desktop. The rest of the work went on either at the keyboard-and-screen or in the privacy of the individual scientist's brain. "It's all a matter of the digital and the dialectic," Dara liked to say, "software meets wetware."

Getting out into the field was for anthropologists and sociologists, for geologists and archaeologists. Since there were no ETs making house calls, the astrobiologist's job was to work with astronomers to scan the stars, to explore the universe through the external eyes of technology and through the inner eyes of insight and imagination. The "field" was out there, way out there beyond reach in his lifetime.

Dara felt possessed by the message. All night long, he tried to rationalize the feeling by convincing himself he was coming down with a cold; after all, he had been working long hours and late nights for weeks. He was run down and needed rest. But this time the cool light of reason was no match for the growing heat in his gut—as if the email message contained a subliminal virus and was corrupting the software of his brain, stirring deep memories, activating ancient dreams.

Something in him was about to surface. Something that would change his life forever.

5

Dream in a Blue Universe
(Second Interlude)

Grumbalot was surprised, but not afraid. Surprised that his heart agreed with the girl: He did indeed know who she was and that they had been, as she said, "I-together" for a long, long time. But as soon as he tried to figure it all out, he was totally confused.

"I can see you clearly enough," he said, "and I feel I know you, but I cannot for the life of me think how it all fits together. It doesn't make any sense. If I am me, then who are you?"

"My name is Fanima. I am you, strange as it may seem. I am your other self, the girl in you that you have forgotten. We have come a long way together," she floated down and held her hand out to him. "Go ahead, it's OK, you can touch me."

He gingerly reached out with his forefinger and touched the apparition. He didn't quite know what to expect, but the idea crossed his mind that his finger would pierce the film of the bubble and—pop!—the girl would just disappear. Instead, he was surprised to find that her hand was warm and soft to his touch. He slid his fingers between the girl's and their hands seemed to merge together, yet remained somehow different and separate. A wave of emotion swept through him, pumping from his heart.

"Grumbalot, the journey you are on is a search for something special about yourself. To find it, you will have to grow and change but you will also be returning to what you always were." He listened intently as she spoke, his own thoughts stilled by the mystery, and the warmth in her voice comforted him.

"But before that transformation can take place you and I will have to be I-together again. The way we were many ages ago." He felt the wisdom of her words penetrate his heart, opening it up in a way he hadn't known before. Again, he tried to get it all to make sense in his head, and again he got more confused.

He felt something pulling him toward the girl, something coming deep from within his own emotions.

"This is very strange, Fanima, as if you and I are one and the same person, and yet clearly we are different in many ways. It doesn't make much sense to me. In fact, I can't make head or tail of it at all."

Grumbalot looked into her eyes and saw an opening to another world. He wanted to dive inside.

She stood silently for a while, holding his fingers in her hand, offering the invitation of her virgin blue eyes. Her gaze flowed over him and down through his veins like rivulets of melting glacier ice carrying ancient messages.

"This is not something you can make headway with if you try to figure it out up here," and she touched his temple with her other hand. He felt a bolt of energy shoot right through his skull.

"This is a matter for the heart." And she gently placed the open palm of her hand on his chest. Again, he felt the bolt of energy, except this time it did not shoot right through him. Instead, he felt it circulate inside, filling him with a warm mysterious glow.

"Every time you touch me, I feel a force surging through my body," Grumbalot said. "How do you do that?"

"I'm not doing anything to you. I-together is creating this. I feel the same energy inside me whenever we touch. It is not my power and it is not your power. It is not even our power. Let me tell you something you will need to know if you are to complete your journey . . ."

He interrupted: "You mean this isn't a dream, then? I really am on a journey?"

"Yes, it is true you are on a great adventure, and your destination is as far away as the stars beyond this universe and as close as the breath in your body. But to say that this is not a dream . . . well, that's not for me to decide. But let me continue. What I am about to show you will be extremely important one day. You may never understand all or any of this, and that doesn't matter much. But you will need to feel it when the time comes. And that time will come when you meet the Visitor."

6
Stories Matter

The phone rang loud enough to break through the black fog. One pill had been sufficient to knock him out, and neither his body nor his mind wanted to wake up. Half asleep, he fumbled for the alarm clock, but the tone kept ringing. His knuckles brushed against the phone, knocking it off its base onto the bed. He pressed the button.

"Hello. Who's this?"

"Hi Dara. It's Graham Bechtel. Sounds like I woke you. Sorry, old chap. But I got your email and the data. I've run the tests, and you're right: something doesn't fit. I don't know what to make of it. I'd like you to go to Mauna Kea to look into this further. They've picked up the strongest signals . . ."

"Graham? What time is it?"

"Eh? Oh, it's seven-thirty. Sorry. Thought you'd be up."

"Why do the English always say 'sorry,' and still go ahead and make a nuisance of themselves anyway?"

"I'm terribly sorry, Dara. You sound awful. Are you okay?"

"I've come down with something. Nothing much to worry about. What did you say, you found the anomaly, too, huh?" He stretched his legs beneath the covers, and pushed back against the pillows.

"Yes. I checked your calculations and they seem to be correct. This could be momentous, old boy. A shift in the Big Bang echo would turn science on its head. Someone—or something—must be creating interference. Think we're on to something?"

"It's too early to tell. But to be quite honest, Graham, now's not a good time for me to talk about it. I'll call you later."

"Sorry, Dara . . . I mean, okay, chum. I'll be out all day visiting some business associates in the city. Call me on my mobile if you like. And remember, we need to get the full report to the top brass before the eclipse." Dara had no time to ask questions; his boss quickly changed the topic.

"By the way, did you hear from Maya Santos?"

"Who? No. Should I?" He propped his still unconscious body up on his right elbow, as though the added elevation would help him remember. The soft mattress sagged beneath the bone.

"She's working on the dolphin thing in Hawaii, remember? Called me last night, very excited. Thinks she's finally made a breakthrough. While you're checking things out at the observatory, why not pay her a visit? Thought you might be interested, since alien language is more up your alley. I told her to call you."

"Thanks, pal. That's just what I need: a trip to Water World." Dara was upright now, and brushed the matted hair back off his face.

"It's the University of Hawaii, old boy, not some godforsaken backwater. Anyway, sounds like you could do with a break. She's on Oahu, just a short hop from the Big

Island. By the way, she said she liked your book *Mind in the Cosmos,* and has used some of your theories. I think you should go."

"It depends on what she's found."

"Check your email. Said she'd send you her transcripts. It's probably just another false positive, but I'd like you to investigate all the same. You know how much I value your analytical skills; you've got one of the best noses for sniffing out baloney. Just see if what she has to say stands up to good old logic and reason. If she's gone off the deep end, I'm sure you can persuade her to pull the plug. In any case, I'd like to see your report on her project, too."

Dara ignored the manipulative compliments, partly because Bechtel was right—he did enjoy wielding the scalpel of logic to cut through sloppy thinking. But he wondered why on Earth Bechtel kept pushing him for reports before the solar eclipse. True, his boss had a reputation as a compulsive A-type, with an almost obsessive addiction to schedules. No doubt Bechtel had his reasons.

Dara felt better and more awake after he showered. His headache was gone, but his stomach still felt tender. Instead of breakfast, he took a glass of water to the den, and powered up his computer.

Now he remembered: Maya Chucana Santos was a young Venezuelan anthropologist who had recently joined the SETI team, and was working on a doctorate in inter-species communication. She was trying to teach dolphins the rudiments of human language. Maybe he could learn something practical about alien communication, beyond the abstract analyses he was used to working with in the lab. Maybe this was a chance to get out into the field? That did intrigue him.

As the screen kicked into life, his phone rang. It was the Earth Mother, calling to schedule a time later that evening to talk with the Marin children. He didn't expect to get much useful information beyond a vague description of the fireball. Nevertheless, he wanted to meet them, even if only to hear their straightforward version of events minus all the New Age claptrap. It might help him judge if there was any possible connection to the radio anomaly from space.

The computer beeped, alerting him that new email had arrived. Two messages caught his interest. The first was from Maya, a long and detailed summary of her progress, with the full report in an attached document. In case he didn't have the time to read it, she offered the highlights:

"My most promising pupil is a dolphin I used to call 'Don Juan'—a pun intended to acknowledge his amorous attentions when I swim with him in the aquarium, and also because I believe dolphins may well be wiser creatures than humans. I think he's a kind of shaman. We've had a breakthrough, and now we can engage in intelligent conversation. Believe it or not, we talk a lot about evolution, so lately, I've been calling him 'Darwin.' I've managed to translate some of his communications, and as far as I can tell he has something quite astonishing to report about the future of our species."

Dara smiled at the irony of a dolphin called Darwin expressing views about human evolution.

"At first, progress was slow. After nine months, I had managed to teach him only a handful of nouns, adjectives, and verbs. He communicated with me and my team in simple sentences. After a while, though, I discovered that when I'm alone with him his ability to understand English improves greatly. Even more surprising, I realized that I, too, can understand Dolphinese quite well. We have begun to communicate in a bilingual dialect. I call it 'Donglish': I speak to him in English, he responds in whistles, clicks, and squeaks. Recently, we seem to be able to communicate with no sound passing between us at all."

Dara was intrigued. He had, of course, heard about other experiments in inter-species communication. Not too far from his Palo Alto home, in the Santa Cruz mountains, a famous gorilla had learned to "talk" using American Sign Language. Working with his caretaker, Koko had mastered about a thousand symbols, matching the vocabulary of a bright young child. But Dara had always dismissed this kind of communication as mere mimicry, training an animal to manipulate a few colored symbols and words. Maya Santos and her dolphin seemed to be operating on a much more sophisticated level. Maybe, Dara began to think, traveling to Hawaii wouldn't be such a bad idea.

Maya's email went on to say she had recorded a couple of sessions, and would have the discs with her at a workshop she was giving at the Esalen Institute in Big Sur. Would he like to meet her there in a couple of days? They could listen to the recordings together, go through her report, and he could decide if it was worth taking the time to fly to Oahu to check out the dolphin in person.

That sounded reasonable. A two-and-a-half hour drive down the coast, perhaps with an overnight stay in Carmel, would make a nice break. And he'd have a chance to hear for himself what she meant by "intelligent" conversation with a dolphin. In the meantime, he could find out more from the full report she'd sent.

He was just about to open it when he remembered the second message that had landed in his inbox. It was from the "mystery writer." He opened it, expecting to see another cryptic one-liner, but instead it ran on for pages, under a bold heading:

'Stories Matter'

"The human mind burns to know and to find meaning. You are rarely content just simply to live and take life as it comes. Something inside you craves to watch yourselves living so you can understand—understand who you are and how you fit into the world around you.

"The one thing all your mythology, art, religion, philosophy, and science have in common is that they are all *stories*. Stories you tell yourselves to make some sense that you are here at all.

"You live in your stories and your stories live in you. You no longer know this, but your species is continually engaged in silent conversations with the world around you. As you take matter in as food, as you breathe it in, as you manipulate and mold it, you are in dialogue with nature, creating stories that shape your bodies and minds. Your stories matter because they determine how you interact with the world. But more than that: Matter tells its own tales. Matter makes stories. The world is not made of atoms; it is made of stories. Nature is in constant conversation with you, sharing its deepest secrets—if only you would listen.

"But for you, the stones have fallen silent. Literally out of touch and out of communication, modern civilization has left you aliens in your own landscape. You no longer feel or hear your once intimate connection with the land and its running, hopping, flying, swimming, burrowing, crawling, rooted creatures. You no longer hear the voice of the Earth, no longer respond to its calling. The loss is mutual and profound: Not only are you disconnected and alone, you have inflicted fragmentation and desolation on a great part of the world around you.

"Your only hope is to *feel* again the pulse of natural kinship. You need to respond to the deep intelligence of the planet and cosmos from which you are born. You need to pay attention to the stirrings of mind *in* matter, to the symphony of universal meaning—to the story of matter itself. Listen: *Stories matter and matter stories.*"

Dara repeated the strange phrase: "Stories matter, matter stories," and he wondered who was sending him these odd messages? Most likely a crank, he thought, a ufo geek, or some nerd who got hold of his email address. He felt claustrophobic, as if the world had gripped him in a vise. He got up and pulled back the curtains, letting the morning light flood into the room. A million dust specks floated in razor-sharp beams, reminding him of the countless stars and planets winding their ways through countless galactic clusters. If even only one stellar speck in a billion harbored life, the universe would still teem with sentience.

He turned back to the computer, and continued reading the email.

"For the earliest humans, stories came in the form of myths, and your few remaining indigenous cultures still pass on their knowledge and wisdom through the medium of myth and dreams. For most of your recorded history, the great stories were found in the teachings of your religions. People turned to their priests as authorities on what to believe. In the Western world, right up to the seventeenth century, the clergy held sway.

"Then came your scientific revolution. And today, the dominant story that shapes your lives comes from the halls of science. You now live in a world vastly different from the Age of Religion, when people accepted without question the existence of gods, spirits, angels, and souls. The Age of Science tells a very different story—a story that has no place for such discarnate entities, a story that doesn't even have a place for the storyteller.

"And because of this, many, many people, including some scientists themselves, feel that science must be leaving something out. That's what we're going to remedy."

That was the end of the message. This time it didn't sound so kooky. It was a sane and concise summary of the role of science in human affairs. Yet all that talk about stories puzzled Dara. And the final line, "That's what *we're* going to remedy," puzzled him most of all: It presumed he was already involved.

In his own book *Mind in the Cosmos,* Dara had written that the universe is probably populated with other species of intelligent beings, though most likely very different from us. Very likely, too, they would inhabit planets or galaxies light years away from Earth. However, now the mystery correspondent was suggesting that perhaps Dara and his SETI colleagues should look closer to home. The message hinted at something even more radical: that nature is intelligent—not just planet Earth, but the very "stuff of the world" itself, the matter and energy of the entire cosmos.

Dara felt lost and confused. What was happening to him? How could he, a Stanford University PhD, a NASA scientist, with degrees in physics, biology, and linguistics, be so mesmerized by these cryptic messages? Why was he entertaining such strange ideas?

Then he remembered his recurring dream about the blue universe, and how deeply it had affected him, feeling it was somehow connected with the mystery email and the idea that "intelligence seeks expression." He shivered. A cold electric jolt shot up his back. Is this what it feels like to be losing your mind? He closed his eyes and recalled more of the dream.

7

Dream in a Blue Universe
(Third Interlude)

"First, stand like this." Fanima took both his hands and pulled him forward slightly, then pushed him back. "Feel where your center is. Feel it below your navel." And she rocked him to and fro a few times.

"Plant your feet firmly on the ground, but be light and flexible, ready to move in any direction. Now, feel the energy flowing between us."

She stood directly in front of Grumbalot, eye to eye, nose to nose, still holding his hands and with the tips of her toes touching his.

"Close your eyes and tell me what you see." He diligently followed the girl's instructions.

He felt a pulse passing from her fingers into his hands, and then from her belly into his. A kaleidoscope of energy shot through him, the same swirling multi-colored patterns he had seen earlier on her body now rippled over his skin. Still with his eyes closed, he felt—no, he could see—her entire bubble-body pulsating with the force. It was expanding and contracting, expanding and contracting, touching his body from head to toe. He felt himself begin to reverberate in rhythm, faster and faster with each pulse.

Soon, he, she, they were vibrating so fast he lost all sense of where his body began and hers ended. He could feel them blending together as one. And now the force grew so strong inside him he thought he might explode. At that moment, he was sure the soles of his feet had opened up and the energy flowed down through him into the ground. He felt solid, immovable, connected to the center of the Earth.

And now he knew what Fanima wanted to show him. He wasn't just connected to the Earth, he was connected in some way with its whole history and with every creature that had ever walked, crawled, crept, or burrowed in it, that ever swam in its rivers and seas, or flew through its air. He was connected to the entire living memory of the planet. As he stood there, exchanging energy with the land, he could see everything that had ever happened since the beginning of time. He knew, then, what Fanima meant when she said they had been 'I-together' through many ages. Yes, in distant times and distant lands they had shared many lifetimes and he knew they would again.

She inched closer to him and spoke in a softer, intimate tone. "I want you to respect and honor me, to acknowledge me for who I am." It was a simple, matter-of-fact request.

"I want to be with you as your friend," she continued, "I am your companion. But . . ." and he shuddered at what she said next ". . . I don't want to be smothered by you. *I want to retain my own identity. And I want you to retain yours.* This is a matter of grave importance—far beyond what you can imagine now."

He burst into tears. They were tears of sadness for all the times he had shut Fanima out of his life, denying their "I-together." They were mostly tears of joy, though, knowing they, he/she, were always together and always would be. As "I-together," Grumbalot was whole, a complete being, a true Grummel. He opened his eyes to thank Fanima for the gift of joy and love she had given him. But she was gone.

8

Dancing with Demons

Alien consciousness was Dara's business. He had devoted his career to searching for intelligent extraterrestrial life. If the dolphin in Hawaii was communicating as dramatically as the doctoral student had implied, then Dara could do worse than check it out. Perhaps, after all, alien intelligence was closer to home than distant stars or galaxies.

"Bechtel was right, I could do with a break," Dara mused as he cruised down Highway 1, just south of Half Moon Bay en route to Big Sur. Besides intense hours working around the clock, he was still trying to pick himself up from the ashes of a traumatic divorce. The separation had left him emotionally vulnerable. For the first time in his adult life, he had been faced with a problem he couldn't solve with careful reasoning. Strong feelings had breached the solid structures of his intellectual defenses.

A year ago, when his marriage was crumbling, long-buried ghosts from his childhood had come back to haunt him, overwhelming his usually clear rational mind with a hurricane of emotions. When Michelle had told him she was leaving, because she was "tired of living alone in relationship," his ordered world of precise logic and mathematics began to unravel. Nothing in his science had prepared him for the emotional storm. The paradox slapped him in the face: Yes, his sharp mind had created the equations that helped him understand the universe. But there was no place in those equations for the mind that created them. Mathematics cannot capture or tame the fires of feeling.

Now, as he breezed along the coast road, warm wind ruffling his hair, and music lifting his spirits, he began to feel more grounded, more at peace. The open vistas gave him a renewed sense of perspective, and he sensed a connection between his childhood emotions and his recent dreams—as if what was haunting might also help him.

It was late afternoon, a hot October sun beamed in through the passenger window. The golden foothills of the Santa Cruz Mountains slipped by on his left; to his right and up ahead, he could see the final fingers of the vast continent reach out into the shining blue Pacific. Beyond, and still out of sight, lay the majestic sweeping hills of the Big Sur coast—a place of beauty and mystery. Once past Santa Cruz, he shifted weight, pushed back against the padded leather seat, flipped to cruise control, and settled in for the ride. Taut muscles in his shoulders still held the weight of his recent past. He turned the radio off, rolled down all the windows, and let the sound and smell of the ocean envelop the car.

His mind drifted in a disconnected sequence of images and thoughts: from ocean waves to dolphins, to quasars, to mysterious emails, to his childhood . . . to Michelle. He hadn't wanted to see a therapist; he didn't think they needed one. Why couldn't they just figure things out for themselves? Seeing a therapist was tantamount to admitting you had lost control of your life, that your own mental resources were insufficient. He couldn't, wouldn't, accept that. But Michelle had persuaded him that the woman they would see was trained, scientifically, to deal with the dynamics of human relations, and so he agreed to go.

He resisted at first, but eventually grew to like the therapist, and to trust her. He opened up, and after the marriage ended he continued seeing her on his own. She called his sessions "dancing with demons." He learned a lot about himself, about how so much of his energy was tied up in his emotions, despite his best rational efforts to suppress them. He was determined to tame his demons, but she told him that that would happen only if he first respected and accepted them. Now, with the distance of a year, he was beginning to get a better perspective, and to understand what the therapist meant.

Dara steered the Jeep around a line of plastic orange cones, moved into another lane, and drove past tanned workmen resurfacing the road near the Capitola exit. He thought about how, in therapy, it was possible to relive and confront his own past, to make peace with it rather than fight it.

As a young child he had been very ill. Hospitalized for nearly a year, his infantile mind had conjured up the story that he was being punished for something—why else would they separate him from his family? He came to believe that he had been abandoned, that he was unlovable, that there was something wrong with him. Later, during his divorce, those childhood beliefs had sprung back to life with a vengeance: He had not fulfilled whatever purpose the long evolution of our species had expected of him. He was a misfit. Evolution is a process of trial and error, and sometimes makes mistakes. He, it turned out, was one of its dead ends.

Nevertheless, the two-year-old kid had learned one important lesson: how to survive. In addition to the terror of being unwanted and unloved, he had constructed an ego strong enough to pull him through, strong enough later in life to bury the raw and incomplete emotions of a terrified and raging child beneath the rigid assurances of hard-nosed science. Strong enough to gain him two doctorates—in biology, and astrophysics. Strong enough to get him a senior role in NASA and the SETI team.

But in therapy, he learned to see that unless he danced with his demons and made peace with them, he might well be doomed to repeat the emotional hell-fire over and over throughout his life.

He feared he was running out of time. He felt it rushing past him, speeding up, contracting more and more with each passing year. As a child, and even as a young man, life seemed to stretch out before him endlessly, an unfolding panorama of infinite possibilities. Then, in quick succession, two events shattered that sense of boundlessness: the death of his father, followed by his divorce. The emotional impact snapped the elastic time of youth, and left him with a knot of torn and shriveled strands. Now he feared there wasn't enough time to fulfill his dreams.

The car shuddered as Dara shifted gears and accelerated to overtake a heavily loaded Mack truck, looming too close for comfort. Heart beating faster, he gripped the steering wheel to steady the Jeep in the crosswind. The adrenaline triggered a familiar anxiety: Would he end up spending his entire career searching in vain for extraterrestrial intelligence? In a universe so vast, the immense distances and time spans seemed to mock his feeble explorations. The odds were heavily stacked against first contact happening during his short eighty or ninety years.

"I feel like I'm living in a bubble universe," he had confided to the therapist. "A relatively tiny region only some eighty-light years across. Beyond that, the infinite stretches of the cosmos remain forever out of bounds, forever incommunicado. Almost the entire universe is out of reach. I can never be in contact with it. Never know what life or intelligence might be out there."

When she asked him what he meant, he explained: "Let's say the average human life is about eighty years. Well, if all information depends on the transmission of light signals through space, as Einstein proved, then, at the fastest-possible speeds the only contemporary signals that could reach our planet during my lifetime would come from, at most, eighty-light years away. All the rest, from fifteen to twenty billion light-years distant, would arrive only after I'm gone. All I can hope to pick up are ancient signals from worlds that may have ceased to exist millions, or even billions, of years ago. That's what I mean: cosmic isolation. No cosmic connection. No hope of making contact. No possibility of live intergalactic communication. All I will ever hear are dead messages—or worse, eternal silence. Yet I've dedicated my life to this search."

She had looked at him without saying anything, silently inviting him to feel his way into his own words. But he thought she was waiting for further explanation.

"Most of the universe is 'off limits'—we cannot know what is out there *now!* All we have are electromagnetic echoes of what used to be, a long, long time ago. We are confined, or condemned, to isolated event horizons, trapped in our 'bubble' universe."

He felt the isolation again now, sitting behind the wheel, shut in behind the windshield, a self-contained world speeding down Highway 1 past other people, trapped in their own bubbles of metal and glass, people whose stories he would never know. Fellow travelers forever out of reach. "Life is a series of glancing encounters," he had said to the therapist, and he repeated it now to the passing traffic. "We glimpse only surfaces, never really touch each other's deeper selves." He was thinking of Michelle. "Relationships are like billiard balls: We bump into each other, make connections, and before we know it ricochet out of reach."

This feeling of alienation had been growing in him ever since his divorce. Coupled with the death of his father, his sense of isolation had collapsed into sharp focus. He recalled telling the therapist how one night the rapid-fire ticking of the desk clock inherited from his grandfather pounded on his nerves. He stared at the second hand jerking its way around the face, each insistent tick-tock snipping at his future. Time was slipping away. Without anyone close in his life anymore, the "bubble universe" was closing in. He had lost his wife because of his obsession with work, and now he feared it might have been all in vain. What was the point of wrecking his marriage and losing his family if at the end of his life all he had to show were a bunch of computer data and charts reminding him over and over of the eternal silences of space?

He had grabbed the clock and flung it across the room. It hit the wall and shattered, spewing mechanical entrails on the floor. The image disturbed him: Yes, the clock had stopped ticking, but the end of time came only at the end of life—even clockwork life. The only way out of time was through the nothingness of death.

As he dodged the sand dunes creeping onto the road near Monterey, he caught the eye of a passing driver, and realized he was speaking out loud. He shook off a momentary embarrassment, and continued his reverie, as if telling his tale to passersby would make a difference.

He raced on in a kind of trance, overtaking cars and trucks, hardly noticing them. The speedometer pushed past ninety-five, and the quickening pace of his heart, revving in his chest, brought him back to his senses. He eased off the gas.

Having to deal with his feelings in a mature, responsible way was, he thought, perhaps the most valuable lesson of his life. Yet, ironically, for the past year since his divorce, he had thrown himself headlong into his work at NASA. But something had shifted, he now realized. As he drove through Carmel, the sun was dipping behind the horizon, casting an ochre tint on the hills. He was beginning to see the difference between obsession and passion. He no longer felt totally driven by his work; devoted, yes, but starting to open up to something more.

With the last outskirts of the Carmel Highlands behind him, and nothing but the curves of the open road ahead, he drove into the descending twilight. The looming hills of Big Sur beckoned. The pulse of city life and the pressure of the university had fallen away. He felt his shoulders relax and his chest expand as he filled his lungs with the evening air. He realized he was looking forward to meeting Maya, and learning more about her work with the dolphin Darwin.

9
Gateway to the Universe

I t took Dara three hours to drive down to Big Sur from his apartment in Palo Alto. Usually, it's a little more than a two-hour trip. But because of the aftermath of the 8.0 earthquake, Highway 1 was detoured at San Gregorio, and he had to switchback inland along 84, through the mountains to Route 9 down to Santa Cruz, where he picked up Highway 1 again, and detoured some more around stricken Watsonville. It was pitch dark when he arrived at Esalen, the world-famous institute for exploring human potential.

Somehow the added time it took to get there increased the sense that this place was further away from the ordinariness and hustle of civilization. He got out of the Jeep, stretched, and drank in the dark heavens. The sky, awash with the Milky Way, was a billion glittering points in every direction. He hadn't just driven to the mid-California coast; he had reached a gateway to the universe. Even as an astrophysicist, he had rarely seen such a clear night sky with so many stars. He was mesmerized by the immensity, by the depth, by the horizon-to-horizon canopy of lights, by the sheer volume of space, by the sense of eternity. He filled his lungs with the universe, and it was a pure and sweet taste, of country night air flavored with the smell of eucalyptus and the kelp-abundant waters of the Pacific Ocean.

Esalen is famous for its sulfur baths. Natural hot springs have blessed this spot since before the Esalen Indian tribe, and their ancestors, first inhabited it—thousands of years ago. The workers in the institute gardens still turn up artifacts from these ancient people, confirmed by archeology and carbon dating to be the products of human hands as long ago as a couple of millennia before the birth of Christ.

Even in those far off days, a time that invokes fantasies of a planet-wide Eden, this must have been an especially attractive spot. Particularly if the climate was in any way similar to what it is today: virtually year-round balmy Mediterranean. There are nights, and some days, especially when the mists roll in off the ocean, when the temperature drops to a chill. How inviting those hot springs must have been to the Indians on those rare nights when the frost bit into the land. Apparently, the rest of the coastline in this region does not show signs of similar ancient habitation. The hot springs, then as now, pulled people like a magnet to this stretch of coast.

But it is not just the ancient flowing springs, steaming from subterranean fires that mark this place as special. It is the place itself, the blend of land and sea and sky, of rolling hills and woods, the incomparable layered silhouettes of cliffs punctuating the ocean as if by the hand of a master artist. The air is thick with spirit, and the beauty stuns visitors to a stillness that allows the heart to speak and the soul to hear the whispers of eternity.

Today, Esalen is hidden from the quiet, winding Highway 1, on a narrow thirty-acre seaward strip, landscaped to enhance the natural beauty. The houses and cabins seem to grow out of the land, so that the presence of humans, for once, is as natural as the trees, the creek, the hillsides, the cliffs, and the beaches below. A small network of miniature aqueducts channels the waters of the hot springs, boiled in the molten belly of the Earth, to stone tubs perched high up on the cliffs above the kelp-rich Pacific.

The night Dara arrived he was greeted by the Santa Anna, an unseasonably warm wind gently blowing up from Mexico. For a late October night, this was a pleasant surprise. After checking into his room, and a meal in the main lodge, he made his way in the dark, guided by the low, dim, yellow lanterns that lined the footpaths, down to the hot tubs. Since it was night, and the moon had not yet come out, he couldn't see much in front of him as he stepped into the stone tub. It was large enough to hold probably as many as six people comfortably. His eyes had not yet accustomed themselves to the dark and he couldn't tell if there was anybody already in the water. He didn't want to call out and break the silence. Just as he was about to step in, he made out the silhouette of a couple in the far corner, and whispered, "Do you mind if I join you?"

"As long as you don't make a splash," came the hushed reply.

He eased himself in, and the displaced water gently lapped over the edge vanishing into the darkness. As his eyes adjusted, he noticed another figure in the tub, floating face up, with the distinctive curves of a woman.

He, too, floated there in silence for a long time, alternately looking skyward at the swath of the Milky Way lit up by an occasional shooting star, and outward at the dancing reflections of dim light on the smooth ocean. Down below, he could hear the waves breaking on the rocks. The couple in the corner, entwined around each other, moved slowly and soundlessly in almost imperceptible, sensuous rhythms. Dara was surprised he didn't feel like an intruder. The darkness, the silence, and the place itself evoked a sense of privacy and freedom. He slid beneath the water up to his chin, cocooned in its warm embrace, enjoying the beauty of the night.

Behind him on the rocks, just above the opening where the spring steamed out of the mountain, a stone Buddha meditated, holding burnt offerings of incense and melted candles. As the moon rose over the looming dark hills of the Ventana wilderness, it washed the scene in a silver light, coating the ocean in a film of reflected mystery. The pool turned to liquid mercury, brushing the floating naked bodies with the same metallic android hue. The only sound, besides the crashing of the waves far below, was the lapping of water against stone as someone adjusted position in the tub. The aura of spirituality was new for the NASA scientist, and he soaked his bones and his soul in the sacred silence.

* * *

The next morning after breakfast, Dara met Maya outside the Big House, where they both were staying. In her early-thirties, she carried herself like an Amazon priestess, strong, determined, yet with an air of natural grace and compassion. Her large brown eyes sparkled in a face sculpted with high-cheekbones and framed by long, flowing black hair. Vitality flared not only from her eyes but also from every gesture. She radiated an ageless paradox of youthful maturity. About five-six, she strolled toward him barefoot, smiling, and with a friendly wave. Her dark slender arms contrasted with her snow-white T-shirt. He noticed a small rainbow-colored web embroidered over her left breast. Something about her was very familiar. He had a distinct feeling that he'd seen her before. But he couldn't place it.

They walked together along a narrow path past a fishpond, across a small wooden bridge, and sat down beneath the shade of a tall cypress on soft manicured grass, overlooking the sparkling ocean. It was a perfect cloudless day. By eight-thirty the temperature was already in the low seventies.

Thousands of monarch butterflies flitted around them, dancing like delicate leaves from bush to bush and tree to tree. They leaned back against the cypress, enjoying the spectacle.

"This is a remarkable setting for a science meeting," Dara broke the silence.

Maya laughed, "Yes. Today, this is our office!" she gestured with a sweep of her arm in a wide semi-circle.

"So tell me about Darwin, the dolphin. When can I hear the recordings?" Dara noticed a shadow cross Maya's face. Then she told him what had happened.

On her way to the airport in Honolulu, she had stopped by the university for a final check-in with Darwin. Two strangers, dressed in dark suits, had locked the aquarium from the inside. They refused to let her in. She banged on the glass, and eventually one of the men came out. He told her to follow him to the administrator's office. The provost asked her to sit down, and handed her an official-looking document. Maya recounted the event, word by word, to Dara:

"'We've been ordered to move the dolphin,' they said."

"I shouted: '*Whaaat!* By whom? Where? *No way!*' and even startled myself."

"Then the provost pointed to the letterhead on the document the men had brought with them: 'It's government business,' he said. 'As you can see, these gentlemen are agents from the Federation of Energy Workers.'

"He reminded me that my research is funded by government subsidy, and that means it comes with strings attached. I've always felt uneasy about that." Maya flicked a hair away from the corner of her mouth. "Whether I like it or not, politicians are my paymasters. As the provost said: 'They call the shots.'

"'But why? What do they want with Darwin . . . with *my* dolphin?' I protested. And then I turned to the man who had walked me to the provost's office "What do *you* want with the dolphin?' I demanded.

"True to form, he replied: 'Sorry, Ma'am. We're not at liberty to reveal that information. Our orders come from Washington. From the top. We're just sorting out the paperwork and logistics. The moving team will be here in a few days.' That was it. Then they left."

A butterfly landed on the grass between Maya and Dara. She looked at it for a moment, then turned to him and sighed:

"I tried to call you before I left Honolulu, to say not to come." She sounded anxious and confused. "I was going to cancel the workshop. But I couldn't reach you. Then I thought that with your NASA connections you might know someone in government who could help me find out what's going on. Who, or what, is the Federation of Energy Workers, and what could they, or the government, possibly want with a dolphin?" She paused. "That's why I'm here. Can you help me? We can't let them take Darwin. Not now. Especially not now."

She spoke urgently and with an intimacy that caught Dara off guard. "*We* can't let them take the dolphin." She was already including him. He was surprised by her intensity and how deeply it penetrated, carried as much by the light in her eyes and her animated hands as by her words. She looked into him, past the surface, in a way that left him feeling the same sense of urgency. He was struck by how alive and purposeful she was, by her fiery beauty. He wanted to help. But, by nature, he was cautious.

"I'm not sure I can do anything, Maya. I'll make a few calls."

"Dara, we've *got* to do something . . ." She was breathless now, and spoke in disconnected sentences, accentuating key syllables by nodding her head.

"Darwin's breakthrough is obviously even more important than I thought. . . . Word must have leaked out . . . but I haven't published anything yet . . . What do they know? How did they find out? And why are they so determined to get hold of Darwin? No-one but me has heard these recordings. . . ."

She reached into her purse and pulled out a couple of small plastic-encased discs. "These are copies I made for you." She handed him the unlabeled minidisks, along with a key.

"I've got a player in my room. You can borrow it while I'm at the workshop. I think you'll be astounded; not just by the fact that these are recordings of a talking dolphin, but even more by what he says."

Then she pulled away. "I'm late for my workshop. You've got my full report with transcripts, yes? Please go through them carefully and with an open mind. You'll see what I mean."

She paused, held out her hand and tenderly took his forearm. He noticed her fingers were long and graceful, the tips of her bright red nails lightly touching his skin for emphasis.

"I'll be leaving for Los Angeles immediately after lunch to catch a flight back. I've booked a ticket for you, too."

She dashed off, disturbing a cloud of butterflies as she moved through the bushes.

"Pull some strings. Listen to recordings. Read the report. Fly to Hawaii. Tangle with authorities. I've known this woman less than an hour, and she's already directing my life," Dara half-joked to himself. But her breathless passion and Latin charm had a captivating magnetism.

Maya's room was on the second floor of the Big House, a recently renovated turn-of-the-century mansion, surrounded by expansive green lawns, built on a cliff edge overlooking the immense Pacific. Dara let himself in with her key. A sweet fragrance lingered in the room. Her clothes were folded neatly in an open suitcase lying on the bed. He found a small, three-inch square, digital player on the dresser, slipped in a disc, and connected the headphones. Her voice announced the date, time, location, and subject of the interview. She began with a short preamble about the training history of the dolphin, how long she had worked with him, and a brief synopsis of progress to date. Her questions sounded scripted, as if prepared for a market research survey.

Dara sat on the edge of her bed and looked out the window, listening to the recording. A monarch, the size of his hand, flitted between the overhanging branches of a tall cypress. He turned up the volume.

Maya asked a series of questions, and the dolphin responded with typical squeaks and clicks. He hit the fast-forward button. Again only squeaks and whistles. He pushed fast-forward again. More squeaks. He tried the second disc, but again all he heard were the same unintelligible squeaks, whistles, and clicks. "What on Earth was she thinking?" he muttered as he pulled off the headphones. "There's nothing here! What did she mean 'Listen carefully with an open mind'"? No-one could understand any of this, except another dolphin, perhaps. Dara tried to suppress a growing frustration. He hated the thought that this was yet another waste of the precious time he had left.

He went upstairs to his own room and took out the report she had sent him. It included translations of the dialogue sessions with the dolphin. He flipped to the back and soon found the section he was looking for.

"Although Darwin speaks only in Dolphinese, with the usual combinations of pulses, clicks, and squeaks, I hear what he says in English, and sometimes even in Spanish. This is true whether we communicate face to face or whether I'm listening to a recording."

She went on to explain she was not just adding her own interpretations to his communications. Years working with other dolphins had taught her a lot about cetacean language. At first, she wondered if Darwin was telepathically sending messages. However, after she listened to the recordings, she ruled this out. Even though the discs recorded clicks and squeaks, she *heard* him speak in English.

After many sessions, and many recordings, she had come up with a theory: Darwin intentionally encodes a frequency modulation into his squeaks and whistles, and these subliminal vibrations trigger appropriate speech centers in human brains. She assumed that any human brain could decode the dolphin's part of the dialogue, and that the ability is not unique to her. The theory could be easily tested, she noted, by simply letting others hear the recordings. If anyone else heard and understood, her theory would be confirmed.

However, the report went on, since she had been working with Darwin daily for more than a year, it could be that the added modulations have a cumulative effect. There might be a learning curve. This was certainly true in her own case. In the early days, she had heard only clicks and whistles, but gradually, these sounds melded into intelligible English. If the dolphin's subliminal codes worked to train the human brain step by step, then anyone else listening to the recordings for the first time would hear only dolphin sounds. To cover for this possibility, she had included a translation of Darwin's Dolphinese in the transcript.

Dara was disappointed that he couldn't actually hear the dolphin speak. He had come all this way for nothing. But as he read through the transcript he became more and more fascinated by what it said. If Maya's translations were accurate, and if her theory were true, then, finally, he had stumbled on the first real evidence for alien consciousness, a form of non-human intelligence.

As he closed the report, a single line of dialogue caught his attention:

DARWIN: "INTELLIGENCE SEEKS EXPRESSION. IT CANNOT BE DENIED."

10
Word Games

When the plane touched down, Dara opened his eyes. The flight attendant announced "Aloha. Welcome to Honolulu and the Hawaiian islands." He picked up his bags from the carousel, and headed straight for a taxi. Maya had told him to meet her at the university once he'd showered and unpacked. She had invited him to stay at her place, but he opted for a hotel overlooking Waikiki beach. He still wasn't sure what he was getting into, and wanted a clear and fast retreat if he needed it.

Maya had left immediately after the workshop, as she had planned. But before leaving, she had persuaded Dara that if he came to Hawaii, even for a few days, Darwin would communicate with him, too.

As an incentive, she threw in, "You know, Darwin would love to meet you. He's very interested in your work at SETI, and I've read him sections from *Mind in the Cosmos*. He said he found it amusing that you should be looking for intelligent life billions of miles away, when actually it is all around you." And she added, almost as an afterthought, "Alien consciousness exists in ways and places you might not even dream." He wasn't sure if this was part of the dolphin's comment, or her own speculation.

But it didn't matter. He agreed to follow on in a day or two. When he got back to Palo Alto he made arrangements to visit the Mauna Kea observatory on the Big Island, stopping over for a few days in Honolulu to check in on Maya. She intrigued him, and how could he pass up the opportunity to meet a speaking dolphin that liked his book. An alien consciousness that shared his interest in alien consciousness was just too much to miss.

* * *

When he arrived at the aquarium, a big and well-lit space lined with white tiles, Maya was already in the water with the dolphin. They splashed about playing, chasing each other in the large pool. Dara was slightly taken aback. The sight of Maya in a bikini didn't fit his image of "scientist at work." She noticed his distraction, and picked up on his thoughts.

"One of the most important things I've learned as an anthropologist is that building relationships is fundamental," her words echoed off the tiled walls. "I'm not a follower of the school of thought that says anthropologists should protect their objectivity at all costs. When you're dealing with people—including non-human people," she threw an arm around the dolphin's neck, "you cannot avoid interacting with them. That is both one of the blessings and the curse of this science—actually, of all science. Objectivity is a myth."

Dara kicked off his shoes and moved to the edge of the pool, stepping around a portable blackboard covered with scribbled phrases and half-erased words.

"Very controversial statement for a scientist, don't you think? Where do you draw the line? How do you know what you're studying: a dolphin as a dolphin, or a dolphin viewed anthropomorphically by a human researcher?"

"Does it really matter?" she replied in that carefree way that comes naturally when swimming, when body and mind are refreshed by the freedom and buoyancy of the water. "It's all useful information. It's just a question of what you think is most important. Sure, one kind of science can treat animals, and people, as objects, and that way produces a certain kind of knowledge. But actually, I think it is abstract knowledge. It tells you very little about the living nature and experience of the subject you are engaged with."

"You like to get inside your subjects, eh?"

"Yes. I'm a big believer in participatory science. Except in this case, it's more like the subject gets inside me."

Both dolphin and woman swam to the side of the pool where Dara was standing. Maya lifted herself out, and he handed her a towel from the back of a white plastic chair. Water dripped from the ends of her shiny hair onto the blackboard by the chair, washing away the few remaining legible words.

"I like to do both kinds of research," she said, tilting her head sideways to let her ears drain, then bundling her hair up inside the towel. "I make use of technology to record objective data." She paused, and sat down with her long legs dangling over the side of the pool.

"But for me, the most important research is not what I can write in my notebooks, or record on tape. It is this." And she called out to the dolphin,

"Darwin, come and meet Dara. He's flown all the way from San Francisco to hear your critique of his book." She laughed, and then a little more seriously, looking at the NASA scientist:

"Actually, he already knows why you're here."

Dara assumed she meant that she'd told the dolphin about their meeting at Esalen, and that he had come to verify for himself that the cetacean could communicate more than mere clicks and squeaks. But, as he was to discover later, she meant a whole lot more than that.

"We don't have very much time," she said. "If you wouldn't mind, my recorder is over there in my briefcase." She pointed to a tan leather bag lying on top of a slatted wooden bench against the wall. "It's cued up, ready to go. I'd like to start right away to see if you can pick up on the meaning of Darwin's responses."

Dara crouched by the side of the pool and switched on the recorder, waiting to hear if Darwin would speak. He had never been close to a dolphin before, and was surprised at how large the animal was. Its sleek, blue-gray skin looked both leathery and soft. "Kind of like a wet suit," he thought. The dolphin's face, in particular, intrigued him: two attentive dark eyes, located forward on each side of a long and rounded snout, much smaller than he expected. They seemed to be smiling. Upturned curves on either side of the beak, reaching from the tip all the way back to the eyes, enhanced the effect. The wide smile was almost human. Dara felt a little unnerved. The dolphin wasn't just looking at him, but *into* him.

Maya began asking simple questions, such as, "Darwin, this is Dr. Dara Martin. Can you show him that you can count to ten?" The dolphin emitted ten clicks. Gradually, she moved on to simple instructions: "Please, tell Dara what time it is," and she pointed at the large-faced clock on the wall over the door. The dolphin let out three long whistles followed by a short whistle. Dara checked the clock: It was three-thirty exactly.

"Now, Darwin, please say something to Dara in English." She turned to see if the recorder was running. The dolphin expelled a complicated series of clicks, whistles, and squeaks, and rounded off by squirting a precisely aimed jet of water that hit Dara in the middle of the forehead.

"Did you get anything?" Maya asked.

"You mean besides being shot between the eyes," he replied. "Yes. I got wet!" He sounded a little indignant. "That's all. Just the same old whistles and clicks."

Dara wasn't sure whether the failure to get the message was his or the dolphin's. Maybe it was Maya's. Maybe there was nothing out of the ordinary to witness here anyway. They kept trying different techniques over the course of the afternoon. Maya asked Dara to close his eyes, to visualize a blank page where the message might appear in English. She had Dara get in the water, and coaxed him to address Darwin in a friendly tone, while touching his forehead against the dolphin's. Nothing worked.

By the end of the session, Maya realized this was a clear case of communications breakdown. In Dara's presence, not only did the dolphin stop showing signs of understanding simple instructions, Maya herself gradually lost the ability to understand Darwin's utterances. When Dara left the pool for a few minutes to go to the bathroom, Maya was surprised to find that she and Darwin were able to resume their conversations. Darwin, she realized, was prepared to communicate only when alone with her.

Over dinner that night, Maya confided this to Dara, and said she thought Darwin was testing him.

"Dolphins are very intuitive," she said, "and Darwin more so than any others I've worked with. He knows that powerful forces are moving in and trying to end our work together, and so he needs to be able to trust you. Please be patient. And please try to be open. Let go of your skepticism; I'm sure that's what's causing the block."

Dara was about to say how ironic it was to hear one scientist tell another to abandon critical reasoning and evidence in favor of intuition, but he decided against it.

"I am trying," he said instead. "I didn't come all this way just to get my face wet." They both laughed.

After dinner, she drove him back to his hotel. He invited her up for a drink, but she declined saying she'd like to get an early start in the morning. Would he be ready by seven if she came by to pick him up? He kissed her on the cheek, and said goodnight.

* * *

For the first time in weeks, Dara woke up feeling he'd had a great night's sleep. Back at the aquarium, the first hour or so went pretty much like the day before. But this time, Dara was good-humored about the lack of progress. They experimented with different strategies for communication, including his leaving the aquarium to give anthropologist and dolphin time to rebuild their connection, which she followed by giving him summarized translations of what Darwin said. Over lunch, she mentioned that he seemed more relaxed, and it was helping her and Darwin find their groove. By the time they returned to the aquarium, he felt a growing bond with Maya, and, by proxy, with Darwin.

Dara agreed to spend the afternoon in the pool with the dolphin and his colleague. Little by little, Darwin began to take the stranger into his confidence. The breakthrough came around four o'clock when Darwin announced to the NASA scientist "I hear that your center is clear. Now we can begin. What do you want to ask me?"

Dara, delighted that the dolphin understood English (or did he understand Dolphinese?) was still a little cautious. He wanted to test the mammal's IQ, and proposed a series of simple and progressively more complex arithmetical and logical puzzles. He was continually surprised by the dolphin's mental abilities. He tried a simple test in logic: "All men are mortal." And Darwin replied, "I know. All men die. Dolphins, too."

"Yes. Yes," Dara continued, "but I'm not interested in the *fact* that all men are mortal. I want to see what you can do with what philosophers call a syllogism." He explained: "I'll make two statements, and if you accept that both of them are true, your job is to tell me what conclusion logically follows."

"Okay," Darwin said, "that seems easy enough. But why do you want to play a word game that has nothing to do with real life?"

"The point is not about real life, about what happens out in the world," Dara said. "It's about how we use our minds. The way we use words shows the way we use our minds. If there's a flaw in the words, there's a flaw in the mind that speaks them. And if there's a flaw in the mind, sooner or later that will show up as an error in how we deal with real life. So, you see, logic, thinking clearly, can be important for survival. If we make the wrong connections in our mind, we will make mistakes in our actions. The beauty of logic and abstract reasoning is that we can run mental tests in the privacy and safety of our own heads. As long as we confine our mistakes to the mind, nothing will happen in the outer world."

Maya threw Dara a glance: "Quit the lecture, Professor." He stopped, and reminded himself he was talking to a dolphin.

"Excuse me, I got a little carried away."

All this time, the dolphin bobbed his nose just above the surface of the pool, focusing on the visiting scientist. He listened patiently, and then spoke:

"I understand what you said, Doctor Dara. But I don't agree with all of it. You have made some assumptions I would question, assumptions that could indicate the way you use your mind might not be all that useful out in the real world."

"For instance?" Dara said, adopting his best professorial tone.

"Well, for one thing, we were about to play a word game in logic. You said that 'All men are mortal.' And your next statement would be 'Socrates is a man.' Am I right?"

Dara was astounded. "How on Earth . . .?"

The dolphin interrupted, playfully splashing a little water onto the scientist's face. "I have a very good memory," he said. "Maya already played that word game with me. And, of course, the answer is 'Therefore, Socrates is mortal.' The conclusion naturally follows if both of the previous statements are true. But here's my question: Just because the conclusion follows in words, does it mean that it is also necessarily true in the real world?"

Dara paused for a moment. "You're asking me?" The dolphin nodded. Dara thought through the logic of the syllogism. "Of course, it must be true. If there's a contradiction in the logic, it would be impossible in the real world."

Darwin snorted. "Are you sure? You think the world must conform to the logic of your ideas and your words. Have you ever heard of a paradox? How does your logic help you there?"

"That's just my point," Dara replied, but feeling a little unsure now. "Paradoxes don't happen in the real world. They are just imperfections in our ways of understanding."

"Precisely," said the dolphin. "Logic is limited. It cannot penetrate the mysterious. Paradoxes exist only in your mind, but mystery exists in the real world. Paradoxes are the mind's way of telling us that mystery exceeds the power of logic."

Dara felt uncomfortable. Was this really happening, was he having a philosophical dialogue with a dolphin, and being cornered by superior logic? But Darwin wasn't finished.

"You implied, did you not, that 'As long as our mistakes are confined to the mind, they will not cause errors in the outer world'?"

Dara agreed he had said something like that. It was well accepted in evolutionary theory that abstract reasoning came into being precisely because it enabled humans to think things through without dire consequences. He wondered where the dolphin was going with this.

"I'm sure you believe what you said," Darwin continued. "But that kind of thinking is itself an error."

"What do you mean?"

"Well for one thing, it's a very good example of poor logic and highly questionable assumptions," the dolphin snorted in a way that Dara took to be a chuckle.

"Even if abstract reasoning gave your species a survival advantage, it by no means follows that mistakes made in the mind could have no effect on the outside world. That kind of thinking assumes, on one hand, that the 'outside world,' as you call it, is *outside the mind*. How could you know that? On the other hand, you assume that the 'outside world' does not also possess mind. If the world does in fact possess mind, then what is there to stop what goes on in your mind from affecting what goes on in the outside world? I would say your logic is leading you into a muddle—and possibly a very dangerous muddle at that."

Dara was silent for a long time. He was trying to deal with the startling surprise of communicating with a dolphin, and on such a sophisticated level. But he wasn't just talking with a dolphin; Darwin was getting the better of him in a philosophical debate.

How, indeed, could anybody ever know if there was a world 'outside the mind'? The only way you could know anything is by knowing it *in the mind.* All knowing, of course, takes place in some part of the mind. That is inevitable. If a world existed outside the mind, it would by definition be unknowable. That much was clear. But the dolphin was saying something more. He was suggesting that the world itself might also possess mind. In Dara's academic training, that kind of suggestion was dismissed as primitive superstition, a hangover from pre-scientific beliefs in nature spirits.

"The world doesn't possess mind beyond the brain," Dara finally replied, now regaining his self-assurance. "Every scientist worth his salt today knows that mind is produced by the nervous system and the brain. Wherever there's mind or intelligence—here on Earth or elsewhere in the cosmos—you can be sure there are creatures with brains."

"So mind is squirted from brain cells," the dolphin interjected, "like this?" And again he squirted a snoutful of water at the scientist.

"Something like that," Dara said, wiping the water from his face with the back of his hand. "No brain, no mind." For emphasis, he slapped the water with the open palm of his right hand. "Everyone knows that."

"I don't know that," Maya said. "At least I'm not so sure about it." She was holding onto the dolphin's fin as they swam circles around the NASA man.

"There," said Darwin, "another mistake. *Everyone* does not know it. Not even every scientist. And certainly *I* don't know that brains squirt out minds. But perhaps I don't count, since I'm only a dolphin?"

He continued: "Tell me this, Stanford Scientist, if minds are just thoughts produced by brains, how far do they reach? A few centimeters, a few feet, a few miles, a few thousand miles . . . to infinity?"

This time without hesitation, Dara retorted: "We can't measure consciousness, but it's pretty certain that each mind is confined to the brain that produces it."

"So mind is kind of like the sogginess of a wet sponge, contained within the brain?" Darwin asked.

"Yes. Or at least within the skull."

"Oh? Then how do you explain that I'm speaking in clicks and whistles, which I know are just meaningless sounds to you, yet you seem to understand me all the same. How might that be?"

Again Dara fell silent. It was true: He did not understand the clicks and squeaks, yet he understood perfectly well what the dolphin was communicating.

"Might it be that your mind is somehow picking up what's going on in my mind?"

"It could be that," Dara stammered.

"Could be? Obviously that *is* what's going on, wouldn't you say?

"Yes, I suppose so."

"Which, if I understand your logic correctly, would mean that what's going on inside your head must also be going on inside my head. Right?"

"How do you mean?"

"Well, you said just a moment ago that mind is like the sogginess produced by a wet and spongy brain, and all of that sogginess is contained inside its host's head. Yes?"

"Something like that."

"That's what you said. Well, then, if my soggy mind is inside my head, and your soggy mind is inside your head, and yet you are 'hearing' what's going on in my mind, and vice versa, then your soggy head must be inside my soggy head, and my soggy head must be inside your soggy head . . . And wouldn't you say that that's just impossible? How can one thing be inside another thing, if the second is also inside the first? It's like saying two beach balls are inside each other. Kind of a paradox, huh?"

Dara was lost. His mind reeled trying to keep up. The one thing he was sure of, however, was that he and the dolphin were indeed communicating through some kind of telepathic link. And if that were the case, then clearly he was wrong about the mind being confined inside the brain or the head. Mind was more mysterious. That's what the dolphin was getting at.

"Glad we got that much settled," Darwin said. "That's enough for one day. The mind can absorb only so much at one time—no matter how spongy the brain may be!"

Before he let him leave, the dolphin insisted that Dara keep their conversations private. Neither Dara nor Maya knew it yet, but Darwin had a plan—something that would catapult the two scientists into a world beyond belief. Today was just a preamble. Tomorrow the real journey would begin.

11

Knowledge is Power

"I've got some news," Dara shouted to Maya as he entered the aquarium for their morning session. "Some good. Some not so good." His words boomed off the tiled walls.

The "dolphinarium" was actually an Olympic-size swimming pool the university had adapted especially for Maya's research. There were also a couple of smaller tanks on the beach where other students worked with three more dolphins. But Darwin had clearly shown the most promise early on, and Maya had requested a private setting to pursue her interspecies training sessions away from public scrutiny. She had brought in the funding, and so the university agreed. But now the funding source was calling in its "collateral"—they wanted Darwin.

Maya was already in the pool, and swam over to Dara. He dropped to one knee and offered a hand to help her out of the water. She declined, shaking her head.

"Go ahead, give me the good news first."

"Well, last night I got a call from Graham Bechtel. Before I left California, I had asked what he knew about the Federation of Energy Workers. He sits on the joint "Space Security" committee of NASA and the NSA, advising them on the use of satellites for global surveillance work. He seemed surprised I'd heard of the FEW, and said he'd get back to me. Apparently, they're a division of the NSA, deeply involved in SIGINT."

Maya's eyes widened. "Hold on there, amigo . . ." she tried to hide a pang of concern. "That's too much of an alphabet soup for me so early in the day. I know of the NSA, of course, the government's National Security Agency, right? But 'SIGNIT' is new to me. And who exactly are the FEW?"

"I'm getting to all of that," Dara said, kicking off his shoes, and sat down on the edge of the pool, dangling his feet just inches from the water. "It's SIGINT, by the way, short for Signals Intelligence. Essentially, they're a cadre of federal technology eavesdroppers and code breakers. They cracked Japanese signals during World War II, helping the US outsmart the enemy. Lately, they've focused on international terrorism—and, no doubt, on domestic targets, too."

"What does my work with Darwin have to do with national security?" Maya's voice crackled as she pulled herself up out of the pool next to Dara. Her face flushed red from neck to cheeks, highlighting a look of disbelief. "National security? Code breaking? Terrorism? I don't get it."

"I don't know what they want, nor does Bechtel," Dara continued. "But their stated mission is, and I quote," he pulled out a slip of paper from his jeans pocket: "to understand the secret communications of our foreign adversaries . . ."

"Do you think they've been wiretapping my calls, listening in on our conversations about Darwin?" Maya interrupted. The dolphin swam up to them, nudged Dara's ankles with his fin, and then slowly glided away.

"I don't know," Dara repeated. "All Bechtel could tell me is that they're the most important center for foreign language analysis and research within the US government. They have the world's best mathematicians and the highest-powered computers to analyze data for breaking and generating codes."

He absent-mindedly rolled the piece of paper between his fingers, and flicked the little tube into the air. It landed in the pool.

"My first guess—assuming they somehow know about your work—is that they want to find out about the translation code you use for communicating with dolphins."

"But I don't have a code," Maya sounded defensive. "It's something that Darwin does." She hesitated and sucked in a deep breath. "Is that why they want him . . . ?" Before Dara could answer, she did it for him. "Yes, I know: *You don't know.*"

She stood up and reached for a towel hanging on a hook attached to the wall.

"And what about this other group . . . the FEW? You said you had good news and bad news. What's the good news?"

Dara looked a little sheepish. "I'm afraid *that's* the good news. I mean, at least I have *something* to report to you. It's a slim lead, but it gives us a direction. Something to do with national security and code breaking. I think that's a start."

"And the bad news . . .?" Maya's eyes narrowed.

"Well, as I understand it from Bechtel, the FEW—eh, the Federation of Energy Workers—is supposedly a top-secret arm of the NSA with a special mission to spy on individuals and to infiltrate groups the government deems culturally subversive. Apparently, this includes non-conventional religious organizations such as New Thought churches, Scientology, and other New Age movements. Internally, they refer to themselves as 'PsychOps' or perhaps it's 'PsiCops.' Very 1984."

Dara was also standing now, face to face with Maya. He explained that while the NSA prides itself on using state-of-the-art high-tech surveillance, the FEW focuses on what the government considers "dangerous ideas" or "menacing memes," as Bechtel calls them.

"Their mission is to 'patrol' new ways of thinking and using the mind," he said, "keeping track of any new developments that might pose a challenge to social stability."

Dara took a moment to recall more details he gotten from Bechtel.

"Apparently, the FEW came into being during the 1960s when the widespread use of psychedelics inspired a generation with new visions for a better world, spawning the counter-culture movement."

Maya's growing puzzlement was clearly visible. She opened her mouth to speak, but then stifled it with a gasp. She moved in closer to Dara, and asked:

"Did you show *anyone* the transcript of my experiments with Darwin—even Bechtel?" Her tone was hushed, as though she wanted to keep her words from echoing off the walls.

"No. No one's seen it. But funny you should ask about Bechtel. He asked me for a copy of the transcript. Said he wanted to see if there's anything there that might have triggered the FEW to come knocking on your door."

"Well, you know that's not possible," Maya snapped back. "Darwin made it very clear that under no circumstances must anyone besides the two of us be privy to the details of our work."

"Yes, I know. But we need to trust Bechtel, too, if we want to find out more about what's going on."

"It's not a question of trust," Maya said, softening. "It's about honoring Darwin's request that we not let word get out about his communications. Not yet, anyway. If we don't keep our promise, Darwin will stop working with us."

"But that puts us in a bind. We don't have much time to figure out what the FEW want before they come for Darwin—in a few days. And, if we're going to move fast, right now Bechtel is our only link to the NSA and the FEW. This is top-level stuff . . ." Dara's voice trailed off.

"Look, I don't mean to scare you, but Bechtel made a point of letting me know that once the FEW are involved—especially if they've revealed who they are—they really mean business. He said if they want Darwin, they'll stop at nothing to get him."

He fell silent for a moment, thinking. His eyes rolled up under their lids as he tried to remember something.

"Bechtel told me that the NSA motto is *'Knowledge is Power,'* and the motto of the FEW is *'Get it. Use it.'* It seems, they're out to get whatever knowledge Darwin has about communicating across species. That's all I know. That's all I could find out from Bechtel."

Darwin leaped high in the air and fell back to the surface of the pool with a loud smack, splashing the two researchers. The dolphin let out a series of high-pitched whistles.

"He wants us to join him in the pool," Maya translated. She dropped her towel and dived in right away. Dara undressed and followed. The water felt cold, and uninviting. But his curiosity to find out more about the dolphin soon took over. Darwin swam between them, weaving in and out, creating waves that forced Maya and Dara to swim vigorously.

"He's helping to get our energy flowing," Maya said. After a couple of lengths, Dara stopped to catch his breath.

"Yesterday, you said my center is clear?" Dara reminded Darwin. "What did you mean?"

Darwin told him that when he and Maya are in the water he can hear through their bodies, and that he has learned to recognize when they are disturbed in any way, especially by fear or anger. Their work could now proceed, the dolphin announced, because he could hear or "feel" that the NASA scientist was opening up, and that he intended no harm.

"Yes, your center is clearer today, Doctor Dara, so let's begin. We have much work to do, and very little time."

12

A Meeting of Minds

"Where is my center?" Dara asked. "Is it here?" and he touched his heart.

The dolphin laughed. "The center is no special place, it moves about. No, it is not your heart, although that organ vibrates with the condition of the center. Sometimes the center is all over the body; then the whole body is the center. Some of your psychologists call that 'being in the flow,' or 'being in the zone'. Sometimes, like today, it is near the heart. Sometimes it is in the stomach. And sometimes it is in the genitals." He laughed, and splashed a snoutful of water at Maya. Dara felt his face blush, as she smiled at him.

"Sometimes it is in more than one place at the same time," Darwin continued. "I can hear that seems to bother you most."

Dara was full of questions this morning. He was eager to exchange ideas, but Darwin seemed happier playing about and joking. Between games, answers did come, and Dara and Maya realized that Darwin had been training them more than they could teach him. He repeated that no one else should know about their work until it was ready—including Bechtel. They'd have to find another way to sidestep the FEW.

Today, Darwin's attention was on more immediate issues.

"I'm afraid your theory is partly wrong," he communicated to Maya. "Although I do add a subsonic vibration to my sounds that conditions certain nerve pathways in your brain, our most effective communication takes place through a direct extrasensory channel. The inaudible modulation prepares your mind to receive my messages by altering your brainwaves. It opens you up. Instead of the usual chatter of beta waves, I facilitate receptivity by inducing more relaxing alpha and theta waves. For really important messages that need to come through dreams, I tune your brain to delta waves."

Darwin nudged the NASA scientist aside, and whispered confidentially, "Remember a certain dream you had recently about an imaginary childhood friend of yours named Grumbalot?"

Dara's entire nervous system shuddered. "How . . .?" He couldn't finish the sentence.

"Do you mind if we let Maya in on our little secret?" Darwin asked.

The astrobiologist's sense of reality began to crack, he felt as if reason itself, along with the structure of the starry heavens, was caving in on him.

"I can see your center is all over the place. That is good. You are opening up, and we have very important work to do."

Maya saw Dara's distress, and swam over to him. "It's okay, Dara," she said reassuringly, "I know Darwin has been in communication with you by, shall we say, extraordinary means. I just don't know all the details."

"We need each other in this," Darwin said to Dara. "I will need your assistance shortly, but first I need to prepare you, to bring some balance to your lop-sided consciousness. All that scientific training has really limited your ability to harmonize head and heart."

Dara's state of mind shifted progressively from anxiety to fear to borderline terror. His heart thumped against his ribs, so loud he was sure the others could hear it. The pounding filled his ears and he felt the muscles around his eyes and mouth tighten as he strained to understand what was happening. Everything began to swirl in a blur around him, and he could barely keep afloat. For a moment, his head slipped beneath the surface, he gulped in a mouthful of water, and struggled to keep from drowning.

"It's okay to be afraid," Darwin said. "But you will live through this, I promise. I can see you are afraid of losing your mind, afraid I'm going to take it over. Part of what you fear is correct. Yes, you are losing your mind—at least I hope you are. No, I'm not taking it over. That would be no use to me at all. Actually, I'm helping you get back the mind you lost a long time ago."

Darwin raised a flipper indicating to Maya to move away. He wanted Dara to feel he had space to retreat if he needed to.

"Your mind is so out of balance you can't help me yet. You will be a liability to my plan—unless we can get you back on track. We don't have enough time to get you fully realigned, but we can begin the process. It's time for you to listen deeply as we explore your story. Are you ready to understand that your stories matter—and that matter stories?"

By now, the NASA scientist's state of mind was so raw nothing more could threaten it. He had no more energy left even to be surprised by that last remark. As far as he was concerned, *anything* could happen.

There was a long silence. All Dara could hear was the pulse of his own blood pumping through his temples. He waited for what would happen next. The silence continued. Then he realized that Darwin and Maya were waiting for him.

"Oh . . . I'm ready. " He said it, but it felt as if the words were spoken by a character from a dream.

"Welcome aboard," Darwin said. "We've been waiting for you for a long time. Soon the real journey can begin. And yes: As you will come to understand, the 'you' that spoke just now is in a way a character you dreamed up. I want to talk to you about your dream. I want you to listen carefully. I want you to listen with all your centers wide open."

"I'm ready." Suddenly, he felt detached as if a part of him were floating in a bubble of clear space outside his body. His heart still pounded in his chest, yet he no longer felt afraid.

"Let me begin with the one thing you need to know more than anything else. Maya told you that I said you are looking for alien consciousness in the wrong places. Well, actually, there is no 'wrong' place. Mind is everywhere in the cosmos, as you have long supposed. But you've been looking in the most difficult places. The intelligence you seek is much closer to home. Do you know what I'm talking about?"

Dara nodded, "I think so. You're referring to cetacean intelligence, to other dolphins and whales like you."

"No, my friend, I'm not. Of course, we have our own consciousness, and to you and others like you, it will appear 'alien.' But that's not what I'm referring to. It's closer than that."

Dara felt his strength coming back, and his mind begin to clear. He pondered for a moment, and said: "I imagine you're talking about the intelligence in matter, then. Since you seem to know so much about my dreams, and since my recurring dream is somehow connected with the mysterious email messages, I suppose you know about them, too?"

"Yes I do. Both messages come from the same source. After all, intelligence does seek expression." This last remark confirmed Dara's suspicion that Darwin was involved in the mysterious emails.

"But that's not what I'm getting at, either," the dolphin continued. "Yes, it is true that 'stories matter' and that 'matter stories'—we'll come to that later on. But right now, I'm trying to get you to see something much more personal."

If dolphins were not the alien consciousness, and if Darwin wasn't referring to the intelligence of the world itself, then what could it be? What could be closer? Dara was stumped.

"You don't mean . . . you couldn't mean . . . you're not talking about Maya?" She was the closest to him right now, next to Darwin. The thought of her as an "alien" was just too absurd.

"You're getting warmer, but moving in a very circuitous route. I'll need to guide you more directly." Darwin asked Dara to close his eyes, and to recall the images from his dream—images of Grumbalot and Fanima, the "bubble girl" in the blue universe. Dara sensed a connection between the dream phrase "I-together," being "All-One," and being alone—being abandoned, first as a young child, later by his wife. But perhaps there was another meaning to all of this, another way of interpreting his own stories. Maybe his story of abandonment was true, but not the way he had imagined it.

Another long silence, and then Dara burst out quizzically: "You mean the alien consciousness is *mine?*"

Darwin let the realization sink in for a few moments. Then he said to Dara:

"Yes, your consciousness is split, fragmented, so that the greater part of it is alien to you. You are a stranger to so much of who you really are. A long time ago, you abandoned an important part of yourself. You became estranged from the core of your own consciousness."

Dara closed his eyes, turning his attention inward, letting his mind open up. It was a new and unfamiliar experience for him: a sense of expansiveness and peace that deepened the more he became aware of his own consciousness. Darwin, too, could sense that his student's mind was shifting and settling. He continued:

"What you haven't realized yet—something that will become immensely important to you later—is that Fanima, the feminine apparition in your dream, is a personification of your own intuition. In fact, your own intuition created that story. Like every human being, you carry around a cast of characters in your consciousness, a gathering of sub-personalities and higher personalities, and they all seek expression through you. Your intelligence and creativity depend on them. Fanima was reminding you not to smother your intuition with reason, which is what you've been doing for most of your life."

As Darwin spoke, flashes of the dream came back to Dara. He saw Fanima, the bubble girl, reaching out to him, her face morphing back and forth between his own and Maya's. He saw the surrealistic image of Fanima melt into the figure of Grumbalot, who was Dara himself. He heard her voice from deep within him say, "We have been I-together for a very long time. . . . This is not something you can figure out with your head. It is a matter for the heart."

Darwin let the flashback unfold. He could see it, too, and he knew that the message from the dream was moving deeper into the scientist's awareness. "In your lifelong search for knowledge and wisdom—about yourself, about your world—heeding the caution from the feminine in your dream will turn out to be one of your most precious gifts. It will, however, prove to be a lesson you'll have to learn over and over again.

"As you move deeper into this story, your search will involve repeated encounters between alien forms of consciousness within your own being. And you will see that the lessons learned from these encounters will have great importance far beyond your personal story." He gently tapped the top of Dara's head with his beak, and then did the same to the center of his chest.

"The struggle between intellect and intuition in your consciousness, you will discover, is a replay of a much more dangerous encounter played out in the history of your species. If you fail to integrate intuition and intellect as you continue your journey, it will threaten your sanity, even your life. And if your species fails to accomplish a similar meeting of minds—a true return to I-together—the future of your entire civilization, even of your planet, will be at stake."

"You mean a meeting between human minds and dolphin minds?" Dara interrupted, sensing the significance of the events that led him to this aquarium in Hawaii.

"Not quite. A meeting of minds between species is indeed a wonderful thing, destined to enrich both partners in the meeting—*provided it is done with the utmost respect and empathy*. But the challenge facing humans is within your own species. You are rapidly losing the last few opportunities to have a true meeting of minds between the vanishing ways of knowing of your indigenous peoples and your modern culture's obsession with rationalism.

"Unfortunately, in all the meetings I know of between your civilization and indigenous cultures, the overpowering surge of rationalism has met the 'alien' consciousness with anything but respect. Reason is a *conquistador*."

Darwin's words echoed inside Dara's head, and vibrated in his heart. The scientist's long-cherished faith in the power of reason, as enlightening savior to the world, began to crumble piece by logical piece. He felt as if his own reason was clinging to a cliff, and Darwin's words were gently lifting one finger after another.

When he finally let go, only then did he grasp the full significance of what the dolphin was saying.

"Yes," Darwin affirmed, "it is a shock to wake up and discover the depth of the dark forces at work in the world. Even more so, to find out that these dark forces are within us. But these shadows are not inherently evil."

Dara listened intently, floating at the edge of the pool. He watched Darwin glide in small circles a few feet away. Then the paradox hit: "I use reason to understand why too much reason isn't rational."

"It's like trying to dry yourself with a wet towel, isn't it?" He heard the dolphin chuckle at the back of his head.

Darwin's voice trailed off, and without warning he jumped up out of the water and landed right between Maya and Dara, sending waves splashing over them and washing over the sides of the pool.

"That's enough for today," he said. "Look what happens when I take on the view of reason. It gets gloomy very quickly. But it really isn't all that bad if you adopt a different perspective—the perspective you were actually born with. Look at your indigenous peoples: In the face of destruction, they continue to laugh, to sing, and to dance, to commune with their spirits. Their dreams, in the end, are not threatened by your illusions. But this is the domain of anthropologists. I'll let Maya take over the story from here. Go out, have fun. Eat, laugh, and be alive. We have more work to do here tomorrow."

13

Conquest of Dreams

Maya and Dara took Darwin's advice and went out dancing and dining in a club on top of Diamond Head, overlooking one of the most spectacular beaches in the world. The DJ pounded out old favorites, and they delighted in discovering a mutual love of Reggae and the music of Van Morrison.

They ate a supper of fresh seafood, washed down with cool dry wine, and danced late into the night. Hours later, exhausted, they escaped the high energy of the nightclub and headed for the solitude of the moonlit beach. Barefoot, they strolled along the water's edge; Maya danced and splashed in the shallow waves, no larger than ripples. The sky, ablaze with stars, enveloped them in its infinite mystery. Without a word, they reached out and took each other's hands.

Dara felt like a teenager on a first date. He turned to Maya and told her how beautiful she looked in the moonlight. Her eyes glinted as she turned her head and smiled at him over her shoulder. Instinctively, they moved closer together, and continued walking in silence. It was one o'clock by the time they got back to her car.

"I've had a wonderful night," Maya said, hesitating before opening the door. "I'm really glad you are with us.

Darwin had singled you out months ago, after I told him about your book. He had me send those emails—his words, my fingers—and, in ways you will not yet understand, he also communicated with you through your dreams. He could tell you have a good heart, but that you also have a very strong rational mind that might be hard to crack. He needs both of those qualities to accomplish his project." Maya twirled the car keys around her finger, and changed the topic.

"Back at the club, you asked me to tell you more about myself. I'd be happy to. Would you like to come back to my place for some coffee?" She smiled up at Dara.

"Too late for coffee, for me," he said. "But I'd love one more tequila."

* * *

They drove inland for about twenty minutes. The stars seemed to be procreating, filling the sky with new forms. He pointed out the constellations through the open roof of her car. They sang along as the radio blared out *Wild Night*, their voices rushing away behind them into the darkness.

"The Hawaiians sure have a grave sense of humor," he quipped as they sped past a cemetery. "Did you see that road sign: 'Dead End Street' right there outside the gates?"

"Yeah. I've always wondered about that. So happens, my house is just down the road. We're home."

Inside, she poured drinks, lit a small fire and some candles, and pulled the sofa nearer to the hearth. Instead of sitting in it, she threw some cushions on the floor and indicated that the sofa was their backrest.

They settled in front of the fire and Dara turned to Maya. "Tell me how you got involved with this work, researching language and intelligence in dolphins?"

She smiled, and said "I won't bore you with the anthropology curriculum I had to slog through. But I will tell you why I know—in my bones—that nature tingles with the spark of spirit and intelligence."

She told him about growing up in the rainforest in Venezuela. Her father, a Ye'kuana shaman, still lived with the rest of her family in the time-honored ways. Like other tribes in the region, the Ye'kuana were renowned for their compassion, empathy, and deep soulful connection to each other, the land, and the creatures around them.

"We are a peaceful people who prize collaboration and understanding over profit and progress."

Maya, who was also a shaman, was the first member of her family to leave their tribe and get a Western education. She had decided, early on, to take advantage of the tools of Western culture—to integrate her natural intuitive abilities with formal academic training. Her goal was to bring this balance to a rigorous study of intelligence everywhere—not just in humans, but in all creatures—and to become an ambassador for "all nations," as she put it—for the sacredness of nature. She had witnessed first hand what happens when Western values encroach on native lands and ways of life.

"There's a basic aggressiveness in the Western character that seems to be deeply rooted in the European mind. It's there in your religions and in your science and technology, too. I've seen native wisdom and culture threatened, and in many cases destroyed, by what anthropologists call conquest consciousness."

"'Conquest consciousness'?" Dara queried.

She explained: "Remember today—eh, *yesterday*—when Darwin referred to reason as a *conquistador?* He meant that reason and logic suppress the body's natural intelligence. After the Spanish arrived in my land it was only a matter of time before my people were conquered. We were overpowered not just by their superior weapons, horses, and disease. They literally colonized our souls through a much deeper and insidious kind of domination—*a conquest of consciousness.* They undermined our ancient ways of life like a virus invading our minds. It still goes on today; the tyranny of reason over feeling and intuition."

Maya fell silent, connecting to an ancient memory of the old ways. Her face revealed a mix of emotions—a profound peacefulness tinged with sadness—familiar to Dara from other Native Americans he had known. Then, returning to the present moment, Maya continued:

"For anthropologists who study indigenous cultures conquest consciousness is a real problem. . . ."

"Not in your case, I imagine," he offered.

"That's true. I've been educated in the West, but I've never lost my indigenous soul. I was chosen by my people to go to the city to learn the ways of the Europeans. Our shamans could see the coming destruction in their dreams. One path of hope, we believe, is to open dialogue between your people and ours. We need to understand how you see the world, because your way of seeing is so very powerful." She paused: "Darwin has corrected me: He says that the

Western way is 'forceful,' the indigenous ways are powerful. I think he's correct."

Maya went on to explain that indigenous consciousness flows in that fluid borderland between dreams and wide-awake logic. It produces a very different kind of logic, utterly unlike Western rational thought.

"It is a logic of feeling rather than a logic of ideas," she said.

A logic of feeling. Dara knew now what she meant. He snuggled closer to her, not with erotic intent, but simply out of an urge to share closer human contact. She responded by wrapping her legs around his, and continued:

"In all cultures, consciousness is shaped by the way adults relate to their children. In tribal societies, caregivers keep infants and young children in close contact for the first two or three years of their life. The young grow up literally feeling a caring presence right next to their skin."

Dara listened attentively, looking closely at the perfect geometry of her face as she spoke. Their eyes connected. She smiled, but he noticed a shadow.

"In our culture, communal body contact and shared sensuousness is a way of life. We are naturally attuned to the feelings of the people around us. If any one of us feels bad, we all feel it. Consequently, we instinctively respond to others in ways that make them feel good."

And then the shadow began to make sense.

"This is a problem when we meet the force of reason. Conquest consciousness is rooted in confrontation. Reason *has* to be right. It dominates. Arguments are won by one idea conquering another. Reason strives to win, feeling aims to please. That's the problem."

Dara responded defensively, unwittingly illustrating Maya's point: "Yes. But when ideas collide, they can lead to new insights. It's a creative process. That's how knowledge grows and evolves. It's how we got from wobbling wagon wheels to the precision of rockets."

She pulled back slightly to get a clearer view of his face, looking to see if he was serious. He continued:

"We're talking about progress. And progress isn't necessarily evil or destructive. For something new to emerge, the old must give way. Life survives only because it feeds on other life—and death. It's how nature evolves."

"That is partly correct," she agreed, allowing him his view, yet still wanting to honor her own. "However, from the indigenous perspective, the old provides a strong foundation for the new. Reason works best with nature when thinking is rooted in feeling. But modern Western civilization has driven a wedge between these two ways of knowing."

Dara then asked Maya if the gap between reason and intuition affects us in real life.

"It *blocks* you from real life." Her voice was stronger, more emphatic. "Look, you may not like what I'm about to say, but it has to be said: Western civilization is deeply dysfunctional. I don't think it's too far-fetched to say it's an evolutionary error."

Dara's eyes lit up, surprised. He shuffled to readjust position, stretching, so that his chin was now in line with the top of Maya's head. "That's a pretty harsh judgment.

What's your evidence?" He probed for more precision. "Please explain."

She gently pointed out that his very mode of questioning was a prime example of conquest consciousness—an unintentional attempt to squeeze feeling-based knowledge into the straightjacket of reason.

"This may take a little time, so please bear with me. It's the main topic of my doctoral thesis." She paused as she collected her thoughts. "I'll try to summarize."

"I'm all ears," Dara replied. "Really, I want to hear this.'

"Okay, you asked for it . . . . Western civilization harbors a deep and shameful secret—a systematic campaign of terror directed at your own babies. It's unintentional, of course, but it's pervasive nonetheless. It happens to just about everyone in your culture."

She sat up, her face now level with his, and then explained further: "For generations, educated 'civilized' society has robbed its children of their evolutionary in-arms birthright, and the consequences for you and the rest of the world have been disastrous.

"Just think about it: For millions of years our common ancestors carried their infants with them, body-to-body, as they went about their daily routines. Babies felt secure and protected as they encountered the multitude of sounds, sights, and sensations natural to their world. *We all evolved to expect this.*"

She emphasized the last few words, looking Dara straight in the eyes to see if he got the point. He did, and she continued:

"As newborn babies, deep down in our cells, we are programmed by evolution to expect close physical contact with our mother from the moment of birth—to be held in her arms, to access her breast, to feel the warmth and security of her skin against ours *for as long as we feel we need it,* usually for the first year or two of life.

"When these expectations are fulfilled, the child grows up with a natural sense of 'rightness.' She is okay, the world is okay, and the child behaves accordingly. An evolved expectation like this lives in us as a *certainty,*" she paused, ". . . until it is betrayed."

Dara's mind flashed back to his own infancy when, struck down by illness, he was separated from his mother, and missed out on precious in-arms experience. Now, for the first time, he realized why he was so driven. An unnamed longing oozed from his cells—a life-long quest for what he could not find. Even his chosen career, searching for alien intelligence, was another forlorn cry from deep within his deprived flesh.

Maya noticed her guest was letting her words sink into a place inside his own private world. A log rolled and crackled on the fire, as an owl hooted in the dark trees outside, its lonely voice carried away on a cool Pacific breeze. She continued to explain:

"Modern society betrayed this expectation when it replaced instinct with reason as the guide for how to bring up baby. Advised by books and medical 'experts,' parents stopped carrying their infants with them. Reason worked against the better judgment of instinct. Result: the evolutionary continuum snapped."

Dara sat upright: "I see what you're getting at. You could say we broke our agreement with evolution when reason decided we should put our babies down rather than carry them. Perhaps we should be up in arms about being put down?"

Maya agreed and elaborated:

"Because of the rupture in evolution, because your birthright expectations have not been fulfilled, generations of Westerners have grown up with a deep sense of something missing, of something wrong. As adults, you spend a great deal of your lives trying to fill that void with substitute experiences: successions of mother figures, lovers, status symbols, religions, careers, drugs, the drive for something new, something better—for *progress.*"

"I think I'm beginning to grasp how pervasive the effects are," Dara interjected. "Our social and economic institutions are built on unstable psychological foundations."

"That's exactly it," Maya agreed. "Ruled by intellect, driven by thwarted emotions and spiritual longings, 'civilized' humans live in evolutionary error. As adults, you spend your lives vainly striving to fulfill stunted expectations—starving for the missing in-arms experience."

"Sometimes evolution makes mistakes," Dara spoke the words slowly, offering them to the fire.

"This error may be responsible for both the greatest glories and the deepest shame of civilization," Maya continued. "It explains everything from the rampant failure of relationships and marriages, to the unrelenting need for progress and novelty; from the effectiveness of advertising, to criminality and addiction; from the drive for adventure and extreme sports, to the need for sexual conquest; from the desire to be noticed, to the creation of heroes or the compulsion to be martyrs; from the insanities of war, to frustrated quests for peace."

They fell silent for a few moments, as Dara tried to absorb the full impact of Maya's thesis.

"But how can this 'error' be corrected?" he wondered, breaking the silence. "The social implications are enormous. I just don't see governments and businesses willing to give up the drive for progress that has built fortunes and cities, that has driven scientific and technological achievements to almost miraculous heights."

"That's the nut of the problem," Maya agreed, and explained further: "Completely fulfilled people, guided by intuition and instinct and at home in their own skins, would not be so competitive. They would not be driven by an ever-growing need for new and better gadgets. Contented people make poor fodder for a consumer society mesmerized and manipulated by advertising and mass media."

"I see that now," Dara acknowledged, shifting his position. "If our evolutionary expectations were met as children, we wouldn't grow up driven by an unquenchable thirst for novelty and progress."

And then Maya offered a vision of a different world:

"With a proper balance between instinct and intellect, people can retrain themselves to live in a very different way—where the paranoia of competition is replaced by a more humane spirit of cooperation; where obsession with progress at any cost is replaced by a realistic respect for conservation; where aggression is replaced by tolerance; where dogma takes a back seat to dialogue; where power and greed are less attractive than service and contribution; where the intelligence in evolution is given full expression; where science is no longer at odds with the sacred."

Dara stared into the flickering embers in the hearth. Maya reached out for his hand, and looked at him with a mix of vulnerability and compassion that caught him off guard:

"The problem with Western reasoning is that it thinks it is the whole story. But it is only a part—a very, very small part—of the Great Story. The myth of reason is that in order to be right it must conquer, negate, annihilate or destroy all other stories, other ways of knowing."

She inched in closer to him, and said: "It is not just the indigenous peoples of the rainforest who see this. It is true for people living the old ways anywhere in the world. I have studied other cultures, too, and have found that we all share the same power of dreams."

She picked up a folder lying on the coffee table next to her, and pulled out a small document of about a dozen stapled pages.

"Let me read you an example, from an elder speaking for his people, a vanishing tribe of sea-faring nomads living in a remote region of the Malay Archipelago off southernmost Burma. They call themselves the Mawken, which means 'The Sea Drowned'—the Europeans called them 'Sea Gypsies.' One of their shamans described what happened when the British arrived with science and missionary zeal:

When reason meets dreams, the dreams evaporate, the dreams retreat. Reason is like a burning light, the harsh glare of the sun on the open ocean, without the shade of trees. In our little boats where we carry our tribal dreams, like cool, fresh water in fragile gourds, the incessant sun dries them up. And we perish. That is the way of things.

But what reason forgets, or doesn't know, is that although our tribal dreams may be destroyed, although our gourds dry up, our little fishing boats are still surrounded by the waters of the great ocean, and our dreams retreat there. Reason, even burning as the sun, cannot penetrate the ocean where the great dreams lie.

"Reason cannot penetrate the subliminal depths of dreams?" Dara wondered out loud.

"That's right," Maya replied. "And since all knowledge and all stories begin as dreams—including the stories of reason—when reason burns up the little dreams, when it obliterates feelings, it can no longer draw sustenance from the deep reservoir of the Great Dream. It is then, like a mad dog, that reason runs wild. This is what is happening today."

A burning log shifted and fell into glowing embers. Sparks flew into the room and vanished before hitting the floor. They both sat there in silence, watching the flames. After awhile, Maya spoke, still staring straight ahead at the fire:

"Do you see now what Darwin meant when he said that finding a balance with alien consciousness is so important?

It's not just each individual reconnecting with deep intuition and instinct. Our species as a whole needs to reclaim and honor the wisdom of the dream world. For so long, the indigenous peoples have been its custodians. But the power of reason is marching nearer every day, on track to obliterate the last vestiges of the dream. We need to connect with each other, with our dreams, before it's too late."

"Yes I understand that," he said. "And I see that something precious from humanity's heritage would be lost with the vanishing aboriginal dreamtime. But I don't yet see why that threatens the real world—I mean, the rest of the world. It would be a sad loss, to be sure, but wouldn't Western civilization continue to plod on its merry way?"

"Western civilization doesn't just 'plod.' It stampedes." Maya's tone was uncharacteristically sharp. "It wipes out everything else in its path. But make no mistake; the loss of indigenous wisdom—our knowledge of the living systems that keep this planet flourishing—will spell disaster not just for our way of life, but for yours, too. The force of conquest will eventually be its own demise. The signs are all around. You cannot have missed them: global warming, rampant pollution, population explosion, water scarcity, famines, disease epidemics, wars, terrorism, civil unrest, crime, economic collapse, ecological devastation."

"I've always thought of those problems as a phase, a kind of 'growing pains' civilization is going through. I've had faith that with advances in science and technology we will pull through," Dara said, trying to reassure himself as much as Maya. Her face darkened, and her eyes pierced into him.

"Then Darwin is right. We have a lot more work to do with you. He has planned an intensive session tomorrow. A staging post before our real journey begins."

Maya leaned over his shoulder and blew out a sputtering candle. "It's past three. Time to get some sleep. You are welcome to stay here if you like. Or I can call you a taxi." He looked at the sofa: "That looks mighty inviting right now."

She pointed him toward the closet where the towels were stacked, and told him to help himself to breakfast in the morning if he was up first.

He thanked her. Then, as she headed out the door: "Do you mind if I ask you something? I've been puzzled all week why an anthropologist would be involved in inter-species communication with dolphins."

She smiled: "You've probably begun to understand that I don't make hard distinctions between Earth's creatures. In my culture, we wouldn't know how to think about humans without also knowing the animals and plants that live with us and give us life. That knowledge must not be lost. The intelligence that seeks expression is in the world—in the animals, in the plants, in the stones, in the mountains, rivers, lakes, and oceans. You no longer understand that language. We do. Without us to teach you, the stones will always remain silent for you, the seas will keep their secrets, and the skies will never talk. That lost wisdom is what can save your world. But first, your world will have to change."

She winked at him as if to say, "Sweet dreams, amigo. It begins tomorrow with you."

14

First Awakening

D ara couldn't sleep. He tossed and turned all night as the events of the past week began to slide into focus.

It all started a couple of months ago, when he first noticed a radio anomaly streaming in from a very remote quasar. Then, when he double-checked the data, he discovered the strange radio waves were coming in from all over the universe—pointing to something highly unusual in the afterglow of the Big Bang. It seemed to contain an impossible pattern, as if the moment of creation was sending out a hidden message—a whisper from the birth of time.

And what about those strange lights in the sky the children saw? Where did they come from, and did they have any connection with the signals he was picking up? Then he'd gotten those weird emails. At least now he knew they'd come from Darwin via Maya; and, according to Maya, Darwin was somehow implicated in his recurring dreams about the Blue Universe. Everything seemed to have a common theme: *intelligence seeks expression.*

But another connection to Maya didn't quite fit. Dara thought back over the sequence of events. A few months ago, Bechtel had told him about a young doctoral student working on interspecies communication, and that she had joined the SETI team. What Dara hadn't known until last night was that Bechtel had made the initial overture to Maya. He had invited her to join the team, when they'd met at a conference. Nothing out of the ordinary there, Dara reminded himself. Bechtel was a consummate networker, always promoting the work of NASA and SETI.

Even so, why had Bechtel been so insistent that Dara go out to Hawaii to investigate her breakthrough with the dolphin? And why did he keep pushing for a report before the eclipse? The timing made no sense.

And then there was Bechtel's association with the FEW. Dara had known for years that his boss was an important link between NASA and the NSA. After all, he had a unique background in both space science and security intelligence. Before coming to NASA, Bechtel had held a high-level position in MI6, Britain's Secret Intelligence Service. It made sense that he would sit on the special joint NASA-NSA committee for space security and surveillance. But how deeply was Bechtel involved with the FEW and their mission to infiltrate and subvert groups committed to the evolution of consciousness?

Until meeting Maya and Darwin, Dara had shared Bechtel's passion for the Western mind. They both celebrated the power of intellect, and benefited from the triumph of reason. No doubt Bechtel had assumed—with some justification—Dara would side with reason and science in the paradigm wars against superstition and intuition. Both men had even joked that "Knowledge is power, intuition is ignorance. Therefore intuition is powerless."

Had Bechtel, then, sent Dara to Hawaii as an unwitting agent, on behalf of the FEW, to gather intelligence and help subvert the interspecies breakthrough? Is that what his report was intended to achieve?

But now, having met Darwin and Maya, he was beginning to see things in a new light. Governments and big business thrive by manipulating emotions that swirl out of the black hole in every unfulfilled soul. They don't want people to think or feel for themselves, and would do anything to protect the status quo—including ending interspecies research with a dolphin. All in the name of reason and progress.

When he finally stopped trying to sleep, Dara woke up to a disturbing realization: The FEW, no doubt backed by the might of the military-industrial-government complex, want to silence Darwin because he offers an alternative vision for the world: humans living together in peace while honoring all species. And, more to the point, *he seems to have a special code to help make that dream come true.*

He didn't know yet how they found out about Maya's breakthrough or Darwin's code, though it is common knowledge that the NSA spies on phone calls and emails of ordinary citizens. It was quite possible that the FEW had snooped on communications between Dara and Maya, or that Bechtel had read Maya's emails on Dara's computer. Either way, he knew now why they wanted to stop Maya's research. Tomorrow he would tell Darwin what he'd discovered.

15

A Threat to Reason

It was Darwin's last day. When Dara and Maya arrived at the aquarium the university administrator was waiting for them on the steps. He broke the news: An official had called to say a US military aircraft was on its way, and a transport team including a veterinarian would come by tomorrow with a truck to pick up the dolphin. Would they please make sure everything was ready.

As Maya's boss, and concerned about the dolphin's welfare, the administrator had asked a string of questions. He had called the FEW agent from last week, in a vain search for answers. Why did the government want to shut down Maya's research? Where would they take the dolphin? What would happen to him? Why the cloak and dagger secrecy? But the square-jawed voice at the other end of the line was noncommittal: They would ship the dolphin to some place in southern California, where he'd be taken care of. That's all the university needed to know.

"Oh, he did say that you should be here when they arrive, Maya. They want to ask you some questions about his eating habits."

Maya glanced at Dara.

"Sure," she said, turning back to her boss, "of course I'll be here. I want to make certain they treat him well."

They didn't want or need to talk to her about Darwin's food regimen, she thought. They had something else in mind. But she wasn't planning on being there—and she was damn sure Darwin wouldn't be either.

As soon as the administrator left, Maya pulled Dara inside the aquarium and locked the door behind them.

"What are we going to do? Has Bechtel found out anything more about what they're up to? How we can stop them? We've *got* to do something, Dara."

Maya was visibly anxious and impatient.

"I called Bechtel again this morning and left a voice mail. I asked him to get back to me with anything. I'll call my hotel in case he's left a message." Dara reached into his pocket for his cell phone . . .

"But it's already too late," Maya stamped her foot, the sound echoed off the tiled walls. "They're on their way as we speak."

"We've still got time," he said, trying to sound reassuring. "I think I know why they want Darwin, and I think we can turn that to our advantage."

"What do you mean? How?"

"Well, it seems pretty clear to me that the FEW want to separate you and Darwin because somehow they've found out about your breakthrough."

Maya's brow furled, showing her concern. She sighed and slumped into one of the white plastic chairs lined up against the wall. Behind them, Darwin glided silently in the pool. Dara continued, trying to sound reassuring.

"But I don't think they have any idea how far advanced you are. They probably think you have trained a dolphin to count, do some simple math maybe, read a few words on your blackboard, and possibly engage in a childlike conversations. They want to get him before he grows too clever, and word gets out to the public. That would be catastrophic for the guardians of reason, and a huge distraction for the government and its corporate backers."

"Really?" Maya wasn't convinced. "I don't see why my work should upset anyone in the government."

She stopped for moment, searching desperately for a way out.

"Look, Dara, I need to find out from Bechtel who is behind the FEW. If I can just talk to them, have a sincere heart-to-heart, maybe I can get them to see we pose no threat." She did her best to sound hopeful.

"Even if you could get to them, which I very much doubt," Dara said, trying to be understanding yet practical, "these are not the kind of people who respond to 'reasons of the heart.'" He paused, then continued his train of thought.

"More likely, they would feel threatened if they discovered their way of thinking is limited, that some other form of consciousness might trump logic. That would weaken their hold on power. The whole infrastructure of the political and corporate world stands or falls on the rule of reason—or at least their twisted version of it . . ."

"You could be right," she said sounding unsure. "But how does that help us, here and now?"

"We can switch dolphins, use one of the others you've had minor success with. When they test him, they'll get the results they expect. Meanwhile you and I will move the real Darwin somewhere safer. What do think?"

Still not persuaded, she said, "Dara, please don't take offense, but I think your theory is full of holes. For instance . . ."

He broke in: "I admit there's a lot about this whole affair that's a mystery to me. But there's one thing I do know."

"What's that?"

"It's not really Darwin they want."

"What!"

"Well, yes. They do want him, but they want something much more important to them . . ." his voice trailed off, as he tried to find the right words.

"I'm listening," she said, with a mixture of impatience and hope.

There was no easy way to say it, so he took both her hands, looked her straight in the eyes and said as calmly and as neutrally as he could:

"They want *you.* They want to stop you publicizing the results of your research." He paused. "I don't want to alarm you. But we need to get you away from here, too. Who else knows about your work?"

"I haven't published anything, Darwin made me promise not to." Suddenly she stopped, and slapped her hand over her mouth.

"Oh my God! *"That's* it! When I met Bechtel at the conference in Tucson last year, I told him about my work with dolphins. I didn't go into details, just that I was working on the hypothesis that, unlike humans, dolphins use intuition instead of reason. I even speculated that the dream world of indigenous peoples has its counterpart in the oceans. I remember telling him that I call dolphins and whales the 'guardians of dreams'."

"Well, clearly Bechtel is aware of your work. In fact, he's the one who told me about it. But I still don't see why he would be implicated in all this. True, he's connected with the FEW, but I can't imagine why he'd want to sabotage your research."

Maya pulled Dara closer.

"I also remember telling Bechtel about the Mawken Sea Gypsy, and I showed him the quote I read to you last evening, where he spoke about reason being unable to penetrate where the Great Dream lies—remember?"

"I do. But I don't quite follow you."

"Don't you see, Dara, reason cannot penetrate the *ocean?*"

"Now I'm really lost."

"When the Mawken shaman said that the Great Dream has retreated to the ocean he didn't mean that metaphorically. He meant it *literally*. The deep intelligence of the dream world has taken refuge beneath the surface of the seas. That's what I write about in my dissertation, *Conquest of Dreams.* That's what my work with Darwin is really about."

"You mean that cetaceans, the dolphins and whales, have become the custodians of indigenous tribal wisdom?" Dara struggled to put the clues together.

"That's only part of it . . . When I was in Malaysia with the Mawken, the shaman N'bai told me of the dream power stored in the ocean, and Darwin has spoken of the same thing." Her voice turned to a whisper:

"Dara, there's a power beneath the sea that dwarfs the force of reason, and would eclipse the power of governments if it ever surfaced."

And then with a noticeable tremor: "Someone in the government knows enough to link my indigenous fieldwork and my breakthrough with Darwin. *They've got my manuscript.*"

"That's why they're after you."

"Yes. Somehow they got wind of it, probably through Bechtel. But now they know the details of my work. They know how close Darwin and I are to discovering the last few steps that will lead to releasing the dream power from the ocean. They suspect, correctly, that Darwin is the critical missing piece." She stopped, now looking vulnerable and scared. "They're really serious about getting me, aren't they?"

He pulled her close and held her. The only sound breaking the silence was a gentle lapping from the pool, as Darwin slowly nosed through the water. Dara could feel her heart beating furiously through the softness of her breast. The fear was not hers alone: The FEW's storm troopers were closing in on all of them.

"It's all beginning to make more sense," he said. "At first, I thought your ideas on the natural instinct in children had spooked them, because tapping into that intelligence would undermine the culture of materialism. But now I see Darwin's involvement takes things a whole lot further. And I think they see it, too. The combination of your experiences with indigenous wisdom and your breakthrough with Darwin is the critical mass. They're afraid if they don't stop it, it will explode out of control and shatter their empires of power. But there's one thing I don't understand . . ."

"Oh . . .?"

"How can the deep oceans store intelligence? Oceans don't have brains, right? How could *water* threaten the corporate stronghold on the world? I just don't get it."

Impatient, she responded: "First, the dream power in the oceans doesn't 'threaten' governments and corporations. It would purify them. Yes, those obsessed with greed may be in for a shock, but once they let go of the fears that fuel their selfishness, they will experience the joy of liberation." Her tone sharpened more:

"I'm surprised to hear you say that the only place to store intelligence is in brains. I thought your dialogue with Darwin had poked a hole in that idea. Remember your emails: *Intelligence seeks expression.* And *matter stories.* The intelligence, the deep wisdom of the world, resides in nature. Matter itself tingles with the spark of spirit—*all* matter, including our bodies, the bodies of other animals, plants, rocks, mountains . . . and, yes, the oceans, too."

His eyes widened, as her reminder sank in. "Ah, so in some strange way, and for some unknown reason, this intelligence that you are calling ' the power of dreams,' the vanishing wisdom of indigenous peoples, is now accumulating in the oceans. Have I got that right?"

"Yes. And without shamanic training, I don't think you can fully grasp how it happens or what it means. Darwin can help you understand."

"Good." He took her hand, leading her to the edge of the pool. "I just want to make sure I'm connecting all the pieces. Let me run my theory by you and Darwin."

* * *

The dolphin greeted them with a high-pitched whistle. "You both need to settle down," they heard him say. "Your centers are dancing wildly like shrimp."

"Darwin, I think I know why they're after you and Maya. At least, I've got some of the clues. It came to me after a long conversation we had last night. Maya told me about the Great Dream stored in the ocean, and although I don't really understand it, it sounds like that could be a crucial missing piece. Maybe you can explain it to me."

"Tell me what you know, Stanford scientist," Darwin said. Dara thought he detected a touch of mock sarcasm.

He began listing what he knew, tapping out the main points of his theory one by one on the tiles: "First, Darwin, you said that the 'alien consciousness' I have been searching for with SETI exists in everyone of us—our repressed instincts and intuition.

"Second, Maya has pointed out that this 'preconquest' intelligence has the full power of millions of years of evolution behind it.

"Third, add to this Maya's experience growing up with the indigenous Ye'kuana: When preconquest intelligence is *expressed,* it is fulfilling, nurturing, satisfying. It doesn't leave people with a sense of 'something missing.'

"Fourth, if people naturally access and express their intuitive consciousness, they will experience themselves as whole human beings, and will not be driven to be consumers of endless products.

"Fifth, if that happens, the driving force behind corporate-dominated societies, the entire capitalist system, would be seriously threatened.

"Sixth, if corporate dominance fails, the most powerful governments in the world, which depend on corporate financing, would also fall—and governments will not peacefully give up their life-blood.

"Seventh, now follow the trail back: Governments will fall if corporations fall. Corporations will fall if consumerism falls. Consumerism will fall if the people feel fulfilled (no longer driven by an endless desire to fill their lives with needless products). The people will feel fulfilled it they follow their innate, instinctive wisdom in childrearing. They will achieve this if they dethrone reason as the only guide to action by cultivating their innate intuitive capacities. But the forces at the top will not let this happen. Their survival is at stake.

"Bottom line: The myth of reason is under siege—and the crucial link is *children,* who have not lost connection to their dreams. If we stop treating our children as dumb blank slates, and instead relate to them as bearers of millions of years of intelligent evolution, then they will grow up into psychologically healthy adults *expressing that intelligence.*"

He glanced over at Maya to let her know he'd "got it."

"As these children grow up, they will not be driven to fill an unfillable void at the center of their lives. They will not need, nor will they support, the consumer system that keeps corporations and governments in power. *That's* what the government is afraid of. They're scared that if Maya's work gets out to the public, people will turn away from the god of reason that drives the myth of material progress. The wielders of power rely on the divisive nature of dialectical reason to keep the masses mired in the illusion of needing more, *perpetually* needing more." Dara threw his head back and pushed his chest forward, looking pleased with himself.

"That's quite a speech, Mr. Spaceman," Darwin said, and again Dara didn't quite know how to take the comment.

"You've clearly come a long way since we first met. You are a fast learner—of course, you've got an exceptional teacher," Darwin nodded toward Maya. "But you are still missing some very important pieces. For now, know you are right about this: What's driving the government's interest in our work, and why they're sending men to stop it, has everything to do with the conflict between different forms of consciousness. And this, in turn, has everything to do with the quality of relationships between humans and their children. But there's more to it."

Dara leaned forward, listening.

"The publication of Maya's work alone would not be enough to turn around the minds or change the behavior of ordinary people in sufficient numbers. Many books already criticize the consequences of over-reliance on reason and the myth of limitless progress, calling for a new kind of consciousness. Much of your popular New Age literature is precisely about that. But more than revolutionary words and ideas will be needed. And not just more or different actions. Something else is needed to bring about a fundamental shift in perception—and that something is now incubating in the oceans. The piece about the dream world and the ocean *is* the critical missing element in your scenario. But we have more work to do before filling in the gaps will mean anything to you."

Darwin spurted a jet of water across the room to the clock above the door. "See. We really don't have much time left. Let's get cracking, as you say."

Dara stoop up, thinking Darwin meant for him to get out and start doing something practical—like finding a truck for the getaway.

16
Maya's Hypothesis

"*How do you know what is real?*" Darwin launched right into the big question, directing it at Dara, who was distracted by Maya tugging playfully at his toes under the water. She surfaced and swam over to the side of the pool to listen and watch her two friends in dialogue.

"Well, that's precisely what science has been exploring for hundreds of years," Dara responded confidently. "Previously, people believed whatever the Church told them, based on ancient myths from the Bible. Then science replaced religious superstition and wishful thinking by using a rigorous method for investigating reality . . . "

"Oh, and what is that?" Darwin asked.

Still confident, Dara replied with an emphatic single word: "*Testing.*"

"Please explain."

"Science doesn't accept anything without evidence. We *look at the world and ask questions.* In short, we do *experiments.* That's the scientific method: begin with a hypothesis, then test it by observing the world closely. Whatever shows up is nature responding to our questions. We then publish the results so other scientists can double check what we've discovered. In other words, we test the results of our tests. That's how science is done. That's how scientific knowledge accumulates, pushing back veils of ignorance. *That's* how to find out what is really real." Dara sounded please with himself.

"Nice try, my friend," Darwin applauded by slapping his flippers together. "I'm all for testing beliefs to see if they truly match reality. Anything else would be delusional. But tell me this: *How* do you observe the world?"

Dara was surprised. "Well, isn't that obvious? We observe by using our senses. We look, we listen, we touch, we smell, or we taste. There's no other way to gather information."

"Ah, just as I thought," the dolphin replied. "Your scientific method relies on the five senses. Unless you can detect and measure something, it can't be real. Is that it?"

"Well, to be quite honest, I'm not sure about that." Dara sounded less confident. "I suppose it's possible that something could exist beyond what the senses can detect. But then it would remain forever unknown. Science is about knowledge. We focus on the parts of reality that can be known. Anything else is left to poets and mystics or worse, to magic and superstition."

Darwin moved in, nose to nose, with the scientist. "'Knowledge is power. Intuition is ignorance. Therefore, intuition is powerless.' Is that what you mean?"

Dara's faced blanched in surprise, and before he could reply to this latest example of mind reading, Darwin continued.

"The first statement is accurate, but the rest couldn't be more wrong. Yes, knowledge leads to power. But only if what you know is real. So, let me ask you again: *How do you know what you know is real?"*

Dara felt uneasy now, suspecting he was being led into a trap. The dolphin eyed him intently, as though peering through his body into his soul. The scientist felt a strange, paradoxical, sensation like a block of ice boiling in his gut. Simultaneously, he felt both excited and unnerved by what might be coming next.

"I'll give it to you straight," Darwin announced. *"Science is the greatest superstition of all."*

Dara was flabbergasted. He expected to be challenged, but didn't expect such an extreme condemnation of science.

"Surely, you must be joking, Mr. Dolphin," he quipped. "You can't be serious." Dara was confused.

"I'm very serious," Darwin replied, and you're not as confused as you might think." The dolphin chuckled; taking another opportunity to remind the NASA scientist that communication can take place directly from mind to mind.

"In fact, I'm quite sure you already know what you need to know. It's just that you don't know that you know. My job is to help you discover the difference between what you know you know, what you know you don't know, and what you don't know you don't know." Darwin laughed, as Dara jumped through mental hoops trying to keep up with the philosophical gymnastics.

"It's always a good thing to stretch the mind," Darwin joked. "Nothing like a good mental workout, especially early in the morning. Now that you've limbered up, let's continue. I want to know *how* you get knowledge through the senses."

"That's easy enough. Psychology and neuroscience show us how the senses feed information into the nervous system and then up to the brain. Once in the brain the signals are processed and transformed into experience. The senses act as windows on the world."

"Well, you've just committed a basic scientific fallacy," Darwin exclaimed. "You think you have explained something, but you've only pushed the problem deeper. You haven't even begun to explain *how* the brain 'transforms' nerve signals into *experiences.* And that's crucial. How does that miracle happen? Can you or your science explain that?"

In his heart, Dara knew this was coming. After all, he had been forewarned in yesterday's conversation about assuming that events in the brain can produce mind.

"I admit I cannot explain the transition from brain processes to conscious experiences. That's really a question for philosophers, not for scientists."

"Exactly my point," Darwin chirped. "Now we're getting somewhere. Science is based on two very shaky *metaphysical* assumptions. First, that reality is made of dead matter. Second, that the only way to know anything is through the physical senses. These two assumptions are hopelessly entangled, and they strangle science when it tries to explore the very instrument of knowing itself—namely, consciousness."

Then he went directly to the heart of the issue: "Look, all of science—*all* knowledge, without exception—must, I repeat *must,* occur in consciousness. There is no other way to know anything. But how do we explore consciousness itself? How can we gain knowledge about the mind?" Darwin paused, allowing his protégé to reorient himself in this borderland between science and metaphysics.

"Think about it: *How do we know how we know?*"

This last question sent Dara's mind spiraling—turning inside out, or was it outside in? He took a deep breath to steady himself. But he'd been through enough by now to realize the trap had sprung. Defensively, he tried to dodge the jaws of defeat by drawing the conclusion himself.

"Ok, I get the point. We can't use any of our senses to observe the mind, yet science relies on the senses." He hesitated, as if he was about to commit blasphemy: "Consciousness is *extrasensory.*"

"You've got it! Science can tell us *absolutely nothing* about the mind because the mind is not a sensory object. We cannot measure consciousness." Darwin wriggled through the water, flapping his tail wildly.

"Let's see if I can wrap this up," he said, "using the logic I've learned from humans: Science is based on the senses. All knowledge resides in the mind. But the senses cannot access the mind. Therefore scientific knowledge is inaccessible to science. It's a paradox: *Scientific knowledge has no foundation in scientific knowledge!*"

Dara felt thoroughly disoriented. His mind refused to digest this information. He heard the words all right, but their significance melted away. Nevertheless, the message was getting through at some level. He felt that the entire wonderful edifice of science, and all that he valued about it, had now fallen under a cloud of uncertainty and suspicion.

He let out a long sigh as a familiar handhold gave way—his belief in the supremacy of science. The loss, however, came with a sense of liberation.

Poolside, Maya, who had been silently witnessing the interchange, paying close attention to Dara's emotional state, finally chimed in.

"Science is superstition because it believes that the senses are the only true guides to knowledge. And there is absolutely no scientific evidence for such a belief."

Not since his graduate studies at Stanford had Dara's mind been stretched and challenged to its limits. He felt mentally exhausted and exhilarated.

"So, where do we go from here?" he addressed both Darwin and Maya. His resignation was obvious. Then, sounding almost desperate, he followed with: "Where do *I* go from here? As a scientist, what am I to do?"

Both Maya and Darwin swam over to the NASA scientist in a gesture of comradeship.

"Just as well you have decided to join our little troupe," she reassured him. "Darwin has plans for you. And when you're through, he says you will have become a true scientist—equally at home in the world of spirit and matter."

* * *

The dolphin beckoned the two swimmers toward him with a tweak of his snout.

"This morning's session is just a steppingstone to what I really want you to understand. We're about to enter territory familiar to Maya because of her training as a shaman. But you, my NASA friend, may have more difficulty opening up to the profound implications of what I'm about to reveal." He gave Dara a reassuring nudge to the chest.

"Again, I'll begin with a statement that may shock you. Just listen. We do not need to work out all the twists and turns today. In fact, it will be much better to let the insights simply percolate in your dreaming mind."

Dara readied himself for Darwin's next message.

"*Reality is an illusion.* The world you think you live in is not the real world. It is a mirage, a system of images and ideas generated and manipulated by the people your society turns to for leadership—the powerbrokers who hold the reins of government, businesses, education, and the media.

"I call the scenario 'Maya's hypothesis,' because she was the one who told me about 'The Reality Illusion'—referring to the systematic brainwashing of the masses by a combination of biased history, government propaganda, politically-correct academics, organized religion, controlled news media, the entertainment industry, and, of course, advertising and PR. Not only is your science built on a false foundation, but your awareness of reality itself is shaped and distorted by invisible Powerbrokers. Your civilization is hypnotized. Duped."

Darwin checked in with Dara to ensure he was getting the message. The NASA man listened with an increasing sense of revelation and unease as he imagined a vast orchestrated conspiracy operating behind the scenes on a global scale.

"Modern Western culture–mistakes the shadows in the cave for what is real. The 'cave' is your collective trance, your paradigm, and the 'shadows' are the images, sounds, and ideas that bombard you from the moment of birth, all the way through school and college, and throughout the rest of your life as you absorb the distortions of television, radio, and the Internet, feed off the packaged reports in newspapers and magazines, and turn starry-eyed at the movies—all designed to make you obedient consumers of the never-ending stream of new products and gadgets you never really need in the first place."

Darwin paused again to let the message sink in. Then he said something that surprised Dara even more.

"I know this all sounds like one great global conspiracy. But that's part of the illusion, too. I'm not denying that certain groups of people do conspire and manipulate to serve their own selfish agendas. That's been going on for as long as human history. No, what I'm talking about goes much deeper than conspiracy. *It's a conflict in consciousness itself.* A battle between two opposing psychic forces." Darwin extended a flipper, touching Maya's arm, and elaborated.

"As you know, Maya recently completed her thesis *Conquest of Consciousness,* where she explains how Western civilization is infected by a virulent mental virus called postconquest consciousness—*reason.* It has robbed generations of children of their evolutionary birthright, turning your civilization into an evolutionary error. That error now threatens the welfare of all other species on the planet. We need to correct it by balancing over-zealous reason with preconquest feeling and intuition. But the psychic battle is an illusion, too. It's unnecessary. It doesn't need to happen. There is a way to integrate reason and intuition, head and heart, by learning to *feel your thinking.* The modern West needs to listen and learn from the ancient wisdom of indigenous peoples."

Darwin indicated that Maya should take up the story of conquest consciousness at this point.

"One of the most subversive accomplishments of tyrannical reason," she began, "has been the manipulation of emotions by the mass media. It is common knowledge that they are little more than mouthpieces for their corporate owners. In cahoots with governments, the media have systematically deluded the masses using compelling hypnotic images and other consumerist distractions—all aimed at keeping the people from cultivating their own evolutionary potentials. Instead of thinking for themselves, instead of trusting in their own native intelligence, entire generations of an emerging global civilization have been lulled into a false sense of security believing that reality is what science and the mass media tell them it is."

It was tough to hear this, but Dara did his best to let it all in. Maya had more to say.

"My hypothesis is that the reality you now live in, believe in, fight for and die in, is a massive illusion. Yes, it may seem highly rational and even emotionally satisfying—at least on the surface. But if you were to stop and pay attention to what you are truly feeling in your heart, you would realize that your lifeblood, your vitality, the energy that charges your soul, is being sucked out of you at every turn—from childhood to old age. You don't live your lives. You live *their* lives, the facsimiles and illusions fed to you from cradle to grave. And that illusion is destroying the world. It is unsustainable."

"I understand that civilization cannot keep going at the current business-as-usual pace," Dara finally interjected. "But what have the Powerbrokers in government and business got to do with the psychic battle between reason and intuition?"

"The Powerbrokers are the servants of reason," Maya explained. "They are caught up in the illusion as much as anyone else. That's what makes this problem so difficult to solve. They are masters at manipulating the illusion *from within the illusion*."

At this point, Darwin took over again: "They have made you believe in a topsy-turvy world, where reality is but a dream and dreams have no place in reality. Given such a paradox, it is not at all surprising that Western civilization is headed for catastrophe. The irony is that in order to get back in touch with reality, your people will have to turn to their dreams for inspiration. Not the manufactured desires so often portrayed as 'The American Dream'—which is really an unattainable nightmare."

Darwin spun around the two swimmers, emitting loud chirps, for emphasis. He continued:

"No, the dreams you need to heed and cultivate are the deep whisperings from your soul, the dreams that speak to you at night, or in alternative states of consciousness. The *real* reality is the world you enter through the dreamtime. This is the deep wisdom of indigenous peoples throughout the world. It is the natural consciousness of my people, the dolphins and whales. Our mission is to restore reality back to the dream, and dreams back to reality."

He fell silent, and his two companions joined him in a wordless aquatic ballet. All three floated together in the pool, letting the words that had been spoken seep into their cells and activate their souls.

* * *

But underneath, something troubled Dara. He recalled that Darwin had said this morning's session was just a steppingstone to a deeper revelation. How much more could his already strained mind take?

17

Deep Knowing

Darwin opened the afternoon dialogue, with Maya and Dara seated by the edge of the pool. He addressed Dara:

"Our first task, my friend, is to undo years of scientific brainwashing. As long as you are dealing with the mechanics of the world, science has great value. But now it is time to deal with the noetics of the world. This is true not only for you, it is true for your culture as a whole."

Dara admitted that the word "noetics" was new to him.

"Yes, I'm sure it has not been part of your scientific training. Nevertheless, many people in your culture have been open to the noetic way for centuries. I will teach you more about noetics as we get to know each other better. For now, think of it as a kind of super-intuition." The dolphin smiled:

"It's what I use to connect with you directly mind to mind. It's what Maya's people use to communicate with nature." He brushed his dorsal fin against her legs dangling in the water.

"'Noetic' is an ancient Greek word. It refers to a kind of knowledge beyond the normal senses and reason. It is immediate, direct, and powerful—a 'hot line' to spiritual reality."

"So 'noetic' is a way of knowing?" Dara offered, "above and beyond how we ordinarily know things?"

"Well, tell me how you ordinarily know things," Darwin asked.

The NASA scientist thought for a moment: "People use different ways of knowing. Some say *'seeing is believing'*—preferring to stake their knowledge on the evidence of the senses." He slapped the surface of the water, as if to say, "There, if you can see it and touch it, it's real."

"However, the senses can be fooled—for instance, in optical illusions or hallucinations. So some people prefer to build up knowledge by *thinking clearly and coherently* according to the rules of logic. We call this kind of knowing 'reason'."

Maya chimed in: "Then, again, some people feel that both the senses and reason—even when used together—are very limited ways of knowing. The senses can reveal only shapes, colors, sounds, tastes, and so on; in other words, quantities and qualities of external, physical things. But so much of what we know belongs to our interior lives—for instance, our pleasures, our pains, our meanings, our values, and our loves. These cannot be grasped by the senses. And the best reason can do is give us abstract concepts *about* our interior lives—frozen snapshots taken from the flow of living experience itself."

"That's correct," Darwin agreed, leisurely swimming back and forth just beneath the feet of the two scientists. His sleek body, gliding through the water, generated small waves that fanned out and encircled the three of them.

"Most of the knowledge derived from the senses and reason is about *doing* things. Philosophers call it 'instrumental' knowing. It is usually focused outwards, on manipulating the external world to suit your purposes. That's not bad. It plays a great part in your day-to-day survival. Doing is important, no doubt about it. But knowledge about how to do things is only part of what you need to know in life."

The dolphin came right up to Dara and pointed his snout up at him.

"Unless your actions in the world are guided by a deeper—some might say *wiser*—mode of knowing, they will not serve or satisfy your deeper needs, the needs of your inner life. For that, you need a different way of knowing—*noetic* knowing."

He checked to see if Dara was following him. Maya knew exactly what Darwin was saying, even if it was different in her own language.

"Unlike instrumental knowledge, noetic knowing is about *being* or *becoming* rather than doing," Darwin continued. "It is directed inward at the unfolding of consciousness or experience itself. Noetic knowing dives right into the heart of reality by tapping into the universal web of connections."

Darwin noticed a furrow in Dara's brow. "You seem a little puzzled Stanford?"

"I'm trying to get a clear grasp of what this noetic way of knowing is," he said. "I'm not sure how it works."

"How it *works?*"

"Yes. My senses work if I open my eyes or listen with my ears—by picking up light or sound waves. And reason works by linking concepts and ideas together in coherent ways . . ." He paused. "But noetic knowing? Where does it come from?"

"Ah. Good question. First, notice you are trying to understand noetic knowing with words and concepts. That will never do. You've got to *feel* it. Instead of trying to understand what I'm saying, pay attention to the flow of feelings in your body, and to the quality of lightness in you mind.

Dara allowed himself to just *be,* to let his body open up like an antenna tuned into unseen currents and messages streaming through the air around him. For a moment, he stopped trying to figure things out, and entered into a state of "flow" familiar to him from running and playing sports. Darwin continued:

"We need to integrate all ways of knowing—sensory, rational, embodied, intuitive or noetic. To live successfully in the world, we need to unlock the code that gives voice to the silent 'language' of nature. That's our task as seers and shamans. It is my job to teach it to you and Maya."

He stopped, then told Dara he would say more about the noetic code at a later time.

"For now," he continued, "just know that some of your greatest visionaries have understood parts of the code. I can name a handful: quantum physicist David Bohm, renegade philosopher Arthur Young, dream psychologist Carl Jung, Jesuit paleontologist Teilhard de Chardin, as well as William James, the first great psychologist—and far back in your history, a mystic called Plotinus, and before him the great philosopher Plato. In different ways, these people knew that to live masterfully in the material world you have to see beyond surface appearances, into the deep intelligence of nature. For that you need noetic vision. It's the only way to enter the dream world."

Darwin paused. "It's also what you will need to help me escape so I can fulfill my mission."

He called the scientist closer and whispered:

"I never try to shift someone's mental furniture unless I have their permission. Are you willing?"

Dara agreed without hesitation.

18

The Evolutionary Sequence

"Let's begin by putting the story of science in perspective," Darwin announced to Dara.

"Remember the email where I said 'stories matter and matter stories'? Well, all we have are our stories. All of human life, all of *life* itself—in fact the entire universe—is the unfolding of stories within stories. Together, this infinite network of stories is the cosmos singing its own lullaby. Aboriginal peoples speak of it as the 'dreamtime'." He looked up at Dara with a sad smile of compassion.

"But some stories get disconnected from the dreamtime, from the deep wisdom of the world. And I'm afraid the story called modern science is one of those."

Darwin moved in closer and held the scientist's gaze with a single, sharply focused eye.

"Starting from the beginning, then, what would you say is the most up-to-date version of the science story? Use the slate and chalk." He indicated the small blackboard Maya had used earlier in her experiments. "Show us what leads to what?

Maya's eyes widened in anticipation and she turned to the Dara. He caught her glance, but was distracted by a loud noise from outside. He looked up at the skylight: A helicopter buzzed overhead, low enough to fill the aquarium with the roar of its engine. He waited till it passed.

The dolphin remained motionless, not even a ripple lapped against the poolside. The only sound was the almost imperceptible flipping of digits on the large clock above the door, amplified in the tiled chamber—and the low hum of the helicopter that had landed nearby. Time itself seemed to slow down, extending and thickening the present moment.

* * *

Dara ponders Darwin's question, and after a few minutes he chalks on the slate:

quantum ‒ subatomic ‒ atom ‒ molecule ‒ life ‒ mind ‒ science

"Good," Darwin comments. "You have neatly summarized the story of science in seven easily identifiable stages." He pauses and turns to Maya. "What do you notice about this sequence?"

She looks intently at the chalkboard: "Well, I always thought the universe began with the Big Bang. Where's that?"

"You're quite right," Dara acknowledges. "About fourteen billion years ago, the entire universe appeared in a mighty explosion. So yes, the Big Bang is the starting point for science, but the theory has some problems."

"For one thing, no-one knows just what the Big Bang really was," Maya adds, "and certainly, no-one knows how or why it happened."

Darwin interjects: "What scientists do know, however, is that the moment it happened the universe flared forth in a blaze of light. And light, as the great Einstein showed, consists of infinitesimal packets—much, much smaller than the point of a pin—called 'photons.' You can think of photons as points of light. Another word is 'quantum.'"

Darwin turns to Maya: "So, when Dara begins the sequence with 'Quantum' that is not a problem for science." He paused. "What else might be, though?"

Maya studies the slate, and eventually says "You know, putting 'Science' at the end just doesn't feel right."

"Okay, let's look at the sequence," Darwin suggests. He squirts a jet of water at the slate. "What's missing?"

Dara and Maya cock their heads simultaneously, listening. The loud hum has stopped. Outside, they hear voices, someone is shouting, but they can't make out the words. Darwin leaps up and belly flops. The smack of his body against the water wins back their attention.

Maya's eyes sparkle. "*God!*" she shouts out. "Spirit, the Creator. That's what's missing. How does the story of science account for that?"

Dara is quick to respond: "It doesn't. There is no room for God in science. Deities belong in stories told by religions." His tone implies "check mate."

"But surely science must make room for God? Who or what caused the Big Bang?"

"Ah, you're pushing science beyond its limits," he says, without any sense of yielding the point. "Even the most ardent materialist will admit that science cannot probe back beyond the Big Bang. All the laws of science, including everything we know about space and time—*all* scientific knowledge—evaporate once we get to the Big Bang. Science humbly remains silent in the face of such metaphysical unknowns."

"So the story outlined by science is incomplete."

"How so?"

She picks up the slate and chalk and begins writing. "It should look like this:

> ? ▬ big bang ▬ quantum ▬ subatomic ▬ atom ▬ molecule ▬ life ▬ mind

". . . and the question mark is God?" Dara asks rhetorically. "Smart move. But not smart enough. Science seeks *explanations,* and God explains nothing."

Maya looks startled: "I'd say God explains *everything.*"

"Not as far as science is concerned," he shoots back. "To say that God intervenes in the world is to say 'and then a miracle occurs.' But miracles are *gaps* in explanation." He looks at Maya to see if she understands, then continues.

"Look, science admits that beyond the Big Bang is a big mystery. That's all. Cosmologists remain completely neutral on whether that mystery translates into God. According to science, the entire universe, every nook and cranny of reality, began with the Big Bang. In any case, whether or not some divine force caused the universe to come into being, there's no need for the God hypothesis *once it got going.*"

Darwin circles in the pool, generating concentric waves that rebound off the walls creating a distinctive interference pattern of crests and troughs.

"And it all got going from the primordial quantum field—a fiery sea of chaotic, random flashes of pure potential. That's what you're saying?" Darwin asks.

"Precisely."

"So, instead of God to account for the magnificent order we find in nature, science tells us blind, purposeless evolution is the creator of all the wonderful living forms that populate our world," Darwin anticipates Dara's conclusion.

Again the NASA scientist agrees.

Darwin continues: "And the arrows in your sequence represent the process of evolution from one stage to the next. Taking it step by step, does anything catch your eye?"

Maya shifts, looking a little bored. "I've got to say I'm beginning to wonder where all this is going."

"Me, too, I'm afraid," Dara owns up. "I'm getting anxious. Shouldn't we be doing something practical to get you and Maya out of here?" He points to the door, shuffles his feet and begins to stand up.

"I can see your impatience. But I'm asking you to stay with me," Darwin's tone is calm. "I could very easily just say what I think is wrong with your outline of the science story . . . tell you what is missing. But that would rob you of an opportunity to learn something. Learning always—*always*—comes from within. There is nothing here you don't already know. My job is to work with you to uncover your own inner knowing—your *noetics*. I want you to discover this for yourself. Remember, you are here to learn about alien intelligence. And this is the best show in town."

Dara sits down again, and Darwin moves in closer, creating a series of waves and ripples around the scientist's feet: "I know this may be a little tedious for a NASA scientist, but please bear with me. We are moving carefully toward a crucial realization. Are you still with us?"

"Yes," he says sheepishly.

"Good. Step 1: Do either of you have any problem with the notion that subatomic particles, such as electrons and protons, may have evolved from the quantum soup?"

"No. Not in principle, even though I've no idea how it actually happens," Maya admits.

"I agree. I just don't know all the details," Dara nods assent.

"Right. The details are best left to the physicists," Darwin says. "What about atoms evolving from subatomic particles, or molecules evolving from atoms?"

"Nope. That seems pretty basic physics," they agree in unison.

"Okay. And what about life evolving from molecules?"

"That's fine, too. Basic biology seems to have that one wrapped up." Dara adds: "Except for some gaps in the details, biologists have a plausible account of how life evolved from DNA and proteins."

"So now we come to mind," Darwin continues with the sequence. "Do you have any problem with this part of the story: mind evolving from life?"

"Not really. It all does seem to hold together," the astrobiologist is confident. Maya is silent.

"Then you've missed the sleight-of-hand. Actually, it's a slip that many scientists and philosophers make—probably unaware they've basically inserted a magic formula into science amounting to 'a miracle occurred'."

"How so? What's the miracle?"

"Let's see if you can spot it. Tell me in your own words how consciousness evolves from life."

"That's easy: It evolves from the brain." Dara repeats the standard assumption in science. Despite his previous dialogue with Darwin, old habits of mind die hard.

"But where does the brain come from? What's it made of?"

"Hmm. Neurons."

"That's right: brain cells. Basically, the scientific story is that the brain evolved from primitive nervous systems, made up of collections of these cells. But neurons are not essentially different from any other type of cell in the body."

Maya brightens: "What Darwin's getting at, I think, is that if we accept the story of science, then brain cells would have nothing special whatsoever that could lead to consciousness. That's the weakness in your sequence, Dara." She circled the arrow leading from "Life" to "Mind."

"You're circling the bulls-eye," Darwin encourages. "Can you now say why that's the weak point?"

"I think I can," she says. "If consciousness means anything, it means purpose, it means intentionality, it means feeling or sentience. And none of this can come from the story of science if it begins with the quantum as a random, completely purposeless entity. And that's what modern physics says the quantum is—something purely random. Purely physical, dead stuff."

"*Complexity*," Dara announces, as if that one word explains everything. "That's what evolution does: it creates more and more complexity. The brain is made up of about ten billion cells interlinked in incredibly intricate networks and pathways. Nothing else in the entire known universe approaches the complexity of the human brain."

The voices outside are louder now—closer.

"I grant you that," Darwin says teasing Dara, "*if* we conveniently ignore dolphins, whales, and elephants." He squirts a jet in the direction of the two humans, and continues: "But you're still invoking a miracle if you claim that complexity of brain cells produces consciousness."

He pauses, and the NASA scientist sees vague images forming in his mind—highly complex, dynamic networks of axons, dendrites, and synapses enmeshed with billions of connections.

"I bet what's going on is that when you try to imagine the vast interconnections between billions of brain cells, your mind draws a blank, or comes up with a very fuzzy picture indeed. You then think that the fuzziness is consciousness. And that's the error. Your consciousness creates the fuzziness, not vice versa."

Dara's face runs through a series of expressions, from deep puzzlement to a flickering of enlightenment, back to a thoughtful frown.

"So *that's* what you say is missing from the standard scientific story—the link from brain to mind?" Dara concludes, trying to speed up their session. "I should have suspected that, especially after yesterday's conversation." He sounds a little less skeptical, but still unconvinced.

"Yes. Don't you see: If the brain could produce consciousness, then whatever the brain is made of must have consciousness, too. But if brain cells have purpose, intentionality, feeling, and so on, then there's no reason why other cells in the body shouldn't have purpose or consciousness, as well."

Dara follows Darwin's logic, but it clashes with his ingrained belief system. He objects:

"Scientists are adamant that cells, whether in the brain or anywhere else in the body, do not have consciousness. And even if they could bring themselves to admit this, they would certainly insist that the molecules or atoms making up the cells do not have consciousness."

"But exactly the same problem arises at every stage, right back along the sequence," Darwin elaborates. "There must be some kind of consciousness at every stage."

"That is precisely what the standard story does not accept," Dara acknowledges, beginning to see the force of the argument. "Science denies that cells, molecules, or atoms could have even the slightest trace of consciousness or purpose. Scientists think that's absurd. Certainly, they do not recognize any intelligence back at the beginning of the evolutionary sequence."

"And that is precisely why the standard story of science does not make sense," Darwin replies. "That is why 'a miracle occurs' in the gap between 'Life' and 'Mind.'"

He playfully flips a piece of flotsam in the air and catches it on his beak.

"Life—even brainy life—cannot evolve into consciousness *unless some trace of consciousness already exists* in the cells of the brain. And that could happen only if consciousness also exists in the atoms and molecules of the cells . . . all the way down, and all the way back in evolution. The bottom line, as you like to say, is that the quantum must have consciousness, too." He pauses to let the idea sink in. Then adds with emphasis: *"The quantum must have purpose."*

"*And* there must have been purpose at the Big Bang, too!" Maya exclaims, obviously delighted with the insight. She slips out of her jeans and dives into the pool, gracefully breaking the surface, arms outstretched in front, guiding her like a torpedo to the other side. She shouts across joyously: "An *intelligent* Big Bang!"

Dara recalls the pattern he saw in the three-degree radiation streaming into his computer from all over the universe. It certainly *looks like* there could have been some kind of intelligence right at the moment of creation.

"If you want to include consciousness in your worldview," Darwin advises, "then you need to change your story. You need a new paradigm—a paradigm with purpose built in right from the start. And that's the journey we're about to take. Are you still on board?"

He studies the slate, and draws a line with his finger from Maya's question mark all the way to "Mind." He looks up at the clock.

"Count me in."

"Good. The next step is to come up with an outline for our new story. And here it is." The words appear clearly and distinctly in the minds of both scientists.

light — subatomic — atom — molecule — life — self-conscious — spirit

"What do you notice about this? What's different?"

"Well I'm surprised how much of it is the same," Maya says, scooping a handful of dripping hair back behind her shoulders. She walks around the pool toward Dara who was now chalking the revised sequence on the board.

"Only a few minor changes," she observes. "You've put 'Light' in place of 'Quantum,' and instead of 'Mind' at stage six, you've put 'Self-consciousness.' At stage seven, you've replaced 'Science' with 'Spirit.' That feels much better. But I'm not sure I understand why you changed 'Quantum' to 'Light,' or how you get from there all the way to 'Spirit'."

"Remember I said that 'light equals photon equals quantum'? That's the first point. Why 'Self-consciousness' instead of 'Mind'? Well, since we've just seen that some form of mind or consciousness must go all the way back to the Big Bang and Quantum Light, it's not Mind as such that emerges after Life, but a special kind of Mind—a mind that is aware of its own identity. Self-reflexive mind: Self-consciousness."

The dolphin emits a loud tweet. "Your third point, getting from Light to Spirit, is a much deeper issue. It's the adventure of evolution. And that's precisely where we're headed."

Suddenly, a loud, impatient hammering on the aquarium door interrupts the dialogue. Dara jumps to his feet and turns to see Graham Bechtel slapping on the glass. He looks agitated.

19

Liberation

"I've been trying to reach you for days," Bechtel announced the moment they let him in. His blue eyes glared out from beneath a shaggy mop of blond hair. He spoke rapidly, without stopping for breath.

"Left messages at your hotel. Where the hell were you? Look, while you've been fooling around out here with a big fish, the sky has fallen in back home. Literally. That anomaly you spotted is probably not a quasar after all. Nor is it an artifact or equipment malfunction. We still don't know what it is. But it's coming at us from all directions, and it's definitely got some very important people upset—very upset . . ."

"And nice to see you, too," Dara interrupted. "Take it slowly, Graham. First, what are *you* doing here?"

Bechtel pulled down on the ends of his navy blue blazer to straighten it out, and tucked his pinstriped shirt into neatly pressed cavalry-twill pants. His disheveled appearance contrasted sharply with his usual dapper English public-school look.

"That's what I'm bloody well trying to tell you," he snapped. "A couple of days ago, a swarm of Marines or Navy SEALs, or some such, stormed into our place and shut everything down. Slam! They've put SETI on ice, for

Christ's sake! Best I can make out it's connected with the strange lights those kids up in Marin saw crashing into the Pacific."

He hardly paused to take a breath.

"Then reports started coming in from around the world that balls of light were falling into other bodies of water: the Indian Ocean, the North Sea, Lake Geneva, Gulf of Mexico, the Atlantic—everywhere. Never dawned on me those fireballs could be connected with your anomaly, but seems they might be. It doesn't make any sense."

Bechtel grabbed a towel and mopped beads of sweat off his face.

"If they suspect we've been visited by UFOs, then why shut SETI down and turn it over to the FEW? That's *our* territory. You'd think we'd be the first to call in if they really believed it was a 'contact.' Anyway, you spoke with those kids, right? I'm still waiting for your report. I'd like to know what the hell is going on . . ."

Dara didn't even have time to open his mouth, Bechtel kept talking:

"Your name came up. Then I heard them say something about a 'dolphin woman' in Hawaii. They're especially interested in your fish," he nodded breathlessly at Maya. "From what I could catch, seems they plan to take him back to California. I suspect they want to send him out to investigate whatever it was that fell from the sky. I tell you, Dara, *none* of this makes any sense to me."

"You still haven't told us why you're here," Dara said slowly and deliberately, trying to calm him down.

"Oh. Sorry ol' boy. Came to warn you, of course. They didn't seem like a very friendly bunch. Besides, if there *is* a connection between your anomaly and the fireballs, NASA needs to know about it. And what about the dolphin? What have you found out? I need a full report on that, too."

"It's all very complicated," Dara finally got a word in. He was not at all sure about Bechtel's explanation for this unannounced visit. Maya surreptitiously toed him on the ankle. Instead of giving away any details, Dara said:

"But since you're here we sure can use your help. I'll fill you in later. Right now we need to find a large flatbed truck and a winch."

* * *

It was twilight by the time they got hold of a four-wheel pickup with a loading pulley, borrowed from Campus Maintenance. Maya told the provost's office they were moving the dolphin to a smaller tank for easier maneuvering when the collection crew arrived. She explained carefully to Dara and Bechtel how to handle Darwin without injuring him. But getting the dolphin onto the truck was trickier than expected.

After a few false starts, the three of them managed to slide Darwin out of the pool and onto an oilskin tarpaulin. But getting him up onto the flatbed was much more difficult. At one point, the sling holding the dolphin slipped and he nearly fell onto the pavement. They continued to struggle with his slippery bulk, and when, finally, they got him onto the truck the two NASA scientists jumped up front and Maya climbed into the back with Darwin. Dara immediately revved the engine, and they headed off campus.

Once they got moving, Dara informed his boss they were taking Darwin to a safe haven. Bechtel looked surprised, but made no objection. In fact, he encouraged the rescue.

"Just be sure to cover your tracks. You really don't want to mess with the FEW. They are a determined bunch. I should know."

This last remark seemed odd to Dara. "Have you had a run-in with them?" he asked.

"Well, because I'm on the NASA-NSA joint committee, a couple of agents from the FEW paid me a visit after the mysterious fireballs over Marin. Asked if we'd noticed anything else out of the ordinary in the sky lately. Told them about your quasar anomaly, and then they asked to see the report. I said you were working on it, but that you were in Hawaii following up on a possible interspecies breakthrough. They seemed rather interested, and kept pressing me for a report on that, as well."

He glanced over at Dara, and then looked away.

"Said this was top priority and couldn't wait. Then, when I couldn't reach you by phone, they sent me out here to get you. Made it plain I was to find you and get your report to them asap." He paused. "Putting it bluntly, ol' chum, they scared the shit out of me."

Dara listened but didn't respond. They headed straight for the coast, driving north and into the oncoming night. Maya sat close to Darwin, making sure the soggy, thick gray blankets kept him wet and cool. Dara began bringing

Bechtel up to date about his experiences with the dolphin during the last week.

"Clearly, the FEW know about Maya's breakthrough with Darwin, and they see it as a potential threat. Why else would they be on their way here? They want to stop him." He hesitated, not sure how much he should reveal to Bechtel. But since they were alone and on their way to release Darwin, he took the risk.

"Look, no doubt, a breakthrough in interspecies communication would be momentous, likely to spark widespread debate in the academic world. Probably even get the public excited. I can see the headlines now: 'Dolphin Talks to Scientist.' But there's more going on, and I think the FEW have gotten wind of that, too."

Again he hesitated and looked over at Bechtel.

"Go on . . ."

"Well, my guess is they are more concerned about the *content* of Darwin's messages—not just the remarkable fact that he can communicate with humans."

"What content?" Bechtel sounded surprised.

Dara caught Bechtel's eye. They held each other's gaze for a moment, then Bechtel repeated: "What kind of content? Tell me what the dolphin has to say? What could be so alarming?"

"From what you've told me, not only is the NSA deeply interested in all kinds of foreign intelligence, but the FEW, in particular, has the job of keeping tabs on any developments in consciousness—anything that might upset the status quo."

"Yes, that's their mission in a nutshell," Bechtel agreed.

"Well, Darwin's breakthrough with Maya is just the precursor to a far greater shift in consciousness with global implications," he paused, ". . . as you know from Maya's report." Dara fished for signs that his boss had intercepted or spied on Maya's emails. Bechtel didn't take the bait.

"She sent her thesis to you, ol' chum, not to me. That's why I'm here. I need to report the details of her breakthrough to the FEW. Why do you think they're so interested in it? What did you find?"

Still not sure what Bechtel did or did not know, Dara decided to test him a little further.

"I think the FEW, and the government honchos behind them, don't like the prospect of Darwin's message about intuition being more powerful than reason getting out to the public . . ."

Bechtel eyed his colleague, but didn't say a word. Dara stared straight ahead. Both men bobbed in their seats as the red Toyota rolled through the suburbs. Eventually, Bechtel broke the silence.

"Is *that* it? Are you really serious, Dara? We both know that intuition is imprecise—in fact, it's really ignorance and, therefore, has no power at all."

He thought for a moment, then went on:

"Of course, I knew the outlines of Maya's research . . . she told me about it at Tucson. I'm aware of her thesis about intuition and dreams. She even told me about some Eastern shaman who has a silly idea about dreams retreating into the ocean," he guffawed. "But we're scientists, we know better than to take such primitive superstitions seriously. Right?"

Dara decided to go full bore.

"I know it sounds crazy, Graham, but Darwin has supplied the piece that was missing for me on why we're being tracked by the FEW. Yes, it has to do with what he calls the 'dream world' simmering in the ocean. We're about to tap into that power, and when we do it will change the lives of hundreds of millions, perhaps billions, of people who will enter a new state of consciousness."

Bechtel's face widened into a disbelieving sneer. Dara continued:

"Darwin says that a vast evolutionary heritage of buried intelligence will reawaken on a global scale—beginning in the world's children."

The truck rumbled into the night along narrow side roads heading toward the coast. Maya had given them clear directions on how to get to Shelter Cove where they would liberate the dolphin. Through the open sliding rear window of the cab, Dara could hear Maya singing to Darwin, a soft lullaby in her native tongue. He turned back to Bechtel, and elaborated.

"According to Darwin, seems like we're about to enter a whole new phase in evolution. The emergence of intuitive awareness will bring about a radical transformation in the collective mind of humanity—how people experience themselves, how they relate to one another, how they engage with the rest of nature, and how they experience the deep relationship between matter and spirit."

Dara felt his colleague's unbelieving eyes burn into him.

"If I wasn't hearing it with my own ears, and seeing you with my own eyes, I'd swear you've gone off the deep end,

Dara. You still look sane enough, but what the devil are you talking about? You sound like one of those New Age weirdoes that are the bane of our lives in California. As far as the academic establishment is concerned, it's bad enough we should be spending millions of precious tax dollars searching for extraterrestrial intelligence among the stars, but the slightest hint of association with UFOs, or any of that New Age gobbledygook, is just too much to take. I let you out of my sight for a few days, and look what's happened,"

Bechtel held up his fingers and started counting off:

"You're talking to a bloody dolphin. You're 'hearing' telepathic communications. You're talking about an 'alien intelligence' in every one of us. You're talking about some mysterious 'dream world' buried in the deep blue sea about to rise up and swallow us all . . ." He threw both hands up in despair.

"And to cap it all, you're talking about 'transforming the collective consciousness of humanity'—not to mention spooky ideas like 'spirit in matter.' You're a bloody *scientist*, for christsake! Where's your sense of objectivity and realism, old boy? Have you completely lost your marbles?"

Dara's eyes stayed fixed on the bright beams slicing through the darkness, watching for potholes. They'd left the paved road, and the four-wheeler bounced over ruts and mounds. He slowed, checking on Maya and Darwin in the rear-view mirror. Without turning his head, he responded to his companion.

"Has it occurred to you—*old boy*—there's a noticeable shortage of objectivity and realism in your own account of what brought *you* here. You came rushing across the Pacific in a government helicopter to warn me about a bunch of bad guys from a supposedly top-secret government agency called the FEW—all because some kids saw strange balls of light drop into the ocean? Explain, please, how all that ties together."

Bechtel was silent for a moment, then:

"I thought I already did. The FEW want your report on the mystery fireballs and on your quasar anomaly—and when they heard you were in Hawaii investigating an interspecies breakthrough, they wanted a report on that, too. So they sent me to get it."

He shot a glance at the driver: "Use your head, dear chap. Occam's razor, remember? Always look for the simplest explanation."

"But *why*?" Dara threw back. "Why would they want the reports? If they suspect these events are connected, then that suggests they *are* concerned about Darwin's message—about the power of dreams building up in the ocean. *You* may think it's crazy, but *they* don't."

He paused, ". . . and, as a matter of fact, neither do I. I'm beginning to see that reason has its limits . . ."

Bechtel interrupted: "Then I'm glad I found you—hopefully in time to bring you back to your senses before you completely flip out on us."

Dara didn't respond to the taunt. In silence, he wondered what Bechtel was leaving out of his story, and why. Something didn't fit.

An hour or so later, the truck came to a halt in a small, isolated cove on the north shore, miles away from Honolulu. Even with four-wheel drive, it struggled in the wet sand as Dara tried to maneuver his payload closer to the water's edge. An almost full moon illuminated the cove, casting strange shadows. Mighty waves, capped with luminous foam, roared and jostled as they tumbled into land.

Maya, Dara, and Bechtel lowered Darwin into the surf, and without a word the dolphin vanished into the open sea. It happened too fast. Dara wasn't prepared for his new friend and mentor to leave without saying goodbye. He put his arm around Maya's shoulder, and she snuggled in.

"Don't worry, Dara, he'll be back by dawn."

20
Science and Spirit

Maya and Dara spent the night curled up together on the floorboards of an abandoned beach shack. Bechtel preferred to spread out on the seat of the truck. Before turning in, the three sat around a small campfire and debriefed on the past few days' events. Maya was surprised to hear Dara defend Darwin's notion of "alien consciousness," as he argued with Bechtel about the different forms of consciousness that live in everyone of us. The NASA boss insisted that if they were referring to instinct and intuition, these were just either conditioned reflexes or undeveloped forms of cognition. No doubt they still persisted in modern humans, a relic of our more primitive origins, but then reason evolved to give us a much more serviceable handle on the real world.

"Intuition leads us to believe in superstitions," Bechtel declared, "and instinct is just programmed habit, the body on automatic pilot. All it does is free up the mind for the more important business of thinking rationally. You can't be serious about intuition being a higher state of consciousness."

Dara assured him he was serious. If it wasn't a higher state of consciousness it was certainly an "other" form of consciousness.

"In a way you are right, Graham: Intuition is undeveloped—but not in the sense you mean. It is not just 'primitive thinking.' It is a faculty of consciousness we all have, but it's tragically underused. We are *trained* not to use it. Our entire education system conditions us to rely on reason. And that's why intuition is 'alien' to us."

The campfire crackled as Dara threw on another piece of driftwood. He shifted position as the smoke swirled around and stung his eyes. The smell of burning logs mixed with fresh sea air reminded him of childhood picnics at the beach with his family.

"In my case, with my people, *reason* is the alien form of consciousness," Maya stepped in. "In my culture, our most important knowledge comes from the dream world. We see it in visions, when the plants and the animals and the stones speak to us. It is highly practical and serves us in healing, in guiding us to find food, in making decisions for the good of the community. Our dreams are messages from the spirits, and we share them with each other every day. When we dream, we dream for the collective."

Bechtel was curious about Maya's background, and she told him about her childhood among the Ye'kuana in the Amazon rainforest.

"I discovered that the way of the dreamtime is far more powerful than the force of reason—especially when we turn to the plants and animals for help."

Bechtel asked if she wouldn't mind elaborating.

"Have you heard of *ayahuasca*?" she asked. "It is a ceremonial brew we make from special plants. When we drink it, doors open to knowledge that obliterates the limits of the mind. At such times, reason cannot withstand the full impact of the dream world. Ayahuasca restores the clarity of the spirit mind. Many other plants and animals, some toads for example, can guide us, too."

"You mean like marijuana or LSD—hallucinogens?" Bechtel asked, and Dara knew from his tone the question was meant dismissively.

"Perhaps you can find out for yourself by participating in a ceremony sometime?" she said. "You don't have to take my word for anything."

Bechtel didn't pursue the matter. Instead, he turned to his colleague and asked if he was "into all this stuff." Dara said he was "into" the true spirit of scientific inquiry: having an open mind, testing a hypothesis, and being willing to be wrong.

"For instance," he said, "I couldn't say whether a dolphin is as intelligent as you or I without some kind of test. Based on personal interactions with him, however, I am quite sure he is at least as intelligent as we are—probably more. I also know that has been communicating with me in a way I've never experienced before—through some kind of mind-to-mind connection. I don't know how it happens. I don't have to. All I need to know is what I experienced."

He summarized his dialogue with Darwin, and outlined the evolutionary sequence.

Bechtel listened, and when Dara finished speaking, asked: "Do you really believe that evolution begins with light?"

"Yes. And here's why," Dara said, picking up a stick and marking the seven stages in the sand.

"Take it stage by stage, level by level, beginning with what science tells us lies at the basis of reality. Some spiritual traditions also have an evolutionary story—but they use different language. The common term in both, however, is *light.*" He then described the seven stages for Bechtel.

"Stage 1: *Light/Quantum void.* This is what science calls the 'zero-point energy' field. It is the source of everything. First to appear are *photons of light.* A tiny fraction of this is what we see." He wrote in the sand: *"From void to light."*

"Stage 2: *Nuclear forces.* Light transforms into subatomic particles, such as electrons and protons—the building blocks of atoms." He scraped out the words: *"Elementary forces appear."*

"Stage 3: *Atoms.* The universe's creative power blossoms into different kinds of atoms—the first things to exist with individual identities." He wrote: *"Atoms appear."*

"Stage 4: *Molecules.* Atoms join together to form molecules . . . the beginnings of chemistry and relationship." And he wrote: *"Matter appears."*

"Stage 5: *Cells/Life.* When certain large molecules become complex enough they produce the first living cells." He wrote: *"Life appears."*

"Stage 6: *Minds/Self-consciousness.* When cells evolve into brains, self-consciousness emerges—the birth of individual egos." He checked to make sure Bechtel was following him, then wrote: *"Minds (egos) appear."* He paused.

"Maya, you'd better take over from here. I'm really not clear what happens next." She agreed.

"Stage 7: *Spirit.* As consciousness evolves, we experience a greater sense of interconnectedness. Minds evolve from separateness to communion and enlightenment." She took the stick and carefully spelled out: *"Spirit is realized."*

And then she whispered into the fire: "Spirit matters, and matter spirits."

The three looked in silence at the words etched into the dirt. Bechtel seemed to be scanning them for some obvious error. Dara spoke:

"This is the story of cosmic evolution from quantum light to spiritual enlightenment." He scribbled in the sand:

light ← energy ← atoms ← matter ← life ← mind ← (spirit)

"With one glaring exception, Graham, this sequence is based on widely accepted discoveries of modern science. Few scientists would squabble with the general overall evolutionary sequence—though many would, and do, argue over the fine details between any two stages. The glaring exception, of course, is the endpoint of the sequence: *Spirit.* Instead of 'spirit,' scientists want to put something like 'language' or 'culture' or 'society.' Some even put 'science' there—as, indeed, I did initially. But now I'm playing with this new idea."

Bechtel shuffled his feet, burying them in the sand, and inadvertently smudged out the last couple of letters from the word "Spirit."

"So?" Bechtel challenged.

Dara reflected for a moment. "So . . . *the quantum is the source of purpose in the universe,*" he emphasized, then paused as if surprised by what he had just said. "I never thought about it this way before I met Darwin. The photon of light is like a messenger from the gods."

Behind the dunes, the vast Pacific tumbled onto the beach in muffled thunder. Bechtel poked at the seven points marked in the sand. He didn't say anything at first, then: "What's all this got to do with our search for alien consciousness?"

"I'm beginning to understand that science itself must open up to the reality of spirit and intuitive intelligence," Dara said. "That is an amazing turnaround for me. I don't expect you to share it, Graham. But maybe, just maybe, we've been looking too far afield for intelligent 'alien' life. If Darwin is right, then some form of consciousness permeates every aspect of nature. To most humans, certainly to scientists like us, these other forms of consciousness would seem 'alien'." He took a breath.

"The point of all this, Graham, is that we may not need to search for intelligent life beyond our own planet. The mystery of consciousness lies here right in front of our noses."

"More than that," Maya added. "Indigenous wisdom and mystics of all cultures teach us that consciousness, at its highest levels, is universal. That means you can tap into your so-called extraterrestrial intelligence if you first learn to tap into *terrestrial* intelligence—by tapping into the very spirit of matter itself."

"How do we do that?" Dara asked.

"That's what Darwin wants to help us with. That's what comes next."

21

The Noetic Code

"Bechtel's gone!" Dara shook Maya awake. "The bastard's vanished." He pointed through the window to where the truck had been. Maya straightened her blouse and tucked it into her jeans. The early morning light beamed into the beach shack through cracks in the walls.

"I'm not surprised he took off." She yawned.

"What are you talking about? Why would he come all this way to warn us about the FEW and then leave before dawn?" Dara's confusion was visible, accentuated by his disheveled hair.

"I've been watching the two of you together ever since he showed up," Maya said. "There's something about him that makes me uneasy. It's clear to me he's not being honest with you. I was hoping to spend more time with him today to get a better sense of the man."

Dara said he'd known Bechtel for about six years. He was a competent scientist, but his real talent lay in management, wheeling and dealing with anyone who could fund his work—from government agencies or universities to for-profit businesses or private philanthropists. Dara never really liked how Bechtel put personal advancement above the pursuit of knowledge.

"Why would he sneak off like that? He's left us stranded. Abandoned." Dara sat down on one of the remaining planks from the shack's dilapidated deck. He squinted into the early morning sun.

"Maybe he's frightened?" Maya mused. "Perhaps he got a glimpse of what you were trying to say about the dream world?"

"Bechtel? Never."

"Stranger things have happened." Maya threw a knowing glance at Dara. "People do open up, you know—even if they think it's against their better judgment." Dara returned her smile.

"I can tell he values your intelligence," she said. "In fact, you are a beacon for him to follow. But after last night, he realized you have moved into unfamiliar territory. I think that scared him and he had to get out."

She repeated: "He got a glimpse of the dream world."

Dara didn't understand.

"He didn't know that's what he saw, of course. But he had no control over the feelings stirred up in him. And feelings are gateways to the dreamtime. If you are trained in the ways of my people, you can choose to open those gates—or to keep them shut. Without such training, you have no option but to retreat—or go crazy."

She pulled Dara to his feet. "But that's *his* lesson for now—if he recognizes it. In the meantime, *you* are due for your next lesson with Darwin."

* * *

The sun was already above the horizon, casting long shadows as they walked down to the water's edge. The old wooden boardwalk creaked beneath their feet. Patches of the walkway, half-buried by shifting sand, sprouted spiky grasses through the cracks. The invigorating scent of ozone electrified the air and crackled in their lungs.

Maya moved ahead, navigating the remains of the narrow wooden path through the dunes. The curves of her hips in tight jeans excited him, and he remembered the warmth of her body next to his in the night. The more time he spent with her, and the closer he got to her, the more he felt his heart was opening. Something about her, just her presence, was changing him in ways he didn't understand.

When they reached the shoreline, Maya put two fingers in her mouth and let out a loud, high-pitched whistle. As if on cue, Darwin shot up out of the water and swam toward the beach, guiding them over to a small lagoon surrounded by brilliant white rocks. The pool was pure azure reflecting the cloudless sky. His sleek outline perfectly visible against the ribbed white sand carpeting the bottom of the lagoon, Darwin invited the two scientists into the water. They took off their clothes and dived in.

"I'm happy to see *you* are still with us, Stanford Scientist, and that *you're* not afraid of feelings."

He really can read minds, Dara thought. He knows about Bechtel.

"You may call it 'mind reading' if you like," Darwin chuckled inside Dara's head, "but I prefer to call it 'body reading.' Obviously, your friend is no longer with you, that's plain to see. I can 'hear' from your insides that you, too, have some strong feelings going on." Dara felt his face flush as Darwin playfully nudged Maya against him.

"Feelings are a wonderful thing," the dolphin said, "an opening to the light. And that's what we will explore today. But first, I want to talk to you about the noetic code."

"The noetic code?" Dara repeated, wanting to hear more.

"Yes. Last night while your friend was sleeping, I entered his dream world and listened to his memories. The people hunting us believe you already know about the code, and are worried Maya may have already deciphered it. They don't know what it is, of course, and they don't even know what to call it. But they know enough from Maya's notes. For instance, they know I am a custodian of the code, and that I'm working with Maya as my apprentice to pass it along. They know, too, from her records of our conversations that the code is capable of unlocking a power within the sea. And they suspect that all of this is somehow connected with the mystery fire that fell from the skies."

"You know about the mysterious lights, then?" Dara tried to hide the fact that he was surprised yet one more time by Darwin's apparent omniscience.

"What in heaven's name were they? And are they connected with this power in the sea you keep talking about?"

Darwin explained that during the night he had reunited with his soul-companion, a female dolphin he called Cassandra, and together they "tuned into" the ocean to draw from it the power and the wisdom he would need to fulfill his part in releasing the Great Dream. The fire from the sky carried important information. From time to time, the code changes with shifts in the constellations of the stars, and from time to time the Great Dream needs updating—a realignment with our sun and moon. Decoding the message from the sky was part of his task.

"But that is not your concern," Darwin said. "I can take care of that. It is just a matter of correct timing." The dolphin turned to Maya. "But you, with Stanford's help, have the task of taking the code to the people. When the Great Dream rises, the people must be ready." He circled around her, clicking loudly. "Have you got your recorder with you?"

After years working in the field, Maya always carried a pocket-sized recorder, to "catch her thoughts on the wing," as she described it to Dara. Reaching out of the water to her jeans lying on the rocks, she pulled out a small digital recorder, about the size of a pack of gum, and hit record.

"Add this to your manuscript. It's an important part of what the people need to know." And Darwin began speaking:

"What is the noetic code? Well, as you know, the genetic code is the language of the genes, the chemical blueprint for life. It's what makes a mouse a mouse, a man a man, a woman a woman, a dolphin a dolphin. It codes for *'grow thyself.'*

"The noetic code, however, is the language of the soul. It guides the development of our interior life. It codes for *'know thyself.'* One codes for growing, the other codes for *knowing.* Noetic evolution is 'growing through knowing'."

"Remind me again what 'noetic' means," Dara asked.

"It's a kind of super-intuition, a highly evolved state of consciousness." Darwin explained further:

"Stanford, whenever science probes nature, the best it can do is understand the mechanics of the world. Scientists talk about 'unlocking nature's secrets,' as if mathematics could decode the language of the wild. But nature loves to hide. Numbers reveal only one layer of the mystery. The deeper layers must be accessed using noetic consciousness, direct soul-to-soul contact. It opens the way to a new kind of knowledge—*noetic* science."

Darwin fell silent as he let the new information settle into the NASA scientist's mental database. Dara struggled to grasp hold of what it all meant.

The dolphin angled his flippers and flapped them to create a series of overlapping waves. Dara felt the ripples lap against his chest, and they seemed to silently convey messages from the ocean itself. The waters of the lagoon felt alive. In a way he could not put into words, the sea seemed to be whispering to him in a language beyond the grasp of intellect. Wordlessly, his body responded and understood, and Darwin's teaching began to make more sense.

"That's the noetic code," Darwin continued. "It translates the wisdom of the world soul into messages we can understand in our own souls. It is a way of listening through sacred silence. We learn this code by *feeling,* not by figuring." The dolphin gently nosed the NASA scientist in the chest.

"The noetic code, then, is a key that unlocks the relationship between mind and body, between consciousness and matter," Maya sang out, raising her slender arms jubilantly toward the sky. She pirouetted like a nymph, dancing with the water, and Dara, feeling her exhilaration, silently shared the sense of celebration. He could feel, even if only dimly, the deeper meaning of Darwin's teaching.

"Yes," Darwin agreed. "It is a bridge between the spiritual and the physical. Mastering the code will transform your people from lone, isolated selves into full-hearted beings living with a deep sense of connection—with all other people, with nature, with cosmos, and with spirit."

Maya slowed her acrobatics, and glided over to Dara. She put her arms around his neck and, looking him straight in the eyes, whispered softly:

"The first step, then, to cracking the noetic code is to learn about the way mind and body are united through feeling." She smiled.

"Quite right." Darwin said. "Through feeling we open up to the body's own consciousness. We can then learn to understand that language, logic, and the senses are all expressions of the body's native intelligence. And through paying close attention to messages from the body, we can enter the gateway of intuition. Then, we can learn the language of the soul."

Man and woman, now nose to nose, entered each other through the windows of their eyes, and for a timeless instant they held the world inside them. They felt each other's smile.

Darwin swam up to join them, and shared the moment of intimacy. Then he gently nosed his way between both scientists so that they now looked into his eyes. He held their gaze, focusing their attention. He was about to reveal something special.

"When we learn to read the code that translates inner being into outer action, one of the first things we notice is the importance of compassion. Our personal inner being is connected with the outer world through feeling. And this 'outer world,' we soon learn, is actually an inner world, too."

He singled out the NASA scientist with a special look that said, "Listen carefully to what I say next."

"The 'outer' world is alive with its own currents and patterns of feelings. It is populated by other sentient beings with whom we are related by sharing feelings. 'My' feelings flow and mingle with 'your' feelings in a dance of communion. That's the way the world works."

Dara felt something shift inside him. At first it seemed to rise up from the pit of his stomach, then circulate in his chest. He was surprised to *feel* it had a distinctive color—kind of greenish black. It was a knotted ball, about the size of his clenched fist, highly charged with emotion. He recognized it as a painful knot of memories long buried inside from early childhood.

"We are not individuals, alone in the world," Darwin went on, "connected only through physical links. That's just a common illusion." He repeated, "We are not alone and isolated—we are, instead, nodes in an ever-changing web of relationships. Each one of us is a meeting place where the universe converges and takes on a unique identity. And through these connections we actually create each other."

The knotted ball moved up to Dara's throat, choking his Adam's apple. He burst into tears, and sobbed like a baby.

"Relationship itself lies at the foundation of who we are as individuals. We are not simply in relationship—but, in a very real sense, we *are* relationship."

Darwin nudged Maya to one side to let the NASA scientist's sobs do their work. After a while, Dara felt the ball of emotions begin to dissolve, seeping out of his body through his tears. The ocean did the rest. He floated motionless for a short eternity, then heaved a deep sigh, scooped up a handful of water and splashed it over his face. He licked his lips, and they tasted of salt. He laughed. Darwin let the moment of release complete itself, then resumed:

"We co-create each other in a never-ending dance of self and other, of I and you. If you want to find a meaning in life, this is it. You need look no further."

Maya pressed her face against Dara's and kissed him. "We become ourselves when we love."

Darwin agreed. "Cracking the noetic code comes down to this: It is learning the language of love, knowing and living our profound interconnection. It is knowing, ultimately, that all is One."

Darwin fell silent. Maya switched off the recorder and put it back in her jeans spread out on the sun-bleached rock.

"I know that's a lot to take in at one go," Darwin continued conversationally. "Remember, though, these are only words. They prime the rational mind for other ways of knowing."

The dolphin pulled away and swam out to the mouth of the lagoon, performed a backward somersault, and torpedoed directly toward them.

"The body needs to *move*," he announced. "Too much staying still is bad for you. Get out and shake up your centers. Dance in the sun. Make love. Feel the force of your soul coursing through your bodies. Then come back. We have just begun the journey."

* * *

The afternoon sun hung high in the sky, baking the rocks and the sand. They ran along the beach, shouting and yelping, delighting in the freedom of their bodies. Maya sprinted ahead, her long mane of black hair trailing behind. He followed, keeping a steady pace, watching her slim figure dance through the shallow back flow as the tide reclaimed its waves from the slanted shore. An invisible thread seemed to connect them, pulling him along.

When he caught up with her, she had found a shaded alcove under an overhanging rock. They spread themselves out on the warm sand, breathless, hearts thumping, feeling the electricity of life pulsing through every pore. Eyes closed, he reached out and fingered the sand until he touched her hand. A current of energy circulated between them, catapulting him into a wordless conversation with her body.

Time stretched out to a vanishing point, transformed into the eternal rhythm of the waves lapping against the rocks. In deep silence, the cells of his body communicated with hers, and he knew, in a new way, the meaning of communion. Not only with Maya, but with the sand beneath them, with the rocks surrounding them, with the soft air brushing the hairs on his skin, with the ocean whispering its secret messages.

An image flashed through his mind, a sense of incomprehensible vastness. This moment, *now*, held tremendous significance—as if all time were somehow enfolded in this present experience. For an instant, he felt connected with the entire history of evolution, and everything carried a single message—*"listen!"* He listened to the blood pumping through his veins. He listened to the gasping of Maya's breath. He listened to the breeze blowing in off the sea, caressing their bodies. He listened to the sliding of the sand beneath them. He listened to the sky and heard its mysterious echo. And when he listened he heard a now familiar message:

"Intelligence seeks expression."

But this time, it was a message beyond words. He *felt* it. Now he knew that the search for "alien intelligence" must begin closer to home. Not in distant galaxies, but within the depths of the oceans, deep in the matter of the Earth itself—deep within himself. And he glimpsed a continuous connection between this moment and all the countless billions of moments since the first instant after the Big Bang. His task—the task of humanity—was to learn to listen to the echo from the birth of time.

22

Quantum Consciousness

"Your centers are glowing," Darwin said with noticeable pleasure when they returned. "You are well prepared for your first lesson in light."

He explained they were about to enter the quantum wonderland. Most of the experiences would be familiar to Maya from her vision quests, he told her, but much of the terminology would not. To Dara, he said the opposite:

"In your case, Stanford, the terminology will be familiar, but the experiences will be new."

Back in the lagoon, the water was warm and as inviting as a hot tub. The sea shimmered clear to the horizon beneath an almost cloudless sky. A few wisps of cirrus decorated the heavens behind them, high over the island. For all practical purposes, they were alone in the world, yet Dara had never felt so connected. Standing chest-deep in the water, letting his forearms float and drift like tentacles of seaweed, feeling its mighty and friendly power, he slowly turned around to face the land and was dazzled by its picture-postcard beauty.

A carpet of fine golden-white sand spread out in a semi-circle, leading off to the dunes dotted with palm trees, bushes, and tall grasses. The air, purified with ions, and smelling of natural incense wafting from the bushes, was relaxing and healing. "This is Paradise," he said to himself, and for the first time in recent memory, he felt perfectly calm and open, ready for whatever the remarkable dolphin was about to reveal.

"My job is to talk to you on two levels at the same time," Darwin said, "on the level of intellect and the level of intuition. You must listen and *understand* the first; you must feel and *experience* the second. Your job is to balance the two so that blending understanding and experience transports you to a new level of knowing."

He invited his two colleagues to float on their backs, with their faces open to the sky, eyes closed. Without a sound, he glided between and beneath them, supporting the man with one flipper, the woman with his other. Dara had never before felt the flesh of a dolphin against his own skin. It was surprisingly smooth and rubbery, firm, yet strangely gentle. The dolphin turned and pressed his snout against the scientist's forehead.

Darwin picked up on a question lurking in the back of Dara's mind for some days.

"Stanford, I know you've been puzzled not only by the fact that I can communicate with you, but also by *what* I communicate: How does a dolphin know so much about science and philosophy?"

Dara opened his eyes to see if anything about the dolphin—his eyes, his snout, his flippers—might provide a clue to his mind-reading ability.

"The short answer is that for many decades my people have been able to tune into the electromagnetic signals your species sends around the globe and out into space. Much of it bounces off the planet's upper atmosphere and returns to the oceans of the Earth. We've been reading your radio and TV signals all this time, and more recently we've learned a great deal from the data transmitted via undersea cable and by satellite for your Internet and World Wide Web. We have divided ourselves into 'Monitor Pods,' and my pod chose to follow your science and philosophy broadcasts. I've been particularly fascinated by developments in quantum physics."

The dolphin pulled the two scientists closer together. Eyes closed again, Dara felt Maya's arm and shoulder touch his. A tingle of energy electrified his body. The idea flashed through his mind that human flesh embodies the relationship between spirit and energy.

"Yes." Darwin acknowledged the intuition. "There is a connection between spirit and matter. To understand this we need to begin with a basic, simple question: What is a quantum? It is often called a packet of energy, but it's really a bundle of pure *action*—the smallest possible unit of physical existence. It's unsplittable. Always remains whole. You could think of it as the source of everything—an inexhaustible well of potential energy giving birth at every moment to all that is."

Darwin paused, building to a crescendo.

"And how does the quantum perform this miracle—creating the physical world from unimaginable, swirling clouds of pure possibility? The short answer is *consciousness*."

Maya's eyes widened and she turned to Dara to see his reaction. He continued listening.

"The quantum is a very strange physical entity, more like a ghost than anything you are familiar with. It has no mass, no charge, occupies no space, and experiences no time. It exists in a weird wonderland beyond the grasp of reason and imagination—a world where matter seems to evaporate into wisps of possibility."

Dara was familiar with these details from his studies in physics, but he was hearing them in a new way. All the while Darwin was "speaking," Dara felt an unusual sensation rippling through his body, flowing in from the other two and back out to them. At first he thought the current of energy entered him just at the points where his body connected with Maya's and Darwin's. But then he realized they were, in fact, no longer touching. Somehow, Darwin had imperceptibly separated them, so that now each was again floating freely.

"At the quantum level, everything is interconnected. The universe is a unified web of *unbroken wholeness.* Physicists call it 'nonlocality.' Every part of reality is entangled with every other part. This is a stunning revelation . . ."

"For scientists, maybe," Maya added, "but shamans and mystics have known it all along."

"Quite right," Darwin agreed. "But remember millions of people living today have grown up educated to believe the world consists of separate things—from atoms to people. And togetherness, when it happens at all, is either due to chance or hard work."

Darwin dived down away from them, out of sight, yet the next part of his message came through with increased clarity. Dara was no longer "hearing" Darwin's words in his head, but throughout his entire body. He was *feeling* new insights.

"Nonlocality means there is no such thing as empty space separating anything. It's all one entangled web." Darwin explained. As a NASA scientist, Dara agreed that Darwin's description of quantum reality was basically accurate.

"This is not just theory. It has been demonstrated over and over in experiments."

Maya listened attentively. Much of this was new to her. "Let me see if I've grasped it so far," she said, "especially how the quantum connects to consciousness." She climbed onto the dolphin's back, hugging his large dorsal fin, her legs gripping his sides.

"Without mind, there's no matter," Maya summarized. "Consciousness collapses possibilities into the building blocks of the physical world. In a very real sense, we do choose reality because the field of quantum potential, where everything begins, becomes reality only if it's *observed*." She groped for words: "Consciousness shapes the fuzziness and uncertainty of the quantum into actual material forms. We've known this for a long time in indigenous cultures."

Dara pulled away from the other two, looking distracted: "Darwin, as a scientist, I find your summaries intriguing—mainly because you are showing how the quantum is related to consciousness. But what has all this to do with the evolutionary sequence we've been exploring?"

"I'm glad you kept that in mind," Darwin replied. "Remember, we are looking at the quantum because it is the first stage in the journey from Light to Spirit. We wanted to see how the quantum could be the carrier of purpose and consciousness into the world. And if you've stayed with me this far, it's time for a reward."

Maya slid off Darwin's back, into the waves.

* * *

Dara felt the waters of the lagoon cocoon his body in a warm embrace. He lay back, floating, looking up at the sky. Ears submerged, the only sounds penetrating his consciousness were the pulse in his temples and a strange, almost musical, chirping coming from the water. He listened intently, and realized that whatever it was, he was "hearing" it all over his body, deep in his flesh. He sensed filaments extending out, connecting him with a network of tiny, unseen currents slipping between the molecules of the water.

For a moment, he "saw" that the countless billions of atoms and molecules that make up the oceans of the world were *organized*—that beneath the apparent chaos of the seas the water itself contains a deep coherence, a code that would reveal itself only to a certain kind of intelligence. Every point in the ocean "knew" what every other point contained. And more. Every point in all the seas and oceans of the Earth was in contact with every point in the heavens. Messages were constantly streaming back and forth.

At a level of knowing beyond concepts and words, an old feeling now coursed through his body. Dimly recognizable as an emotional echo from his early childhood, and for no reason he could identify, a sense of fear and sadness began to take him over—as if someone close was abandoning or betraying him. Confused, he couldn't tell whether the emotions were rising up from his own deep memories or whether he was picking up messages from the ocean itself. He sensed a connection between his own childhood dreams and something deep within sea. For a few brief moments, he felt as though his own feelings were resonating in sympathy with currents of emotion flowing through the surrounding waters. Behind the chaos and turbulence of the ocean currents lay a hidden purpose.

Next, an image flitted into consciousness, blurred at first, then gradually becoming clearer like a developing photograph. He recognized a familiar face: Bechtel's. His NASA colleague looked anxious and intense—obsessed was more like it. Just as quick, the image faded, and as it did Dara's sensation of oceanic interconnectedness vanished, replaced by a feeling of foreboding.

* * *

Darwin's voice filled his head once more:

"Nonlocality is just a word. It's not something you can understand—it must be felt or intuited. Quantum physics has given science a glimpse into the dream world, where energy and images fuse in a dance of archetypes. It is a vast, infinite, sea of quantum potential that some of your physicists call the 'zero-point energy field'. Emptiness brimming with creativity."

Still disoriented by the image of Bechtel and the sudden, unaccountable surge of emotion, Dara made an effort to refocus on what Darwin was saying. He asked:

"Is there a way the mystery of the quantum can add meaning to our lives?"

"I can see your center is shifting, Stanford. You are opening up to this knowledge in a new way, and asking different questions. That's good. Our work won't always be easy or comfortable, but stay with it," Darwin sounded more compassionate than usual. "There will be times when the world itself opens up to you in new ways, and you will see things that disturb you. It's all part of the great learning."

The dolphin swerved quickly, and the wash from his flanks swept over his two companions. They felt the water suddenly vibrate against their bodies with a new insistence, and knew this was Darwin's way of adding emphasis. He wanted them to pay special attention.

"Tell me where I'm going to move next." Darwin darted chaotically around the lagoon. When neither scientist tried to guess, he came swimming back. "You couldn't predict my next move because there was no pattern. My zigzags were unpredictable, just like the quantum."

Again the dolphin launched into his chaotic antics. "See, it all looks random to you, but to *me* it's the exact opposite. It's choice. Every single move I make happens because I *choose* it." He slowed to a graceful glide. "Chance or choice? Take your pick. Whether it's a crazy dolphin or a weird quantum, any behavior generated by choice will appear random to an observer."

"Okay, I'm getting it," Maya sounded excited. "What *seems* like quantum chance may actually be quantum choice."

"Yes. Don't you see: choice or purpose must be built into the cosmos right down at the most fundamental level."

"Would you run that one by me again?" Dara asked. "Are you saying that when a quantum jumps it's making a *choice?*"

"Do you believe in free will?" Darwin turned the question back to Dara. "Have you ever made a choice, something that made even some small difference in the way things unfolded?"

"Sure, we all do it all the time."

"So free will, choice, exists."

"Seems so."

"Yes, it *does* seem so," Darwin came back. "You're thinking, not feeling. It seems so because it is so. And if you and I can make choices, if we have goals or purposes, then we need to be able to explain how *that* could happen. Quite a mystery, eh?"

Dara's mind was reeling again.

"Your thoughts are jumping all over the place," Darwin announced. "Just like a crazy quantum." And then something happened that completely surprised the NASA scientist. Darwin swam right up to him, snout-to-snout, and whispered:

"So *stop it.* Stop your crazy thoughts."

That just made matters worse for Dara.

"Of course, you can't. The harder you try to stop your mind, the more it runs away with itself. But now just let go. Stop trying to stop thinking. Just *choose* to let your mind do whatever it is doing, and see what happens."

Almost immediately, Dara felt his mind relaxing. His racing thoughts subsided. Like a bubble popping, a wave of peacefulness poured over him. Everything seemed clearer, and a broad smile of realization lit up his face.

"Ah, I see it now," he said to dolphin and woman. I can't stop my mind by force of will, but I can choose to let it be."

"Yes. You've just experienced the paradoxical power of choice—using free will to relax your will. And now that you've experienced it, you *know* it's a fact. It no longer just 'seems' that way. Right?"

"Right."

"So how did you do it?" Darwin asked rhetorically. And continued: "Where on Earth did you get that ability? If you are completely composed of quanta, and they are purely random, where did your free will come from?"

Dara got the message this time.

"It must have come from the quanta. They must have some kind of ability to make choices. I see it now."

"Yes, our free will is a manifestation of the spark of choice embedded in the quantum." Darwin emphasized the point: "*Quantum intelligence finds expression through us.*"

"That's as good a definition of spirit as science could hope for," Dara offered. In his chest, he felt a very different understanding about the role of the quantum in evolution.

Like a homing missile, Darwin shot up from the depths of the lagoon breaking through the surface with a loud splash, rose four or five feet in the air, and landed smack dab in the space between them.

"Very observant," he said. "This, then, is the goal of our journey: from quantum light to spiritual enlightenment." He paused. "It is now time, Stanford, for you to move into an *experience* of the quantum wonderland. To help you along, I've brought you this." And he regurgitated a small ball of tangled seaweed. "It is from a rare species of kelp my people use to open up consciousness. It's been fermenting in my stomach long enough now and should have just the right potency for you."

Dara felt nauseous at the thought of chewing a piece of rubbery kelp laced with a dolphin's gastric juices. But he had already committed to the journey—it was too late to turn back. He took the golf-ball sized object, perched himself on a rock, and began eating.

"I advise you to come back into the water, Stanford. In a short time you will be flying. And since you are a novice at this, I suggest you do your experimental flying in the safety of the water rather than through the air. Don't worry, I will be beside you every inch of the way. When you need air, I'll carry you to the surface." At the last mouthful, Dara dutifully slid back into the lagoon.

23

Lesson in Light

When he finally let go completely he found himself cushioned inside an invisible sheath, sucked up and twirled around a levitating spiral of water. He could see the tiny blobs that were Maya and Darwin far below. His whole body filled with the roar of the vortex, like an entire universe rushing into the jaws of an insatiable black hole.

Spinning like a top, the world of the lagoon became nothing but a luminous blur of neon-blue streaks laced with lines of reds and purples way below. Up and up, faster and faster, he spiraled around the vortex and the closer he got to the top, the more the deafening roar pounded in his ears and filled his head. It grew so intense, there was no room left in his brain to process anything but the assault on his auditory senses. With the noise and the spinning, all his other his senses were numbed and he was about to lose consciousness.

"Hold on to your awareness, whatever you do," Darwin's voice pierced through the tumult. "Pay attention to who you are." And that was the last he heard. An instant later, his mind blanked out—completely. There was no sound. There was nothing to see. With no thought, no feeling, no sensations of any kind, he was as light and empty as a hot-air balloon floating freely in the stratosphere. There was nothing. He was nothing. Yet he knew he was awake, so awake and conscious in fact, that everything else throughout his entire life had been nothing but a dream.

He looked down and saw himself spiraling up to the top of the vortex, but in freeze-frame slow motion. At that moment he realized he was disembodied, and was seeing himself and the world of the lagoon from inside a wormhole in spacetime. He had escaped. He was free.

* * *

Ghostly as pure consciousness, Grumbalot rode the cosmic tunnel like a magic carpet ride. He had lost all sense of time, all sense of space and, for all he knew, was traveling faster than the speed of light for a string of eternities. Just as possible, he was frozen in a single instant, at absolute zero speed, beyond time, beyond space. He was nothing and yet he was everything that ever was, is, or could be. Like a god.

And then a thought slipped in: "What about my body?" Immediately followed by another thought: "I've left my body behind floating in the Blue Universe. What can I do without it? Worse, I don't even know where my mind is. I have no idea where I am. I can't see, or hear, or feel or taste anything. I am just is. I might as well be pure action." Which is exactly what he was just at that moment. For the only impression filling Grumbalot's disembodied consciousness was a sense of primal spinning. As he tumbled and rotated through the vast nothingness between universes, he knew that somehow his twisting and turning was creating space from the void around him and tunneling him back into time.

"I'm not sure I like being nothing but a spin," he thought, as he corkscrewed through the cosmos. "I don't know whether I'm up or down. This is very strange indeed." What would have been an instant later, had there been any such thing where he was, something else announced itself in the wormhole.

"Charming, I must say. Charming." It sounded like a voice close-by in the tunnel, but how could he hear anything, since he had no ears or any senses at all? Yet the voice was speaking to him just the same.

"Hey, Spin, over here. Me and my buddy have been looking for a neat little number like you. Want to join us so we can make something of ourselves?"

"Who's there?" thought Grumbalot as loud as he could. "What do you want?"

"Like my buddy said, Spin, you're just what we've been looking for. What a team we'd make. With me in charge, my buddy's charm and your spin, well, we'd be set to be one heavy particle. Just think of it. A real particle at last. Then we could get out of this wormhole and get into something that really mattered . . ."

"Yeah, like an atom," the first voice said.

"Or a molecule. Maybe even a cell. Imagine that, would you? Being in a living cell. A part of life itself," said the second strange voice.

"We could fission and fuse, generate and replicate, pass from generation to generation. One day, if chance falls our way, we could be in the lips of a famous actor strutting the stage as he speaks the immortal words 'To be, or not to be?' Whooo! Wouldn't that be exciting, instead of randomly bouncing around in the chaos of pre-existence waiting an eternity to hook up with someone like you."

Grumbalot's consciousness shivered, the way his body would have if someone had run an icy finger up his spine.

"You must excuse my friend," said the charming voice, "he's not called Strange for nothing. Whenever he's got an opportunity like this to make something of himself—and believe me they are few and far between—he tends to get carried away and waxes all philosophical and poetical. But I can't really blame him. I think he's got a great idea. You're the perfect little number. Let's get together right now, this is too good a chance to miss."

Grumbalot began to panic. "They want to kidnap me and take me off somewhere, imprison me in a cell. I'd never get back to Grummeldom. If only I could stop spinning, maybe they'd leave me alone."

Fat chance.

"What a magnetic spin you've got," gushed the charming voice. "You're so attractive. I'm Charm, by the way, if you didn't know by now. And this is my buddy, Strange. And you, you've got a most exquisite spin, a right little building block if ever there was one. With your spin, my charm and his strangeness, the world's our orbit."

"I'm no building block," Grumbalot thought rather indignantly. "And stop calling me Spin. I don't know what your game is, or what you've got planned, but I can tell you right now, I won't be any part of it. I'm on a mission from Grummeldom, and I intend to complete it."

He surprised himself with his bravado. Of course, when all you have are your thoughts, you can think anything you like. But just the same, he was glad to be thinking brave thoughts.

"Oh, don't be such a spoilsport. Maybe you find my buddy a little too strange. Is that it?"

"I find this whole shebang too weird for words," thought Grumbalot with such fierceness that he almost stopped spinning. "And if you or your buddy so much as touch me, I'll . . . well I'll simply stop believing in you. Then where will you be?"

"That's a very good question," said the charming voice. "But here's another question: If you didn't believe in us, then where would you be?"

"Where I am has nothing at all to do with whether or not I believe in you," Grumbalot thought confidently. Since he hadn't the faintest idea anyway where in the world he was, or even if he was in the world at all, he had nothing to lose.

"But you must believe in us," quivered one of the little voices. "We're quarks, we're the building blocks of everything in the universe, everything that matters, that is. Without us there wouldn't be elementary particles and therefore no atoms or molecules or cells or plants or animals—or anything. There'd be nothing. Zero. Zilcheroo. If you want to get out of this wormhole you better stick with us. We're your only hope. Otherwise you are in a tunnel to nowhere, chum."

Grumbalot wondered if what they said was true. What if he did need them to get himself out of the hole? After all, he had nothing going for him right now except non-stop rapid spinning in the void. And how far could you get in life if all you could do was spin? He certainly couldn't see much future in that. Maybe he should consider teaming up with them? All the same, this business with quarks didn't sound quite right either. Would you put your trust in invisible entities called Charm and Strange, inviting you to join them so you could end up in an atom or a cell in someone else's body—a Goochie's, for instance? Well, Grumbalot wasn't convinced either.

"I've never heard of such a thing," thought Grumbalot. "If you are quarks or whatever, and you claim to make up everything there is, then what makes you?"

"Nothing. We're it," said the strange voice. "We're not made up of anything but ourselves. Have you ever heard of opening up a quark to find what's inside? How ridiculous a thought! We're the smallest thing there is, too small to be seen by anyone."

"Or anything," Charm chirped in. At that moment, a tiny loop of nothingness quivered inside the quark.

True, Grumbalot couldn't see the quarks, so they must be pretty small. But that didn't mean they were the ultimate rock-bottom stuff of existence. He stretched his mind as far as he could to think of why he couldn't accept the notion of quarks being the root of everything. There was something cockeyed about that. He couldn't make up his mind, he couldn't put his finger on it, even if he had a finger to put on it, and he thought and thought and thought, and as he thought some more he continued tumbling through the infinite tunnel to nowhere, spinning beyond all control.

And then it hit him: "How many quarks does it take to make up my mind? None. I can think 'quarks,' I can make them come and go in my mind, but they can't make me think.

"You guys are impostors," he thought decisively. "Pure fictions, nothing but clever little ideas masquerading as facts. You're no different than those squeaky little creatures lurking under the leaves in the Blue Universe. I don't believe in you."

He thought this thought with such conviction that, poof! instantly the irritating little quarks were gone, rubbed out of existence as surely as if he had canceled a mathematical equation with a minus sign. At least, that's what Grumbalot thought.

And at that very instant, he had the weirdest sensation of his entire life. Although he had no eyes or ears, no senses of any kind, he was overwhelmed by a dazzling spectacle. A shower of infinitesimal points of light zipped all around him—or at least where he imagined himself to be. They zigzagged over and under him and zoomed right through his space. He felt as if he was caught up in a blizzard of dancing tiny angels that filled his universe with the brightest, purest light there could ever possibly be. He felt a warmth and friendliness all around him and he knew these points of light were here to help. But strangest of all was the feeling that he himself was one of the lights. He was part of the dance.

He was a little nervous because everything was so strange. He even began to wonder had he finally gone out of his mind—as well as his body.

"That's it. Let go completely, little friend," he heard a sweet, faint voice as soft as the brush of a feather on his nose. "You have chosen to dance with us, and we are happy to have you come with us, all the way down, all the way down, all the way down, and up again, all the way up to the Final Point."

"What's going on here?" Grumbalot wondered as best he could without the benefit of a regular mind. "All the way down to where, to what? And what's the Final Point? Really, all I want to do is get back to my own world, to Grummeldom. Can you help me?"

Like golden wings swishing behind his ears, the reply came from somewhere, somewhere that was neither far away nor close by.

"You've been spinning so fast that all your energy has compressed itself into the smallest thing there is: a photon of light. You have become a dimensionless point, a quantum. Congratulations!"

Grumbalot had been through enough mind-boggling experiences lately that by now he knew better than to try to make any sense of this latest state of affairs. And he did feel a certain sense of achievement about being a totally dimensionless point of light. He was pretty sure no other Grummel had ever got to this point. He felt as if he was nowhere and everywhere at the same time. In fact, it was just dawning on him that actually he was beyond time and space altogether. That is, the entire past and the full unfolding of the future were instantly available to him. Yes, now he knew it to be true: He was traveling at the speed of light. In fact, he was the speed of light. He was pure action. He was sure he could shoot himself from one end of the universe to the other and back again faster than a flash. He never dreamt he could feel so powerful. All he had to do was effortlessly flip his imagination this way and that and he could be anywhere he wanted to be, at any time in history, in any form he liked.

"I feel like the whole universe is inside me," he allowed himself to think. "Yet I'm so small, that even a quark would be a giant beside me. I'm so small that I'm nothing. And yet I'm everything at the same time."

"You're getting it, Grummel," The Voice echoed inside him and around him. "You're getting very close. You are indeed a 'quantum of action.' You have become a point of pure light. You are now a Quantum Grummel. But be careful. It's true you can be anything you want to be just by choosing it. But you can get yourself into all sorts of tangles and troubles if you blindly rush in. There is a path you must follow. You are at the starting gate, Point Zero, it is sometimes called. And from Point Zero there are as many paths to follow as there are choices to be made. But not all paths lead to the Final Point. If you choose the wrong one, you may find yourself stuck in a dead end, or you may turn back on yourself and wind up where you started."

Grumbalot hadn't heard words like these before, but somehow he knew that what the Voice was saying to him was true.

"How do I know which is the right path to choose?" he wondered.

"Pay attention to what is happening all around you, Quantum Grummel. The journey you are on is from Point Zero to the Final Point. It's called 'evolution' and the path you must follow depends on who you join up with on your journey. So choose your partners carefully. If they do not dance your dance and you do not dance theirs, you will stumble over yourself at every step. And if you keep tripping yourself up, you'll never know where you are. There is one thing it is now time for you to know, so you don't have to keep coming back to Point Zero."

"What's that?" Grumbalot asked the cloud of lights dancing and scintillating inside and around him. He was getting more and more curious and interested in learning about how the world worked.

"You could remain a Quantum Grummel forever, just a pointless point of light dancing up here in the kingdom beyond space and time. But what fun would that be?"

"I kinda like it," Grumbalot thought as privately as he could, not wishing to interrupt the Voice. He wanted to know more, but he had to admit that he was enjoying being a speck of pure light. It filled him with a new sense of peace and power.

"That's just it," said the Voice, letting him know that up here there was no such thing as a private thought. "You are so self-contained, so full of your own power, and that does have its own attraction. But what are you going to do with all that power? As soon as you try to do anything, you will realize that you can't do anything that matters, anything that makes any difference. You are just a little photon, and all you can do is dance the light fantastic. In order to do anything that makes a real difference, well, you will have to create a difference, won't you? And you can't do that on your own, now can you?"

Grumbalot didn't even try to pretend he understood this last remark. Instead he listened with an open mind, since without a mind this was the easiest thing for him to do.

"Up here you can't do anything because you are just a quantum. Just the tiniest little bundle of potential for action. So all that power you think you have is just an illusion, unless you use that quantum potential to make a choice. Try it."

Grumbalot hadn't the faintest idea what to do. So he did the only thing he could: He made a choice. He just simply chose to be completely open to whatever was going on around him. It wasn't really doing anything, yet he felt as if he had just pressed a lever and the whole universe shifted.

"What else did you notice?" the Voice prompted.

Even more than the feeling of the universe moving, Grumbalot was most impressed by what was happening right at the center of his point of being.

"I feel more 'me.' I mean, when I made a choice, I could feel who I was as if I was the center point of the whole universe. I felt ready for action. I had created a purpose."

The wormhole filled with the whisper of wings swishing in applause.

"By Jove, he's got it. That's it, Quantum Grummel. You've started the ball rolling. You've released a spark of consciousness. You've seen that choice is consciousness, consciousness is choice, otherwise it's just blind action. Beautiful.

"Now here's a clue about the path to follow and it's also a map for knowing where you are on the path. You have just taken the first of seven steps on the journey. By making a choice you have begun the long descent down the arc of evolution through the field of potential to nuclear particles, where you will interact with other particles, binding with them through a dance of attraction and repulsion. From there, you'll move into the world of atoms, where you will create a unique identity. Next, you'll enter the complex world of molecules, where you will merge your identity in relationship with other atoms. That's the turning point.

"Then begins your upward journey, through the beginnings of life, becoming part of a living cell. Then on to plants, and later to animals, where you will have the power to move around. Next you will join the family of Grummels, with their minds full of ideas, goals and thoughts. And finally, at the top of the arc, when you complete your journey and learn to glow inside, you will shine again with all the glory of the original light you came from.

"The difference, though, is that at the top of the arc you will have evolved from Point Zero, through the Turning Point, to the Final Point. Here you will shine with the light you share with the rest of the world. You will have transformed yourself from Quantum Grummel to Cosmic Grummel. That is your path. And now you know where you are as a Grummel and what your destination is. When you leave this wormhole, when you get back into your mind, keep this map in it. It will help you if you ever get lost again."

The Voice fell silent and Grumbalot noticed a familiar sensation forming in the vortex of the wormhole. His mind was coming back. And without a moment's hesitation he began to fill it with thoughts, more to just feel what it was like, than to think of anything in particular.

Then he remembered that the Voice had warned him about stray thoughts sending the wormhole off course, possibly to kingdom come. All this thinking about quarks and spin and charm and strangeness, and quanta and photons, and choice and purpose, could have jeopardized his escape. So he quickly exercised his mind to imagine the galactic, solar and planetary levels of his home universe, working his way down to the surface of the Earth, with all its creatures, and even into the tunnels of Grummeldom. At that instant he had the bright idea that if he focused all the way down and imagined himself, imagined his own body, maybe it would be there for him when he returned.

For good measure, he also imagined that Darwin and Maya would be there, too.

* * *

Dara opened his eyes, the world vibrated and radiated with a brightness, a clarity of color, a freshness, a sense of *realness* he had never experienced before. He felt reborn with new sight, with all the toxins of body and mind flushed from his system. In the center of his chest a football-sized clearing allowed him to breathe with an unfamiliar softness and depth, as though he were inhaling light. He was floating—free of all the emotional and intellectual baggage he'd accumulated over the years. And he was literally floating, face up toward the vivid sky, in the warm, blue, waters of the lagoon. He felt like a child again.

"Welcome back, Stanford. I see you've survived your journey through the quantum wonderland," the dolphin's voice sounded reassuringly familiar. "How was it?"

Dara rolled over in the water, dived and surfaced, and rested the back of his head against the dolphin's flank. He continued to float in silence, a broad calm smile beaming from his face, simply enjoying *being there.* Images from the "quantum wonderland" came and went before his eyes. And then he spoke:

"I was transformed," he said. "I was transformed into a child-like creature, the same one from my big dream some time ago. Yet I did not feel as if I was dreaming. It seemed both fantastic and very real at the same time. At one point I experienced myself as a photon, a quantum of pure light. It was beyond words . . ." and he stopped to feel the energy pumping through him.

"Well, my friend, you may not want to call it 'dreaming'," Darwin said, "but you undoubtedly entered the dreamtime. Perhaps we should say you were 'realing'?"

Dara liked that. "Yes. I was definitely reeling and spinning, and it was very, very *real.* But I felt . . ." and again he was lost for the right words. " . . . I felt like I had disappeared into an infinitesimal point in space. But also as if I had gone back in time—back to my childhood . . ." Again he paused, ". . . back beyond before I was born, before I was even a speck in my mother's womb."

"That's exactly right, Stanford. You had to become a child again to free your mind of all your academic training, to free yourself to *experience* your own deeper intelligence and creativity. Only as a child could you possibly open up to what Maya has known all her life. She has never lost contact with her natural intelligence, her evolutionary birthright. You needed to release your own living child—to find your beginner's mind.

"Without that, all this talk about the quantum and consciousness would have remained lodged in your intellect, next to worthless as dry and dead concepts. You had to get beyond your fossilized thoughts, to dive right into the eternal, living flow of quantum thinking itself. Now, at least, you have a foothold in such experience. And that should make all the difference."

Darwin gently glided away from underneath Dara's head, and swam out toward the champagne breakers. Dara lithely followed. They cavorted in the waves, whooping and whistling. Maya felt an urge to join them, but then sensed this was a good time for them to play together. Dolphin and scientist swam together in the open waters, enjoying each other's company in silence.

When they returned to join Maya in the shallows, Darwin said that she had balanced her intuitive knowledge of the quantum wonderland with intellectual knowledge from physics.

"And now you, Stanford, have done the reverse—a much greater challenge, mind you. You now have had an experiential understanding of the first level in the sequence. You have literally experienced what it's like to be pure potential." And he added: "Potential with purpose." He swam between both scientists and extended his flippers to embrace them.

"Congratulations. You have completed your first lesson in light. Now the journey can begin. The next stage takes you into the domain of energy and time—to the forces that hold the universe together. It is time for you to learn about freedom and immortality."

The dolphin pushed them in toward the shore.

"I wish we could continue now," he said, already turning toward the open sea. "But you've got to get off this beach—and fast."

24

Storm Warning

Darwin's parting words startled the two scientists. They dressed quickly, and sprinted back through the dunes to the cabin. A handful of gulls circled above, their cries piercing the roar of the surf. Dara's senses, sharp and clear, illuminated everything around him with an electric presence. He felt energized, ready to meet whatever was next.

He didn't have to wait long. Maya pointed to a dust cloud rising above the dirt road, rapidly heading in their direction. Instinctively, the couple dived into the tall dune grass and waited. Two trucks pulled up in front of the shack. Bechtel stepped out of the first, accompanied by a tall, slender man with a large mustache. A set of large binoculars dangled from his neck. Another four heavy-set men, all dressed in black, emerged from the second truck, and stood in line like bowling pins.

"This is where she said we would find the dolphin," Bechtel explained to the tall man who seemed to be in charge. Peering at the lagoon, the leader said, "I thought we'd get all three of them together."

"Seems you were right about Bechtel," Dara whispered. Maya ignored the comment. Time for that later. They both watched closely, sensing danger.

The men began walking toward the shore, then one shouted out "Is that it?" He pointed at a barely visible dark triangle breaking through the surface. The tall man raised the binoculars, and confirmed: "Yeah, that's a fin all right." He scanned the lagoon some more.

"Seems our dolphin is trapped by the tide. We've got him." He barked over his shoulder, "Bring the gun down here!" One of the men raced back to the trucks, unhooked a rifle from its cradle in the cab, then ran to catch up with the others on the beach.

"Now's our chance," Dara whispered animatedly. "Let's get out of here." And he started running toward the trucks.

"We can't leave. They've got Darwin," Maya croaked after him. A shot cracked through the air. Dara called out to Maya to follow him, but she started running toward the cove. Three men scrambled back up the dunes, chasing her.

"I think we've hit him," someone shouted from the beach. "Make sure of it," another answered.

Maya tried to dodge past the men, but one caught hold of her, pulling her to the ground. The other two kept running for the trucks, guns in hand. Dara had no time to think. He jumped into the first vehicle as one of the men started firing. He revved the engine and kicked it into gear. Tires screamed on the hard dirt, throwing up a blizzard of pebbles and dirt. He could smell burning rubber as the wheels tore up the road. All he could see in his mirror was a cloud of smoke and dust. One more loud rifle shot rang out from the beach.

* * *

When the dust settled, there was no sign of the others. Adrenaline pumped through Dara's veins, and his body shook with fear. He drove for about half a mile, mind on autopilot, before pulling off onto a dirt track. Tall stands of bamboo shielded him from view, though he could still see through the thicket. No one was following. Instinctively, he wanted to go back to rescue Maya, but the more he thought about it the more he convinced himself that was not a wise option.

"A lone man against five armed thugs; six, counting Bechtel. If I turn around and go back for Maya, they'll either shoot or capture me, too. At least this way one of us is free, and that's our best card right now." These were the facts, but emotionally he felt he should have done more. He would *have to* do more.

The sky darkened and the first few splats of rain dappled the windshield. The sound of an approaching engine interrupted his anguished meditations on the morality and wisdom of his actions. As it sped past, he recognized the other truck—too fast to make out the occupants, only that it was crowded. He waited a minute, then eased out of the bamboo grove, pursuing at a safe distance. He figured they would be focused on the road ahead trying to catch up with him.

Dara drove for an hour inland toward the hills. As the road curved into a series of sharp bends, he lost sight of the other truck. At one point, a police car passed in the opposite direction, and he resisted the impulse to swerve into a u-turn. With the FEW involved, he no longer knew whom to trust. He kept on driving.

The rain was coming down fast now, making it difficult to see through the curtain of water washing back and forth across the windshield. He strained to catch a glimpse of red taillights, but they had vanished into the darkness. As far as he could tell, this was the only paved road into the hills, and so he continued the pursuit, still ascending the interminable snaking curves. Time seemed to stretch to a standstill, and each passing minute added to his anxiety and growing sense of urgency. What would they do to Maya? What could *he* do if he caught up with them?

For what felt like hours, he saw no signs of life anywhere in the hills. And then, through the rainstorm, a faint flickering about half a mile up ahead. As he drew closer, he saw the light was coming from a huddle of old wooden cabins, with a lone rusted gas pump standing in the forecourt of one building. He slowed, and turned in, switching off his headlights, wheels crunching over wet gravel. He rolled down the window to get a better view, and was greeted by a low throaty growl. A large dog eyed him suspiciously from the sheltered porch of an old store.

Sanctuary Creek general store was set back off the road in a small clearing between the thick bush of surrounding trees and bamboo. Its rusting gas pump stood like a forgotten soldier on guard outside a ghost camp, in permanent frozen salute to whoever passed this way. The shacks behind had long ago fallen into decay—doors locked with rusty bolts, windows protected only by sheets of punctured plastic and faded moth-eaten curtains.

The store itself was in better shape: a large redwood cabin, in stark contrast to the surrounding bamboo rainforest. A wide steep ramp, flanked on both sides by

wooden steps, led into the store. The overhang of rough
axe-hewn timbers sheltered the railed porch. Dara pulled up
and got out. He opened the heavy double doors and entered
a lobby to shelter from the rain. The dog followed, sniffing
his heels, and shaking itself vigorously. An inner door led
into the store. The smell of strong coffee told him someone
was home. Maybe he could find out where to get a hot meal
and a bed for the night. The road was running like a river
out there.

He pushed the door, and an old bell rattled announcing
his arrival. Inside, the store was more spacious than it
appeared from the road. He glanced around: shelves
stocked with canned and packaged foods, and a wide
variety of hardware from spoons and knives to axes,
chainsaws and auto parts. Barrels of flour, pulses, nuts,
potatoes, fruit and other fresh produce stood in the center of
the room. A wood stove burned on a stone platform in a
nook, surrounded by an assortment of tattered chairs and
bookshelves.

Behind the counter, seated on a tall wooden stool, an old
Asian man with long gray hair and a beard looked up from
his newspaper.

"Hello, friend. Help yourself to some hot coffee or some
spiced tea over there. It can get pretty wet and mean up
here," he gestured outside toward the mountain.

Dara poured himself a coffee from a stainless steel
electric urn, and asked if there was somewhere close by
where he could eat and stay the night if the weather didn't
clear. The nearest motel was about twenty miles back on
the highway, the man said, otherwise the nearest town, if

you could call it that, was Mauna Kula further up into the hills.

"You won't get much accommodation from those folks, though," he said. "It's pretty much a one-family town and they don't take very kindly to uninvited outsiders. The only other habitation close by is the scouts' camp back in the woods. I can't see you driving in there, either.

"But if you hang on here, my wife will be cooking supper soon." The man stood up. He was small, yet lithe and muscular as a jaguar.

From the corner of his eye, through the storefront window, Dara caught the flash of headlights as a vehicle slowly pulled up outside the old gas pump.

"Seems we've got company." The old man threw on a large waterproofed hooded cape and walked to the door.

Low dark clouds, heavy with rain, made visibility difficult, but Dara could make out the shape of a police car. "Same one I saw back on the highway?" he wondered, squinting through the rain as the storekeeper approached the car. Dara stood at the window sipping his coffee, watching the rain beat down. The dog had followed his master into the muddy yard and sniffed around the tires.

"Glad you made it."

Dara jumped at the sound of the woman's voice behind him. She held out a welcoming hand. But Dara, spooked as much by the unexpected appearance of the old woman as by what she said, kept both hands cupped around his coffee.

"Hello, Ma'am," was all he could say.

Noticing the alarm in his eyes, she quickly added, "Oh, I'm sorry. I assumed my husband had told you. A friend of yours came by earlier, and asked us to give you this." She handed him a folded piece of paper. A scribbled note from Maya:

Dara I'm OK. The Tatsuakis are good people. Please trust them. They can help. Bechtel and his men are taking me to Honolulu. You must get back to the cove . . .

The note ended abruptly, leaving him confused and suspicious.

The old woman wore a Paisley buttoned smock reaching from her chin down to her ankles. Her gray hair was pulled back in a neat bun. She smiled and nodded.

"How . . .?" Dara's question was cut short when the door blew open. The old man came back in, pulling the wet cape tight to his chest.

"That policeman took some persuading that we're okay, up here," he said. "The power is out all across the mountain, and he offered to take us down to town in case the storm gets worse. I assured him our generator would take care of all our needs. Ours is the only light visible for miles. Attracting folks here like moths to a lamp." He took off the cape and draped it over a stool at the counter.

"I see you've got Maya's note," he said. "She was hoping you'd follow their truck and find our place."

He approached the visitor slowly. "Permit me to explain what has happened."

Dara felt his eyes dart back and forth between the two old timers, keeping the corner of his eye on the door if he needed a quick escape.

"Please go on," he said trying to sound calm and steady.

"Very well," the old man continued, gesturing to the visitor to take a seat. "My name is Keiji Tatsuaki and this is my wife, Yuka. We are Maya's friends." He explained they had met at the university in Honolulu where he used to teach East-West philosophy.

"She told us you know about Darwin . . . about the noetic code. So we can be candid with you. We've been helping Maya for about a year, and were two of Darwin's early apprentices."

He poured himself and his wife some spiced tea from a black iron teapot, and nodded to the coffee urn offering his guest a refill. Dara shook his head, and took another sip from his steaming mug. The old man continued:

"Like you, I expect, I thought I was there to give this dolphin the benefit of my wisdom. After all, I was a professor of Buddhism, and he was just a curious dolphin. I soon learned, though, as we all do, that *I* was the student. Darwin introduced us to the elements of the noetic code." The old man fingered the rim of his cup, and his wife excused herself to prepare supper.

"When I retired earlier this year, we bought this ramshackle place. We're fixing it up bit by bit. The store doesn't take much work, and makes enough to pay for itself. Right now, our modest library is a center for a small group. We meet here for dialogues, and in time, hope to build a Noetic Center." He gestured in a wide sweep, indicating the complex of buildings. "It's part of Darwin's plan to create a global network of people working for the evolution of consciousness. He calls it the NET—Network for Energy Transformation."

"Maya helped us to tidy up the place when we moved in. She's been a regular visitor sharing recordings and transcripts with us so we could keep up with Darwin's teachings. In exchange, we've been on the mat with her practicing advanced aikido." He paused, then explained: "It's a Japanese martial art that trains us to work with people's energy." He got up to put a log in the wood stove, and beckoned Dara to pull his chair closer.

"When she arrived here this afternoon with six grim-looking men, I suspected something was wrong. She gave no indication that we knew each other, and we played along. We served them lunch, and Maya offered to help Yuka in the kitchen. That's when she told us what had happened. She explicitly asked us not to try to interfere or to involve the police. She said she was in charge—and, of course, we knew at once what she meant."

Dara stared blankly at the old man.

"Oh, Darwin hasn't introduced you to soul charge yet?" Tatsuaki asked. "Maya's gotten pretty darn skillful with it, and used it to lure her captors to our place. They were hungry, looking for somewhere to eat, and she directed them toward Mauna Kula, knowing they would have to pass by here. Evidently they were very open to suggestion—not surprising given their aggression. The storm helped, too, of course. She told Yuka she needed to get the note to you. Meanwhile, she's gone back to

Honolulu as their 'captive' to try to find out who's behind their shenanigans."

"How did she know I'd find this place?" Dara asked, beginning to feel he had been drawn into a conspiracy way beyond his comprehension.

"It's less to do with what she knew," the professor said, "more what she intended." He paused again: "Energy follows the path of purpose."

The Stanford scientist blinked and shook his head as if rattling his brain might adjust reality. He felt his mind split: One part was willing to suspend disbelief and open him up to a world of new, if not bizarre, experiences. The other part, his scientifically trained mind, was still trying to call him back from the brink.

It wasn't just the professor's conspiratorial tone that unnerved him, or even mind-boggling sessions with a telepathic dolphin—not even threats from the FEW. He sensed he was caught up in a web of invisible connections, and that greater forces were at work directing the unfolding of events. Forces unseen and unknown by science.

This unlikely, yet seemingly propitious, meeting with the Tatsuakis was just the latest in a strange string of circumstances—pushing him past the point of no return.

25

Forces That Bind

"Maya told us you have already moved through the first lesson in light. So you know what it feels like to be a quantum of pure potential?"

Dara nodded, waiting for what was coming.

"Well, the next step is to work on the power of intention. You need to build up soul charge." The old martial artist spread an open palm on his belly just below the navel. "This is the *hara,* where we store emotional force." His eyes narrowed into a knowing smile. "But you must give up something in order to gain something. Yes?"

Dara nodded again, though not really sure what Tatsuaki meant.

"You need to learn to work with this force if you are to help Maya. She asked us to show you."

Uneasy about what was in store, and suspicious, Dara asked: "What must I give up to get . . . what did you call it . . . willpower?"

"*Soul charge*. It's a special kind of intention, and it's not at all the same as willpower. Yes, it involves a form of will, but it is rooted deep in the collective soul. In fact, you will need to give up some of your personal willpower in order to create soul charge. That's the trade off."

The old man pulled his chair closer to Dara's and took hold of his hands, placing them against his solar plexus.

"When you use soul charge, you tap into a deeper intelligence that expresses itself from here." He moved the scientist's hands in a wide circle over his belly, then lifted his hands above his head, arms out straight like a radio antenna. Dara felt a noticeable shift in the energy flowing through his body.

"With soul charge, *you* are not willing something to happen," Tatsuaki added, letting all four arms drop. "It's more like something is willing you to happen—if you let it, by getting out of the way."

Dara remembered experimenting with free will and letting go while swimming with Darwin in the lagoon. Instead of tumbling into chaos, he was surprised to discover that letting go was more like surfing on a wave of power greater than his own personal will.

"Was that 'soul charge'?" Dara asked, wondering if that could be the unseen force sweeping him along. Had he tapped into it not knowing what he was doing?

"Soul charge is the expression of collective intention," his host explained. "It is the binding force in all relationships. And the quality of our connections determines the kind of energy or charge we, as individuals, can project."

Dara noticed that Tatsuaki's eyes sparkled as he spoke, and he felt a pulse of energy circulate between them, belly to belly.

"When we tap into soul charge, we activate a sort of chain reaction," Tatsuaki continued. "One person connects with another, who connects with another, and so on, and the whole network feeds everyone more power. It is a self-generating system. Once the process starts, theoretically there is no limit."

This last remark reminded Dara of the "zero-point energy" field in physics. He explained to Tatsuaki that ZPE, as it is often called, is an infinite, universal store of energy below the level of the quantum. A lot of very expensive research—much of it top secret—is aimed at turning the theory of ZPE into practical reality. If achieved, humanity will have plugged into the very force of creation itself.

Tatsuaki stood up and went to a bookcase crammed with hardback volumes. Dara noticed that the old man seemed to glide, his feet barely touching the floor. Each step was so finely balanced it seemed to channel his weight into the earth and at the same time draw renewed energy for the next step. He moved like a cat.

"Some individuals and groups feed energy to others. Some feed off the energy of others. What matters, though, is keeping the energy circulating."

He picked out a couple of books and held them out for his guest. "Here. You may borrow these." Dara took the books and glanced at the covers.

"If someone or some group hoards the power, taking and taking and taking without giving back, the system turns corrupt." Tatsuaki said. "These are the 'Takers,' as Ishmael, one of our initiates called them. The others, those who keep the energy circulating, are 'Leavers' or 'Circulators'." The old Japanese man tapped the cover of one of the books. It was titled *Ishmael*. He held Dara's gaze with a soft focus. A surge of energy shot through the scientist's body, entering through his solar plexus.

"The noetic code reveals how to coordinate soul charge on a global scale."

"Sounds like it could be manipulative," Dara replied. "In the wrong hands, couldn't it lead to world domination?"

"Precisely, and that's the problem. It's what Darwin and Maya and the rest of us want to prevent." He paused, looking Dara straight in the eye.

"A little knowledge is a dangerous thing. And that's as true for the noetic code as anything else. Yes, in the wrong hands, it could be distorted to subvert the course of evolution. We have already seen this happen to living systems with bioengineering, and manipulation of the genetic code."

Tatsuaki now spoke softly, as though he didn't wish to say the words:

"Someone, or some group, in power knows about the noetic code. And they want it." He placed both hands over his chest as though protecting a precious secret.

"Anyone with a large organization behind them can build up immense reserves of soul charge. For centuries, successful religious and business leaders—politicians too, of course—have used it to draw energy from their networks. But without the noetic code, this is only a pale shadow of what it could be."

Tatsuaki's face darkened. "Unfortunately, it is possible to learn enough to amplify soul charge for the benefit of a select few. That's what Hitler did, and that's the problem we face again today."

Yuka came in carrying a large tray with steaming bowls of rice and soup. She added: "Used correctly, the noetic code is an antidote to power-hungry motivations, and attempts to dominate others." She arranged the bowls on the table. "The complete code lights the way to altruism and compassion, and a desire to share power."

"She's right," Tatsuaki agreed. "The noetic code works best when it is shared. And shared power is most effective of all. That's why our Network must get to it first."

He slurped a spoonful of soup and invited his visitor to eat. After a short silence, the husband and wife put down their spoons, and the old man leaned forward toward their guest. He continued:

"In today's world, millions of people are no longer willing to rely on external authorities to tell them what is real and how they should live their lives. They are eager to take responsibility for their own spiritual evolution. They are ready. They are primed. Hundreds of local groups have spontaneously formed in many countries throughout the world."

The woman took hold of her husband's hand, and nodded affirmatively.

"The great mystics speak of 'The Great Turning'," she said "when the people of the world will embark on a spiritual path and open up en masse to the power of higher intelligence." Her face lit up. "And shamans speak of 'The Great Dream Rising', when the people will open up to the natural intelligence of the world."

Tatsuaki interlaced his fingers between his wife's.

"The noetic code is the key to bringing these two great movements together," he said. "Darwin has been working with us to crack that code. Once it is released to the people, they will no longer be at the mercy of corrupt groups who seek to concentrate power for themselves." He paused. "That is why they have hunted him down. That is why they have taken Maya."

Mrs. Tatsuaki began clearing the table. Dara wondered how Maya was applying soul charge with her "captors." The old man said that if she was using it according to noetic principles, then she wasn't forcing them to do anything against their will, but was blending with and guiding their energy to serve the wellbeing of the group. In some way he didn't yet understand, Dara suspected that Maya had also used soul charge to draw him up the mountain. It all felt natural, unforced—even if his scientific mind told him it was impossible.

Tatsuaki glanced at his watch and announced:

"It's time to learn about immortality."

Dara felt goose bumps tingle all over his skin. That was the last thing he remembered Darwin saying. The old man pointed to the other book in Dara's hands: "It's time to introduce you to the great Whitehead himself."

He began flipping through the pages, but Tatsuaki shook his head. "I'm not suggesting you read that now, it's far too difficult to grasp in one sitting. Much better to meet the author himself." Dara looked at Tatsuaki for a sign he was joking. The famous British philosopher had died decades ago. But Tatsuaki wasn't joking.

"Yes, of course, Whitehead has been dead a long time. But he still lives on. And I don't just mean through his books and ideas. You can experience Whitehead *in person* if you are willing to engage in a little experiment?"

Dara, still unsure, nevertheless accepted what sounded like an invitation.

"Good. We need to prepare you first. You will need to reenter the dream world, and tap into the intelligence in your body—that's where you will find Professor Whitehead. Don't worry we will help you get there, and back."

* * *

Yuka poured hot water from the cast-iron kettle on the stove into a small earthenware bowl. All Dara could see was a brownish powder, with some pieces of green stalk. She stirred the mixture and handed the bowl to him.

"Sip it slowly, it's very hot. It won't take full effect for half an hour or so, and in the meantime I will prepare a place for you to sleep. Keiji will guide you through the preliminaries." She disappeared behind a heavy curtain, and Dara heard her footsteps as she went upstairs.

"The drink will help you dream and return to quantum potential," Tatsuaki said. "We've been there, too, and have enjoyed the sense of total freedom, unfettered by space or time or body, or even by the distractions of having a mind. But you cannot begin the journey, never mind complete it, unless you leave the domain of pure potential and move into time and space. And you must make that transition from the dream world."

Dara wondered how dreaming would introduce him to Whitehead and teach him about time.

"Once you have entered the dream state, you will be guided into the very essence of time itself. You will see how time leads to immortality." He paused to let Dara take another sip. "Throughout this session, you will be able to hear and speak, whether it is to me or Yuka, or to Whitehead—or whomever else shows up."

He explained how this exercise would show that every experience anyone has ever had remains in the universe forever. "Experience is immortal. The universe wastes nothing."

Dara paid close attention.

"Every moment, for every sentient creature everywhere, a new experience comes into being. Think about that. The universe is constantly growing richer with countless billions of new experiences. *And we have access to every single one of them.* They live on in every one of us." He paused. "Time is experiences blinking in and out every moment."

The old man smiled, and gently placed a hand on Dara's shoulder.

"But we're getting ahead of ourselves. This is Whitehead's territory, and we'd best leave it to him. I see you're getting drowsy. Let's retire upstairs and begin our experiment with time."

26

An Experiment With Time

T he last thing he remembered was his head hitting the pillow and the sound of a woman's voice carrying him away.

Keiji Tatsuaki, the old Japanese professor, had led Dara up the narrow stairs to a small candle-lit room at the top of the remote mountain lodge. Outside, the winds still howled, lashing rain against the curtained windows. Inside, the room was warm. At one end, a small exquisitely hand-carved table served as an altar, featuring an onyx statue of the Buddha as the centerpiece, surrounded by dried flowers. A stick of incense burned in a wooden holder. Except for the altar, and a couple of round meditation cushions, the room was minimally furnished.

Yuka had laid out a futon on the polished hardwood floor, instructed the guest to strip naked, step into a down-filled sleeping bag, and lie with his feet facing the door. She placed one hand on his chest, the other on his forehead, and began chanting an ancient song.

Dara did not understand the words, but in his dream state he understood their meaning:

It takes time to greet the birth of each new
dawn;

time for day to meet the dark of every night,
time for night to dream into the deep.

It takes time for Father Sun to send us light;
time for light to nurture Mother Earth,
time for Mother Earth to bring forth life.

It takes time for every womb to grow its
seed;
time for life to find its place in death,
time for death to find its place in life.

It takes time to sing the stories of the past;
time to open up for what's to come,
time to close each story and let go.

It takes time to venture from the path of
grace;
time to right the wrongs we give and get,
time to be forgiven and forget.

It takes time for stars to spin from ancient
dust;
time for all creation to return,
time and time again, for all we know.

The song drifted off beyond the reach of his senses, but the echo of its rhythms remained in his body. Then he heard her say, in a quiet, deliberate tone: "The lesson of the song is that we need to honor Mother Time."

Compared to the complete freedom he had experienced as a dimensionless photon, Dara now felt constrained in the one-way flow of time. And from his point of view, that's all he was: *just a string of sensations unfolding from one moment to the next.* He had no sense of space, no sense of his body. He couldn't move. There was nothing to move. He could only feel the passage of time. Going back was impossible.

He spoke to Yuka: "I know I am dreaming, yet somehow I can see you and I can hear you. I can even see my own body down there. But it's not *me*. It's fast asleep, yet *I* feel fully alert and awake."

"Yes, Dara, you are in lucid dreaming."

Yuka stroked his forehead, her cool hand helped focus his attention. "You are now ready for the next part of the lesson." She slowly, gracefully, stood up, blew out the candles, and moved aside.

* * *

Dara heard a disembodied voice enter the room. It seemed to come from far away. No, he realized, it had no distance. It was neither near nor far, but seemed to come from a time many years in the past. Yet he was hearing it now.

"Very pleased to meet you, Dr. Dara," the voice said in a most gentile and friendly tone. "May I introduce myself: I'm Alfred Whitehead. You may well be wondering how it is that I am speaking to you now, since as you know I have been dead these many decades."

Dara tried to open his eyes to see if he could locate the voice in the room. But it was so dark he couldn't tell whether his eyes were open or shut.

"I believe Professor Tatsuaki has explained to you that no experience is ever lost. In fact, every experience that has ever happened, at any time or place, lives on in the memory of matter. And that includes me, too, of course."

Dara felt the voice moving closer, sounding more intimate.

"The kind professor and his wife have been very gracious to prepare a potent catalyst for you. It has activated some very deep memories stored in the cells of your body. You could say I am speaking to you from the depths of your own flesh."

Dara stiffened. Intuitively this seemed to make sense, but rationally it sounded impossible. Right now, he sure as hell didn't want to figure it out. He just wanted to lie there and *feel*.

"I can see you are somewhat unsure about what I'm saying." Whitehead spoke with a soft, cultured British accent. "But I promise to keep my ideas as simple as possible."

Dara tried to shift his body, to reposition it on the floor and make himself more comfortable. His feet kicked inside the sleeping bag as he twisted and turned. Then he realized he was watching the whole scene, including himself on the futon, from a point somewhere up near the ceiling. He could also see the philosopher floating right next to him.

Dressed in a dark gray Victorian frockcoat with short, wide lapels, Whitehead had the look of a typical Cambridge don. A black silk cravat speckled with tiny white polka dots, and held in place by a mother-of-pearl pin, contrasted elegantly with the stiff white collar of his shirt. He looked the perfect gentleman in every way. Bald, except for neat tufts of gray hair on both temples, his round face and soft eyes emanated a profound wisdom and kindness—forged through some silent personal pain. "Here is a man who has seen deeply into the soul of the world," Dara thought, and felt a surge of emotion as their eyes met.

"Perhaps I should begin with a slogan that summarizes the heart of my philosophy," Whitehead said. *"Past matter, present mind."*

Dara's puzzlement was palpable.

"I admit it's a little clumsy. But if that's all you remember, you will be doing just fine." His voice was reassuring. "I could have said: 'What matters is the past, what we mind is the present—what they create together is the future'." His voice trailed off, giving Dara a moment to reflect.

"I don't want you to just hear my words," he said, his tone even softer. "I want you to *feel* them. Don't listen just with your brain. Use your intuition to see if what I have to say matches your own experience." And he paused again.

"It is really quite simple. Just pay close attention and you'll see what I mean." Whitehead raised a hand in front of Dara.

"Every experience comes into being and lasts for a mere blink of time. Isn't that right?" He snapped his fingers. "No sooner has it appeared, than it's over. Complete. Expired. Slipped into the past." He snapped his fingers again, pronouncing each syllable carefully.

"Of course, Whitehead is correct," Dara thought. "The present moment is elusive. You can never grasp it. It's here, then gone. Everyone knows this."

Whitehead continued: "What hardly anybody notices, however, is that *matter is expired experiences.*" The

Victorian philosopher's voice deepened, alerting Dara that what was coming next was crucial. "Matter, you see, exists just a moment ago." He paused, then emphasized: "Matter is what used to be 'now'."

Dara struggled with the idea that matter is in the past. But
Whitehead insisted that this was an important point to grasp.

"What we know as matter is really layer upon layer of past moments of experience. Matter is the way the past persists into the present." He paused, then repeated: *"Past matter."*

"But, in sharp contrast, every fleeting moment of *now* is alive with experience. Isn't that right?" He smiled at Dara. "It is the easiest thing in the world to test this: Just sit or lie quietly and observe the passing of time within."

Immobile in the single dimension of time, it was indeed easy for Dara to do nothing but pay attention to the flow of experiences coursing through him.

"Yes," he said, *"I feel it.* I live in the present, and the present is alive. My past, even my immediate past of just a moment ago, is gone, dead. *This* is where I live, only in this moment do I exist."

"Present mind," Whitehead emphasized. "What else do you notice?"

"Even though my past is gone, it somehow still lives in me, as if my present self scoops up my past experiences and draws them into me over and over with each passing moment."

"That's quite right. Truly, the past does live on in the present. That's the *only* way it can live on." He paused. "It's as simple as that."

For an instant, Dara though he had grasped it: Time is what connects past and present, matter and mind. Could it really be that simple?

Whitehead read his thoughts: "Yes indeed, Sir. That's the great paradox: The *now* is both infinitesimal and yet eternally replenishing. Every moment comes and goes almost as soon as it arrives; immediately followed by another, and then another. There's no end to the process, thank goodness. Mystics have been telling us this for thousands of years: *Now* is the gateway to eternity."

Whitehead interrupted himself: "Am I going too fast?" He stopped and waited.

The windows of the small room rattled as the storm outside picked up fury, breaking the moment of silence. Dara was glad to be inside.

"I think I've got the essence of what you're saying," he answered, "even though I'd probably have difficulty repeating it."

Whitehead remained silent for a few more moments. And when he spoke, his words were more emphatic.

"Your mind, your inner sense of self, does not remain the same through time. *You are a process.*"

Dara made a heroic effort to follow the great philosopher.

"But where does my new self come from, to replace my self of just a moment ago?"

"Every moment of every life, is an act of creation. 'You' are an expression from the 'nowhere' of pure potential—of eternal objects. In this sense, you are indeed a god—a creative expression of purpose and intelligence. And this is true whether the 'you' I'm talking about is a human being, a dolphin, an insect, a blob of protoplasm, a molecule of DNA, an atom, an electron, or a quantum." Whitehead sensed Dara's growing perplexity, and explained:

"The 'you' that exists at this moment never existed before. Yet it could not exist without all the past 'yous'. The past is essential for the present to come into being."

Dara did his best to keep up, but could not hold and connect all the new ideas. There were just too many for him to digest in one go. He was still reaching for something, some vital core at the heart of Whitehead's teaching.

A flash of lightening lit up the room, followed almost instantly by a crack of thunder overhead. Dara noticed that the light went right through the philosopher, illuminating him like a 3-D hologram.

"My point, dear fellow," Whitehead continued without missing a beat, "is that *all* experience is preserved for all eternity. We can call it the Law of Conservation of Experience."

He reached out and touched the back of Dara's hand. A sense of peacefulness rippled though the NASA scientist's body. He could feel it in both locations: on the floor and up near the ceiling.

"Every moment of experience contains the entire history of the universe." Whitehead closed his eyes. His high forehead wrinkled as he searched his thoughts.

"You are eternal, and eternally creative. That's my message." Then, he added an uncharacteristically cautionary note:

"Each of us orchestrates our own future by selecting and literally incorporating aspects of the past. But remember, we are never in complete control—not of our past, not of our present, nor of our future. Always, there are greater forces at work directing, influencing, and luring our creative choices."

* * *

Try as he might, Dara still couldn't fully grasp Whitehead's teaching—at least, not intellectually. In the darkness, he took a deep breath and felt his chest expand. He held it for a few moments, and then slowly exhaled. His mind raced, running around in circles trying to make sense of what the philosopher had told him. No sooner did he grasp one idea than another took its place, and all meaning seemed to evaporate from the words.

And then he felt himself back in his body, and he noticed he was *noticing*. The closer he paid attention the more he realized the "noticing" was happening in the tension of his muscles, in the blood pumping through his veins, in the electricity shooting through his nerves. It gave him a deeper understanding—an insight beyond words. His sense of self pulsed onward, riding the crest of the moment, pulling his past along with it.

His "self" was converging from the past—from just a moment ago, and from a stream of earlier moments trailing back to his childhood, beyond memory. As soon as he noticed it, the noticing itself became an object for another layer of witnessing in the next, new moment. And as he focused more, the flipping back and forth between observing self and observed object dissolved into nothing but a pure sensation of oscillation. He experienced himself *becoming*—coming into being at every new moment.

At that instant, he had the clearest sense yet of what Tatsuaki and Whitehead meant by a moment of experience blinking in and out of existence. His entire body pulsed as he created himself in the moment, then expired, and then recreated himself a moment later.

"So this is the lesson of time and immortality," he thought. "I am a creative, self-replenishing god, an expression of divine intelligence."

"I'm very pleased to hear you say that," Whitehead announced, clearly enjoying the revelation. "Recognizing your own divinity is powerful."

Dara waited through a long, pregnant silence for Whitehead to say something more. But that was it.

* * *

Then he heard Tatsuaki's voice: "Only you can choose to limit your own freedom."

He felt this truth deeply. The mysterious message—*intelligence seeks expression*—that had launched him on his adventure now made more sense: Spirit is present in all levels of matter itself. Intelligence is immortal.

27
Being Space

Dara woke energized and refreshed. The night's conversations still echoing in his head, he came downstairs to a bowl of Yuka's steaming hot chocolate. Tatsuaki invited him to the breakfast table. Bright sunlight filled the kitchen, and through the window Dara saw that the storm had completely blown over.

"That was some dream," he announced, as he sipped the chocolate. "What on Earth did you put in my drink last night? Professor Whitehead came back to life. I saw him with my own eyes, and we talked face to face."

"Indeed, yes, parts of Whitehead did come back to life," Tatsuaki agreed. "The medicine helped you relive some of his experiences and ideas. Now they live on as *your* knowledge. I trust he spoke to you about matter and mind?"

Dara affirmed he had, but that the details were difficult to recall. The old man asked him to put down his cup.

"Take a moment to pay attention to what's going on in your body right now. Notice your weight, any tension in your muscles, your heart beating, lungs breathing, and the various energies pulsing through you. These are physical processes—your *matter*. But there is also a part of you that is *aware*—the part that feels the pumping of your blood and the energy flowing through your body. That's your consciousness—your *mind*." He paused as Dara focused attention on his own awareness, and Tatsuaki added: "You could say: Energy *flows*, consciousness *knows*."

Outside in the yard, the dog started barking. Yuka got up from the table and went to investigate. Her husband turned to Dara: "Your work here is done. You have learned the importance of time and how it connects matter and mind."

Yuka came back in, accompanied by a policeman. The dog nosed his way between their legs, tail slapping against the table with a clatter. "Shhhh. Be quiet boy. Down." Yuka stroked the dog's head. The animal flopped to the floor but kept his upturned eyes on the faces above him.

"Dara, Kenji. Officer Ronway here has something to report."

"Thanks Ma'am. There's been a fatal wreck on the road to Honolulu. Truck overturned. Driver and a passenger killed, another in critical condition. We found your business card on the dead passenger." The cop looked at Tatsuaki, but Dara felt the news was for him. "No other identification. No driver's license. No credit cards." He described the men and the truck, and asked Tatsuaki if he knew who they were.

"Some men stopped by here yesterday and we served them a meal. We hadn't seen them before. How many did you say were in the truck?"

"Three men. Two dead, one badly injured."

"That could be them, all right." Tatsuaki glanced at Dara: Say nothing about the others, Maya, Bechtel, and the remaining two kidnappers. "They must have been in another vehicle," Dara thought, "and kept going rather than get involved with the police."

After a few more questions, the cop thanked them, and left his phone number in case the Tatsuakis remembered anything that might help identify the occupants. As he walked out the door, he turned and said as an afterthought:

"Oh, by the way a dead dolphin was found washed up on the beach at Shelter Cove. Shot to death. People just have no respect for life these days. They say dolphins are as intelligent as humans, you know?"

Dara felt his insides churn. His worst fears had been confirmed. Darwin was dead.

"Funny thing, though, another dolphin was seen in the cove this morning. I guess, like us, they care about their dead." The cop closed the door behind him and left.

* * *

The road shimmered ahead as Dara drove down the mountain. The late-morning sun warmed the wet tarmac and sent plumes of steam rising from the tropical plants growing by the roadside. Dara was torn. He wanted to head for Honolulu and find Maya, but the message she left with the Tatsuakis urged him to get back to the cove. Now it was too late. With Darwin dead, he saw no point in going back. She was the one in danger. Yet her note assured him she was okay—and the Tatsuakis had confirmed this.

As Dara was saying goodbye, Yuka had handed him a small package, wrapped in plain brown paper.

"Maya asked us to give you this. It's a book we borrowed from her, and she wants you to read it." The old woman clasped her hands over Dara's so that all four grasped the package. "She said it will help you understand what N'bai meant when he said their tribal dreams retreat to the ocean."

At the foot of the mountain he turned left without a moment's hesitation. It wasn't a conscious decision. He just found himself heading for the coast. But inside, his ambivalence grew as if two sides of his personality were about to annihilate each other.

When he reached the shack, he turned the engine off and looked in the rearview mirror. The face that stared back at him was familiar, but the eyes were those of a stranger. Dara had changed. He no longer knew who he was.

He was disappearing. He felt the boundaries of his being melting away, and he could no longer tell where he began and ended. He closed his eyes, and tried to imagine his own face, but all he could feel was a vast empty space stretching out to infinity. In place of his head, the entire universe filled the gap between his shoulders. Everything—including his body, the truck, the beach outside, the limitless ocean, the gulls flying overhead, the white-hot sun, the immense blue sky—all existed in the emptiness where his head should be.

Afraid he was going crazy, Dara got out of the truck and walked down to the beach, taking in deep gulps of fresh sea air. Instinctively, he called out to the waves. But the only response was the roar of the ocean. And then he saw the carcass. The tide had reclaimed the dolphin's body, and it tumbled like a log in the surf. Part of its flank had been ripped off by the bullets.

The waves rolled in on the sand, a carpet of foam spreading out, cleaning the edge of the earth. A meeting of two worlds. Out there lay another universe that somehow had the power to beckon humans as if calling them back to their ancestral home. Dara lay down on the sand, turned onto his stomach and stretched out his arms and legs. He felt himself floating, rotating with the planet, and at that moment he knew that humans could "feel the earth" as dolphins "feel the sea."

A high-pitched screech broke his meditation. He jumped up. Another dolphin had entered the cove and was circling around the carcass, touching it gently with its snout, emitting a mournful cry.

Dara watched the private ceremony in silence, wanting to wade in and comfort the dolphin. But he stayed on shore out of respect. After a while, he heard: "They killed her, Cassandra, my soul companion."

Dara looked twice, unbelieving.

"Darwin! I thought you were dead. Is it really you? How . . .?"

Darwin explained that he and Cassandra had arranged to meet at the cove, and that she had arrived first. The men in black had shot her, believing it was him.

"Why? Why are some humans so cold and confused they kill without need, without compassion? What kind of mind turns to such actions?" Darwin's questions had no answers. His pain tore open the scientist's heart.

Dara now felt a different kind of emptiness consume him. He was black inside. Lost for words, he turned away from the dolphin. Warm tears rolled down his cheeks and he lifted his face toward the cloudless sky. He tried to focus on a speck flying high in the air currents, as if the bird could carry away the sorrows of the world. He began to cry out loud, and through his sobs apologized for all the mistakes he had committed, and for the wrongs of human kind to other animals.

"Goddamnit, Darwin, why would you want to save my people when we are so self-centered and destructive?"

Darwin's reply surprised Dara: "Actually, my friend, too many humans are not self-centered enough. Most of your people have yet to find their centers. We wish to help humans only to help the Earth—to liberate the Great Dream and help true intelligence find full expression in the world."

As he talked, Darwin carefully nudged and repositioned the body of his beloved Cassandra, orienting it toward the ocean.

"I do not have anger or hatred in my heart for the men who killed my companion and who kill many thousands of my people every year. I do not even think of them much. My heart center is too full of sorrow to have room for anything else. I will continue to work with you and Maya, and the others, because our centers have grown close." He stopped, and Dara could now feel that Darwin, too, was emptying himself.

"I will now take Cassandra home. I will be back soon. Wait here for me."

Dara stood in silence at the water's edge as Darwin slipped under his companion's lifeless body and made his way out to the open sea.

28

Zero Point

By the time Maya had reached the Tatsuakis, she knew she had to get to the FEW—and that meant going East. While they held her prisoner in the car, Bechtel and his men had let it slip that the "Bosses" were headquartered in Singapore. And, with Darwin gone, leadership of the NET now fell on the shoulders of the old Malay shaman, N'bai. Only he could initiate Dara into the next stage on his journey into consciousness. Maya and Dara had a double reason to get to Indonesia.

As her captors drove her to a hotel in downtown Honolulu, Maya took advantage of the time to get to know them. She told exotic stories about life in the rainforest and how she came to the United States to be educated in Western ways. Self-disclosure, she hoped, might get them to lower their defenses. Playing "coy female" helped, too.

Secure in the belief that she was their prisoner, the two men riding beside her in the back boasted about their escapades as professional mercenaries. They worked for a private security firm contracted to the NSA. Bechtel sat upfront in silence, with the gang's leader behind the wheel. Maya probed with indirect questions trying to find out who their paymasters were, but they revealed no names.

She told them a little about her research, but downplayed her success with Darwin, saying she was just a student surviving on a scholarship. Her job at the University of Hawaii's Center for Interspecies Research was merely academic, learning what she could about cetacean language while trying to teach her dolphins to understand a few words of English. They had made a terrible mistake killing an innocent animal. Yes, she had succeeded in teaching him some "verbal tricks," but could not fathom why the government, or anyone else, might feel threatened by a breakthrough in interspecies communication.

She struggled to hide her grief and anger over Darwin's slaughter, pretending instead to be a submissive captive, willing to cooperate. More than ever, Maya was determined to get to the faceless men behind the FEW, but trying to appeal to her captors' conscience, she realized, was naïve. Instead, she needed to beat them at their own mind games. She hoped that her shamanic training and martial arts skills would give her a decisive psychological edge. She would also have the element of surprise because they would not expect her to "take it to them."

Now that Darwin was dead, she felt a greater responsibility to carry on his mission. N'bai's knowledge would be vital to their success in releasing the Great Dream, and keeping the code from the FEW. Somehow, she would have to connect Dara with N'bai.

"Our work could help others in education," she said, deflecting attention, "especially kids in kindergarten. Doesn't it make sense that a better understanding of how other intelligent animals learn and communicate could tell us a lot about ourselves?"

Her captors showed little interest, but she wanted to impress on them that her project was innocent, even innocuous. Telling them part of the truth, she hoped, would sound convincing and harmless. She continued talking.

"Dolphins are very social creatures. For them, the pod is paramount. While humans rely on thinking, dolphins *feel* their connections to the world around them. They rely first and foremost on their relationships. I think we can learn from them, and develop educational programs to help our future generations. . ."

A loud ringing interrupted Maya, and one of the men guarding her took the call on his cell phone. She tried to listen in, but couldn't overhear.

"A-okay. Everything's set up at the hotel," he told the driver. "We can take her there now." Bechtel punched in the destination on the GPS and they headed for Honolulu to await further instructions.

Maya's attempts to convince her captors that she posed no threat seemed to have worked. The two hired guns in the back seat joked and chatted with her on the drive to the city.

The problem was Graham Bechtel. He reminded her that she was the real target, not the dolphin. Her work—with or without the "fish"—had alarmed the Bosses. When she asked why, he boasted he had downloaded her report from Dara's computer at the Stanford lab, and had passed on the information to the FEW.

Communicating with Darwin had opened a Pandora's box, he told her. Her report indicated she had discovered the existence of a code to unlock "alien intelligence," and they wanted to know more. He had been assigned by the NSA to track and report any unusual developments in the academic world—especially if they involved codes that might prove useful to national security.

"So, you're an NSA agent?" Maya asked.

Bechtel grinned, "No comment. Let's just say I get funding from a variety of government sources. That's my job: to raise money for research, so people like you and Dara can continue your work."

He turned around to Maya, hemmed in by the two burly mercenaries.

"Look, these are complicated times," his tone was serious, "and only fools think in terms of black or white, right or wrong. Many of our traditional institutions are under threat, domestically and globally. Rising crime rates, economic stress, declines in family values and education, corporate espionage, political corruption, terrorism . . . the list goes on and on."

He fell silent for a moment, as though he was about to say something and changed his mind. Then:

"We have to take precautions to protect ourselves. Someone has to take charge."

Maya knew better than to argue, and replied ambiguously:

"Yes, of course, if threatened, we need to understand the situation and act accordingly." She probed some more.

"I'm still in the dark: Just what exactly about my work worries your bosses?"

"For one thing, they don't like the sound of 'alien intelligence,'" Bechtel explained, "and they want to find out who or what these 'aliens' are. Besides Islamic terrorists, we still need to keep an eye on the Communists. After the fall of the Soviet Union they are less visible, but still working behind the scenes in many states. Or perhaps these 'aliens' are something even more dangerous?"

Maya kept quiet, sensing that Bechtel and the FEW had misinterpreted her report about "alien intelligence." She just shrugged her shoulders. He elaborated:

"Since you work on SETI, they wondered if your 'aliens' might even be visitors from outside the solar system." He laughed. "Of course, they don't really believe that. I would be one of the first to know of any contact. But they do believe in hedging their bets. Understandably, they rule nothing out until they have the information they need. Part of my job is to help them get it."

Instead of playing aggrieved victim, Maya decided to play along. As an *aikido* master, she knew how to "blend" and redirect her captors' energies to work to her advantage. The more Bechtel said about why the FEW wanted her, the clearer it became that both he and the bosses were confused about the noetic code. In fact, it turned out, they suspected it might be some highly advanced computer or mathematical algorithm capable of cracking the zero-point energy barrier. She encouraged the misunderstanding.

When they got back to the hotel, Bechtel took Maya directly up to the suite, while the three mercenaries grabbed a snack in the bar. She used this time to work on him some more. He told her the FEW had figured out from her transcripts that Darwin was either in possession of a potentially world-changing code or had some of the key pieces and knew where to find the rest.

"But my dolphin is dead. You killed him," her matter-of-fact tone masked the fire in her gut. "And now I'm the only one who can fill in the gaps." Her best strategy for protecting the code, she figured, would be to step in as a decoy, while Dara and N'bai guided the rest of the Network to complete Darwin's mission.

"I think we can help each other," she said. "But I need to know more about the Bosses."

Bechtel relaxed a little and said he was mostly in the dark about the men at the top, but gave her the gist of the FEW's grand plan. They serve at the pleasure of an international syndicate of corporate and government leaders, he told her. Their aim is world governance and security for all nations. To achieve this, they have taken control of the global economy by "managing" six interrelated industries: financial markets, oil and energy, arms trade, bioengineering, information technology, and mass media. They also work closely with agribusiness and pharmaceuticals, he added.

"Oh my god," Maya thought, "they want it all: energy, weapons, money, media, food, and medicine. Total control of people's lives. Total control of the planet." With evident irony, she said:

"That's a mighty ambitious goal. I'm honored to think my work is viewed with such significance."

Gradually, Bechtel's suspicions waned, and he volunteered more. Maya discovered that the FEW believe the greatest threat to their "Global Security Plan" is the rapid spread of activist consciousness communities.

"Our efforts will work only if we win the confidence of the masses," Bechtel said. His allegiance was clear. "At the very least, we need to ensure they don't resist the GSP, even if they don't actively support it." He added that corporate consolidation of the media was key to winning the hearts and minds of the world's populations.

Maya expressed genuine interest in this strategy, and Bechtel was pleased to elaborate. The FEW focus on two groups in particular, he said: The Greens, Earth-loving environmentalists, who are increasingly more vocal about sustainability and the need to combat climate change.

"They just don't get the big picture," he complained. "Civilization has always marched forward by taming the wilderness and increasing mastery over the natural world—from fire to nuclear fuel. If we don't control the forces of nature, they will control us."

Maya was startled to hear the depth of Bechtel's commitment to human domination. It confirmed for her the chasm between different paradigms. She viewed the world as a network of interrelated species that need to cooperate for mutual survival. Bechtel, and people with his values, believe strongly that "humans are special." One group goes by the principle "caring is sharing," the other by "might is right."

"For the most part, these are well-meaning, but seriously misguided people," Bechtel opined. "The Greens refuse to see that the most effective way to bring progress, peace, and balance to the world is to let the free market decide. Technological innovation is the only way forward."

Maya said nothing. Then reminded him: "You mentioned two groups."

"Yes, besides the Greens we also have to contend with the Lights," he said. "Networks of consciousness-raising spiritual seekers, who believe that humanity and all life on Earth participate in some cosmic unfolding of spiritual evolution." He spoke with distain.

"They are a bunch of navel-gazing nuts, out to undermine the gains of reason," Bechtel scowled. "They reject everything that science has achieved. If they got their way, they would take civilization back to the Middle Ages, when faith and superstition ruled." His voice grew more intense. "Instead of the Enlightenment, that gave us democracy, freedom, and the rule of law, these New Age types seek so-called *spiritual* enlightenment." He rolled his eyes in dismay. "They preach and teach that people should develop their own inner authority. But that way lies madness and anarchy. It can only lead to social chaos."

By now, Maya realized the magnitude of the task she faced. Bechtel and the FEW were by no means idiots—though, in her view, they may well be insane. Their reach is deep and global. Despite their denials, they must know that time is running out for the Earth, as populations continue to explode, and global pollution keeps pace. They must know that economies based on fossil fuel are not sustainable in the long run. But, as far as she could see, they are not interested in the long run. They want as much power and control as they can grab today.

Bechtel explained that the FEW's grand vision for "Global Security" hinged, ultimately, on tapping into zero-point energy. ZPE is so abundant, he enthused, that a cubic centimeter of empty space contains more power than the total amount of energy tied up in all the atoms of the entire universe.

"Now *that's* a power source!" he exclaimed with delight. "Whoever gets control of the 'mining' rights to ZPE will have solved the energy crisis forever. *Permanent Global Security*, that's the dream!" His eyes gleamed with evangelical zeal.

Yes, ZPE would give them all the power they could ever dream of, Maya thought. "A sure recipe for a global nightmare." Silently, she reassured herself that accessing zero-point energy is intimately tied in with the evolution of consciousness. Getting it will involve "unfreezing" light from matter, by aligning with the creative force of the photon. She had learned from Darwin that at that level of reality, we're dealing with the borderland where mind and matter meet. Success would depend on undertaking the photon's journey from light to enlightenment.

"The FEW have not grasped the significance of the evolutionary sequence," she thought. "In a way, that's too bad. If they could see that beyond the rational mind are higher states of consciousness, then they might awaken to the error of their ways. To open up to Spirit, they would have to let go of ignorance and greed, and their obsession for domination."

But it is also possible, she realized, that if they glimpsed the power of higher consciousness, they would strive to suppress it. Instead of opening up to its vast potential, the FEW would be even more determined to prevent the masses from ever gaining access to the noetic code. If Darwin was correct, and Bechtel seemed to confirm it, then the FEW and their paymasters were already controlling the mass media in a coordinated global effort to entrance and deceive the people with false information.

"If the FEW got hold of the noetic code," she speculated privately, "they could learn enough to lead the people astray with a pseudo code. And if a critical mass of people does not master the true code in time, the Great Dream would stay repressed forever. "We cannot let that happen," she thought. "Not now, not after we've come this far."

She had to get Bechtel to convince the Bosses that she had what they wanted—and that she was willing to meet with them. Then she would distract the FEW with a promise to decipher nonexistent code embedded in recordings of Darwin's clicks and squeaks.

"You seem to be an important link in the chain," she coaxed. "I have a proposal: This code is so revolutionary, it should be hand-delivered to the people at the highest levels."

She tempted Bechtel with the prospect of basking in the glory of personally giving the most powerful people on the planet what they wanted most.

"If I help them crack the code for ZPE, you will have assisted in perhaps the greatest scientific breakthrough ever." He lit up at the recognition.

She hoped this wild goose chase would buy time for Dara and the Network. By now, her Stanford colleague should have advanced far enough along the evolutionary sequence to know what to do next.

That was her plan. But she had underestimated the FEW. Bechtel's phone rang with new instructions. Analyzing her report, they had found out about N'bai, the old Burmese shaman, and that he was one of the leaders in the NET searching for the noetic code. Maya had met N'bai many years ago in Burma when she was on sabbatical. She had invited him to return with her to the West, and they had lectured together on indigenous wisdom in European universities.

Now, with Darwin out of the way, N'bai was next on the list. The hunt had shifted to Asia. Bechtel's orders were to take Maya to Rangoon.

29

Bearing Witness

"It is good to be with you again," Darwin told Dara when he returned. "Tell me about Maya. Did she make it off the island?"

Dara recounted the events of the past few days—about how he and Maya got separated; about her note that she was okay; about meeting the Tatsuakis and his encounter with Whitehead.

"I'm glad you are both well," Darwin said. "And I'm glad to hear you took the next step in your initiation without me. Time is running out for all of us."

Darwin moved closer toward the shore.

"You need to reconnect with Maya as soon as possible. She may be using soul charge with her captors, but she remains in danger. Strong forces are marshaled against us. We need all the help we can get to liberate the Great Dream."

Darwin sounded more concerned than Dara had ever heard before.

"Thankfully, the heavens are on our side. The code is distributed around the globe. The lights in the sky over California carried one part of the message. The rest of the code is hidden deep in other seas. The most important part lies waiting in the Indian Ocean. We have a friend there trying to reach it. But I fear for him. He is old, and no match for the forces hunting us down. We need to move fast to do our part."

Dara could feel the dolphin scanning his insides.

"I can see you are much clearer than before. You have been emptying yourself."

Dara told Darwin about his experience on the beach.

"I felt I was disappearing. It's as if everything I have known about myself is changing, and I no longer know who I am anymore."

"Ah yes, this is good news. Like a chrysalis becoming a butterfly, you must dissolve your past identity before recreating yourself anew. This is always so on the path of transformation. Work with me, I can help you."

"I am grateful for your teachings, Darwin," Dara said sincerely, "for opening my mind to other ways of knowing. I am ready now to move on past reason, to develop noetic ways of seeing and being."

Dara felt a ripple in his rib cage, and realized he was "hearing" the dolphin chuckle.

"Yes we need to move quickly, but you are in too much of a hurry, Stanford. I am very pleased that you have progressed this far, but let me emphasize something I should have said before. *You cannot skip any stage in the evolutionary sequence.* Only when you have mastered the domain of reason can you begin to move on to what is beyond reason."

The NASA scientist acknowledged his impatience. He waded out to a rock exposed by the retreating tide. Hoisting himself up, he sat down, hanging ten in the warm, blue water. It felt good. The hot sun penetrated his body, and he relaxed. He pulled out a wet bandana from the pocket of his shorts, wrapped it around his temples, and adjusted his sunglasses to block the glare. The dolphin peered at him from just beneath the surface.

"You have spent many years—and your culture has spent many, many generations—cultivating reason, but you have not yet mastered it. It may surprise you to hear this: The problem with your civilization is that *you have too little reason.*"

This was indeed a surprise to Dara. The last thing he expected to hear from a shamanic dolphin was that humanity needed more, not less, reason. Wasn't the root of the human predicament this over-reliance on logic and the conquest of intuition and dreams? Darwin picked up Dara's train of thought.

"Yes, an *over*-reliance on reason has pushed your species out of balance with the rest of nature. But what you have failed to see is that over-reliance on reason is not at all rational. It is a distortion of reason."

Darwin could see the scientist's growing perplexity, and tried to clarify.

"This is not a new insight. Right back at the dawn of Western philosophy, the great Socrates and Plato knew that reason was limited, and that before anyone could know what those limits were they had to master reason to get there. Only then, could they move to the next stage."

Dara noticed a strange meeting between his thoughts and feelings. As before, ideas came and went through his mind, but now, instead of looping through the circuits of his brain, it seemed as if his thoughts were rising up from within his whole body. His reasoning faculties were still intact, but in the silence he could clearly sense how his thoughts were flowing through him. Instead of being disconnected from the feelings in his body, reason was expressing these feelings, giving them a voice.

"Yes, it is better to feel your thinking," Darwin resumed, "rather than merely think your thoughts."

Dara understood Darwin's words, but this did little to relieve growing anxiety about his disappearing identity. The dolphin responded immediately.

"You arrived here today already shaken loose from your foundations." Darwin paused, and Dara sensed a punch line. "The problem, I hope you are beginning to see, is not whether you are your body or your mind—the problem is whether you are really *'you'.*"

This last remark unnerved Dara even more. And the world seemed to respond in sympathy. A hawk circling high above on thermal currents let out a piercing cry, and swooped toward the dune grasses. Dara stood motionless. In that silent moment, a cavity opened up inside him, as though the middle of his body had vanished. Once, again, instead of his head, he felt a blank space straddling his shoulders.

Darwin encouraged him: "Go on. Tell me what you feel. Tell me where you are."

"This is very curious. I feel as if I'm emptying out, as if my body is filling with nothingness, with space. Yet that spaciousness seems to deepen my sense of who I am."

Darwin instructed him to pay closer attention. "Is it really a deeper sense of who *you* are?"

"I'm not sure I can find the right words." He thought for a moment. "It's as if the space is filled with awareness. There's a sense of *presence* more real than my normal self, and this presence can choose to focus in on whatever it is I call 'me' or my 'self'."

"Excellent. Please continue. Describe what happens when the presence focuses in."

Dara felt his thoughts floating freely in the space. They passed by like images on a screen—being *witnessed.* He tried to focus on the witness, and the flux of thoughts came streaming to a point. The "witness" collapsed into a sense of I-ness, one more thought among all the rest, and created a feeling of individual identity.

"I am the Witness," he exclaimed, excited to have discovered his true self. But as soon as he spoke, the words no longer felt right.

"Good. Good. Now tell me what just happened."

"I tried to focus on the Witness, and the feeling of space collapsed to a point."

"Yes. Yes. Of course. But what happened when you focused? What did you *do?*"

Dara felt the stream of thoughts and images race through his mind. "I . . . eh . . . I thought about the Witness."

"Precisely. You *thought.* You collapsed the Witness by using your rational mind. You turned the *experience* of witnessing into an *idea,* and then you thought that that idea was *you.* But at the very instant 'you' appeared from the vastness of space, 'you' no longer felt as full, as immensely *real,* as the Witness. Right?"

"Yes. I think so. I can't really say what happened, except that for a moment I thought I had found my sense of identity as a point in the vastness of infinite space."

"You did. You did exactly that. That's what reason does. That's what it is so superb at doing. Reason is a form of self-reflexive consciousness. It congeals identity out of the web of relationships in the Presence, in the Whole—like an atom condensing as a particle of matter out of the universal fields of force and energy."

Dara made a mental note: "Identity comes into being like atoms in space."

"Reason is what gives you your sense of individual identity," Darwin confirmed, "your sense of 'me-ness.' It does this by separating 'you' from the rest of the universe."

"Is that such a bad thing?" Dara wondered, feeling protective of his individuality.

"Not at all," Darwin replied. "In fact, building a strong ego is essential for success in the material world. Only by mastering the ego-self can you move beyond to what comes next." He paused, then added with emphasis: "*You have to know your self before you can let it go.* You have to find it before you can lose it."

Darwin's message hit home. After his divorce, Dara's sense of identity had been shattered. For months, he had struggled just to get through the day. He had walked around in a daze, drowning in emotions, feeling wounded and fragile. He couldn't think straight. Trying to drag himself out of this quagmire, he had dived headlong into his work, and concentrated on building up his rational faculties again. Eventually he made it, and developed a secure sense of who he was—a successful NASA scientist.

But then he met Maya and her dolphin.

Now Darwin was driving him to the verge of insanity again, breaking down his hard-won identity as a competent researcher. His precious sense of self danced in and out of existence.

"As you struggle for identity," Darwin continued, "your rational ego forgets that the self is on a journey through many levels. It collapses all of reality to flatland." He paused.

"Your civilization is stuck in the mistaken belief that physical reality is all there is, and that human reason is the end of the line for evolution."

An evolutionary dead-end, Dara thought. Darwin leaped out of the water, eyes sparkling, jaws wide open in what Dara was sure was a beaming smile. Rows of tiny teeth glinted in the sun.

"The way to truly find yourself isn't to obliterate reason. You find yourself by honestly and courageously acknowledging the limitations of the rational mind—by opening up to noetic consciousness."

Splashing around in the waves created by his nosedive, Darwin chirped and chuckled.

"That's our purpose, Stanford. That's the journey we are on."

"But what about all the progress science has made through the centuries?" Stirred by loyalty, Dara was concerned. "How can science and reason be mired in a kind of flatland if they reveal so much about reality?"

"You're quite right to defend your science," Darwin responded. "Indeed it has achieved a lot. But so much of science is remote and meaningless to the masses. Our job now is to touch the people, to connect with what they already know deep within . . ." Darwin paused, then elaborated.

"But even more, we need to connect with what the people dream—with their visions and aspirations."

Dara understood, and asked if, in the end, dreams were more powerful than reason wouldn't that spell the end of science and modern civilization as we know it?

"Isn't that what the FEW are afraid of?"

"The Great Dream will not obliterate reason or science as our pursuers fear. But it will shift the balance of power in the world. That's why we need to move swiftly. If the FEW crack the noetic code they will try to develop a false code—one that co-opts and distorts noetic insights and uses them to conquer instead of connect."

Darwin explained further: "For years, my people have been scanning the oceans for information about the leaders who control your world. We've known about the FEW for some time. Backed by limitless funds, they have penetrated New Age communities—even parts of our Network—posing, for example, as healers and teachers working with subtle energies. They are shrewd enough to realize that explorers in these fields are opening up the way toward a new future. They know that the old paradigm is on its last legs. Their best line of defense, they believe, is to learn enough about the new paradigm and then mislead the people with familiar terminology, and feel-good ideas. But in actual fact, the messages and images they are spreading are meaningless imposters."

Darwin came right up to the rock where Dara was sitting, head bobbing out of the water, snout brushing his toes. His tone was still serious.

"The FEW have just one goal: to suppress the Great Dream. That's what we've got to prevent. That's why it is vital we get to the noetic code first.

Darwin nipped Dara's right ankle, indicating the session was over. "We are moving against a rising tide of masterful deception, and we have very little time."

30

The Turning Point

The sun had dipped below the horizon by the time the lesson was finished. After Darwin left to "feel the waters of the world" for keys to the noetic code, Dara lay on the sand scanning the dome of stars and listening to the rhythmic, eternal motion of the ocean as the waves carried it to the shore. Out there, he sensed the spirit of the sea was communing with the spirit of the skies. Somehow, the sea was receiving information from above.

Before he left, Darwin had instructed Dara to work on integrating head and heart. "Remember, feelings can guide you through changes in time, and reason is your guide through the dimensions of space," he had said. "You need to bring them together to master the world of matter. Only then will you reach the all-important Turning Point. Until you do, you will not be able to help Maya or me, or play your role in releasing the Great Dream."

Darwin had explained that matter is a crucial stage in evolution. Indeed, the density of matter confines Spirit, and by doing so, provides it with opportunities to learn and grow. "Matter is frozen light," was the phrase Darwin had used. It is heavy and massive. But the "drag" of gravity is matter's great gift to Spirit.

"Imagine being suspended in free space and trying to move," Darwin had said. "Unless you could place your hands or feet on a solid surface you couldn't even begin to move. You'd have no leverage, nothing to hold on to. Well it's kind of like that with Spirit. It needs to get a grip on solid matter before it can move itself and evolve." Darwin paused.

"By pushing against the mass of matter, Spirit can pull itself through the evolutionary sequence. In short, Spirit needs the friction of matter for its own self-revelation."

Dara had difficulty squaring this with what he knew from science. Darwin continued:

"Matter is the supreme challenge to consciousness. It hones intelligence."

He went on to explain: "Ultimately, we are all beings of Light, made up of photons. Each of us—whether doctor, dolphin, dog, or diatom—has the potential to realize Spirit. To arrive there, however, we must move through every stage on the evolutionary arc."

Lying on the sand, the warm Pacific lapping at his feet, Dara thought about the stages in the evolutionary sequence and how this knowledge had altered his outlook on science, on the world—on his own life. He had always supposed that whenever scientists finally make contact with extraterrestrial intelligence they would recognize it because it was *rational*. He had been trained to equate intelligence with reason, with intellect. Now he knew intelligence involved a great deal more.

The events of the past weeks had radically changed him. Not only had he learned that intelligence guides the cells of his own body, and pulses through the world around him, but that if—*when*—we make contact with conscious beings outside our solar system, there's every chance they will have evolved beyond the stage of reason.

As he lay on the sand gazing at the stars, he thought about his life and career. For as long as he could remember, he had been looking skyward, searching the heavens for signs of alien intelligence. And now he found that what he had been searching for all this time had been himself. He realized that as long as his own feelings and intuitions were blocked by reason, an important part of his own psyche would remain "alien" to him. No wonder he had difficulty connecting with others; he hadn't even connected with himself.

He turned to look at the reflection of the night sky on the calm lagoon and drifted off to the sound of the waves lapping on the beach.

* * *

Suddenly, the silence of the night was broken by the buzz of an engine in the distance. Dara sat up and looked around trying to locate the source. It seemed to be coming from out over the sea. He saw a moving point of light in the sky and at first thought it might be a shooting star. It was headed directly for land. As the point of light grew larger, a bright beam shot out in front, like a searchlight scanning the surface of the waves. Closer by the second, the noise grew louder until all Dara could hear was an ear-splitting roar of blades tearing through the air above his head. He dived for cover behind the rocks. The air churned like a tornado, whipping up the lagoon and spraying the land with ocean rain. Dara watched, awestruck, as the helicopter touched down, sandblasting everything in its reach.

When the blades stopped turning and the air settled down again, the door to the glass cockpit opened and out stepped a gray-haired old man. Stooped slightly at the shoulders, he wore a brown tweed jacket, with a red silk handkerchief tucked into the breast pocket.

"Sorry if I disturbed you," he said looking directly where Dara was hiding, "but I still haven't quite got the hang of this." He strolled over toward the rocks. Dara hunched down further not sure what to do.

"Let me introduce myself," the old man announced sounding jolly and impish. "Arthur Middleton Young at your disposal. Our mutual friend Darwin said I needed to clear up a few things with you and to guide you through the world of matter."

Dara crouched in a crevice between two large rocks, feeling a mixture of fear and disbelief. It was one thing to have met Alfred North Whitehead in a dream, but this was a dead man walking on solid ground—*and* flying a helicopter! All the same, he felt he should be courteous to this disarming visitor.

"Eh, good evening Mr. Young. What are you doing here?" Dara crawled out and brushed himself down, wiping the wet sand off his face and spitting the grit out from between his teeth. He kept a safe distance.

"I just told you. I'm here to clear up a few points about the evolution of consciousness." He noticed Dara was covered with sand and spray thrown up by the whirlwind. "I am very sorry about that. I'm still a novice at this game," and he nodded toward the 'copter. "Oh, I don't mean flying—I invented that machine—I mean this kind of inter-dimensional travel." He sat down on a rock near Dara.

"I'll try to make this brief, even though it took me many years to master the mechanics of matter. But you have a good start, having studied physics. Though I must say if you want to really understand matter the best thing is to be an engineer."

He took off his horn-rimmed glasses, stuffed them in the top pocket of his jacket, looked wistfully at the sky, and then at Dara.

"As a young student, I was ambitious enough to want to develop a theory of the entire cosmos—including its spiritual dimensions. I was dissatisfied with science because it explored a very limited slice of reality. Pretty soon, though, I realized that I wasn't the least bit prepared to work out a complete theory, and that the best place to start was with matter. Only by mastering the material world could I begin to see how universal laws work in our everyday lives."

His eyes twinkled. "After a few false starts, I decided to design a vertical lift-off vehicle. During my research, I discovered that the idea went back as far as Leonardo da Vinci. What a tremendous genius, by the way—the greatest all-round intellect that ever lived. Anyway, those early designs—including many of my own—all came to grief because the rotating blades shook the body of the craft till it shattered."

He combed his fingers through his thinning hair, pushing it back off his forehead.

"I set myself a goal of fifteen years to accomplish the task. It took eighteen. When I finished, I sold my invention, and so the first successful vertical lift-off flying machine was the Bell helicopter."

He waved his large, bony hands in the air and slapped them on his knees—a gesture that said "So much for that phase." Dara noticed that beyond the ridges of big knuckles, Young's hands were graced with long slender fingers that would have been equally at home building precision machines or performing delicate surgery.

"Having mastered the mechanics of matter, and having learned some profoundly important lessons along the way, I returned to my adolescent dream of developing a theory of the cosmos. From then on, I was free to explore the evolution of consciousness."

He wiped away a spot of saliva from the corner of his mouth. "That was the turning point for me. The rest of my life was dedicated to working out as many details of the theory as my eighty-nine years permitted."

"I am familiar with the general outline of your ideas," Dara said. "In fact, working with Darwin, I have moved beyond understanding the evolutionary arc intellectually, and have been guided, step by step, through an initiation."

"I'm delighted to see you've come this far." Young crooked a finger inviting the scientist to sit next to him. "But what have you *learned?*" He moved over, making room for the NASA scientist, and lit a cigarette.

Dara thought for a moment. "Most of all, I've come to realize there are different levels of reality and different ways of knowing. As a scientist, I always knew the world is going through an evolutionary process, but I was not aware this involves different levels of consciousness and freedom."

"Well I am impressed, you've certainly caught on quickly. However, you've got it only partly correct. Remember, the universal process descends from Light to Matter. This is so consciousness can *use* mechanism to learn and evolve—as it ascends back to Spirit. Being a scientist, you will be tempted to get stuck in Matter. I can understand that. And you can certainly learn many useful lessons at this level. But keep in mind that the lessons of the material world are only steppingstones to higher consciousness. Your journey will take you deep into matter, but you must also retain enough consciousness to *choose* to transcend the pull of matter."

Dara listened carefully. This was a very different view of evolution from what he had learned in science. "First Light descends into Matter, then there's a Turning Point, followed by a homecoming journey to Spirit."

Young smiled at the scientist. "Go on."

Dara's voice rose in pitch as he tried to suppress a slight tremor: "I'm eager to learn about the Turning Point. That's why you're here, I assume? I need to master the level of matter so I can rescue Maya."

Young reached into his inside pocket and pulled out a piece of crumpled paper. He unfolded it, handed it to Dara, and pointed to a diagram of the Reflexive Arc depicting the evolution of consciousness. "This is the map or our journey."

"And the noetic code is our guide for this journey?" Dara asked, as he studied Young's arc of evolution.

"Precisely, my friend. You have to master multiple ways of knowing in order to move through all levels. Humanity has been on this path for many thousands of years. We are at a critical time in the evolution of our species. A great number of people are on the threshold between the stages of Mind and Soul."

Young nodded at the diagram. "Be sure to keep that safe." He stood up, threw his cigarette in the sand, and scrunched it underfoot. "But never mistake the map for the territory."

Dara slipped the piece of paper into his pocket. The old engineer turned toward the helicopter standing on the sand like a giant dragonfly.

"Keep that in mind as a symbol of how mastery of the world of matter and mechanics can lead to spiritual enlightenment," he said pointing at the machine with obvious delight. "It is a physical manifestation of a far more profound principle at work throughout the universe: the *torus*. Think of it as a doughnut shape with energy and consciousness constantly flowing in and out of a hole in the center. But that is advanced cosmology. Our task right now is to get you out of your head and into matter.

"If you are ready, we'll begin by giving you a direct experience of why matter is a necessary stage in the evolution of consciousness."

"I'm ready."

31

A Taste of Hell

"Are you serious?" Dara was sure it was a joke when Arthur Young invited him to take a spin in the helicopter.

"Don't you trust me? I can assure you if anyone knows how this machine works, it's me. I want to show you something." Young began walking briskly toward the craft. Over his shoulder, he shouted with characteristic impishness, "It's a matter of spirit."

Dara caught up with him and demanded an explanation. "If I'm going to go up in that thing with you, I need to know where we're headed—and why. How's that going to help me rescue Maya?"

"This is exactly what you need. It's your next step. Actually, we're not going up so much as going down."

The old man hopped up into the pilot's seat and began checking the dials. Dara blanched.

"Going down? What do you mean 'going down'?

"If I'm not mistaken, young man, you already agreed you were ready for the descent into matter. If you haven't got the guts, better say so now. I can't promise you a pretty ride. I can't even promise you'll pull through. In the end, that's up to you. But I *do* promise if you are going to make it, I'm your best guide for this portion of the journey. Few have ever mastered matter as I have—by seeing right through to its hidden spirit."

He fired up the engine, and the long blades began slowly turning. Dara stood immobile, frozen in indecision. Young threw a sly, knowing look at the NASA scientist. "Are you on the bus, or off the bus?" Next thing he knew, they were soaring above the beach, the blackness of the night sky all around them. Below, the ocean heaved like a sea of thick oil.

"This is notoriously the most difficult part of the journey—by far," Young said, sounding as though this news was meant to be reassuring. "And the greater the challenge, the greater the learning." He adjusted a few dials, and dimmed the light in the cockpit.

"As you know by now, Spirit has chosen to involve itself with matter in order to learn more and more about its own hidden potentials." And he quipped: "Matter is friction. It rubs Spirit up the right way." He chuckled, and turned to his companion.

"Wise men and women through the ages have known this, and have called it the 'dark night of the soul' for very good reason. Descending into the depths of their own personal dark night of spiritual despair, they finally broke through and woke up."

The 'copter continued climbing, and Dara could just make out the curvature of the planet below. "How high can this thing fly?" he asked, trying to sound unconcerned.

"Oh, as high as we need to," came back the pilot's cryptic answer. "You know the old saw, 'What goes up must come down?' . . . well now it's 'The higher you go, the deeper you fall'."

At that instant, the cockpit filled with a terrifying silence. Young had switched off the engine. The rotating blades slowed, and for a timeless moment the bubble of glass and metal seemed to just hang there in the blackness of space.

"Jeezus! What have you done?" Dara screamed.

Young leaned back, hands behind his head, and simply said: "This is it, young feller. Hold on for the ride of your life."

The craft spun out of control, and plummeted toward the Earth like a piece of lead shot. Dara shut his eyes tight. All he could hear were his own involuntary cries and gulps, and the rush of night air as the flimsy craft accelerated through it. His mind buzzed with a million thoughts and images a second. He wished to himself that right now he was a religious man who had a prayer—if not to save himself, then to soothe his terror and put his mind to rest.

Next he heard an almighty crash, and the sound of rushing air gave way to the roar of water. They'd hit the sea. The last thought Dara had was "In one nanosecond I'll be dead." At least, he expected that would be his last thought. But a full second later, then another, and another, he was still having thoughts.

"What the hell is happening? I'm still alive."

He looked over at Arthur Young, who sat there calmly, smiling. "You're alive, too," he said to the old man, then immediately corrected himself: "You're still here."

"Don't worry about me. Just keep your attention on what's going on around you. Take mental notes. You'll need them later."

The helicopter was still intact. That was the first thing he noticed. But they were still falling, or sinking—slower now, descending through the dark water. Down. Down. All the way down. After what seemed like an eternity, they hit bottom. Young leaned forward, and began fiddling with the controls.

"This part could get a little tricky," he mumbled, more to himself than to his companion. "I've never flown through solid matter before." He flipped a switch, and the blades started rotating in the opposite direction. The craft shuddered as they heaved and pushed through the weight of the water. Gradually, the blades picked up momentum, and Dara began to notice sand swirling up past the windows. They were still sinking—into the sea floor.

Everything went silent. Pitch dark. Dara felt a hand on his knee, and he reached down to grab it. Arthur was reassuring him to hold on. He was surprised at the warmth and strength of the old man's touch. Weren't dead people supposed to be cold? The invisible hand gave a gentle squeeze and then withdrew.

Dara could feel the vehicle continue to slowly burrow down, and then he realized the cockpit was filling with sand. After a while, it completely surrounded him. He couldn't move—not his legs, not his arms, not his hands, not his fingers, and even if he wanted to, he could no longer open his eyes. He couldn't feel his chest move or open his mouth to breathe. Yet somehow he was still breathing. Completely immobilized, a wave of panic washed through him. The only movement he could feel was the rapid-fire beating of his own heart.

He waited for something to happen. He waited. And waited. And nothing did. Time seemed to swirl about him in crazy rhythms, one moment seeming to slow to a standstill, another seeming to zip by at the speed of light. He lost all sense of how much or how little clock time was passing. Eventually, all he could do was feel himself existing from one moment to the next. The thought crossed his mind, "This is probably what it feels like to be a rock—if a rock could feel, that is." From a human perspective, the passage of time for a rock would seem to be almost nonexistent, measured in eons, hundreds of millions of years, instead of minutes or hours. But to the rock, it would feel like this: an almost timeless persistence of existence—bare, motionless duration. An eternity in a moment.

The thought of being imprisoned like this, immobilized till the end of time, triggered another surge of anxiety. Dara felt he might last a few hours, or even a few days, but the prospect of being stuck beneath the sea floor for an eternity was more than his imagination could handle. He willed with every cell of his body to find even the slightest movement in his arms. Nothing. If he could even wriggle a finger that just might be enough to begin to dig himself out. Still nothing. He couldn't even locate where his fingers were anymore. The mounting fear became unbearable and he tried to yell, but the most he could do was hear a silent scream reverberate inside his own head.

The terror continued to grow, and each eternal moment fed the next with excruciating panic, building to an inevitable, yet never-ending crescendo. He wanted to die. He wished he had died in the crash. He wished he had never been born. He wished he had never grown up to be a student of the skies. He wished he had never developed a passion for extraterrestrial intelligence. He wished he had never joined SETI. He wished he had never worked with Bechtel. He wished he had never met Maya or Darwin. He wished that along with Whitehead and Young, the Tatsuakis were only figments of his imagination. He wished he'd never heard of the noetic code or the Great Dream. He wished for existence itself to dissolve to nothing.

Each wish and thought just compounded the terror. He had no control over what had happened. And worse, he had no control over what was happening now. Adding to the panic, he realized that whatever would happen in the future would be exactly the same as this eternal damnation of the frozen present. Unbearable anxiety gave way to bleak despair. His mind went blank. His feelings numbed. His last wish, it seemed, might be coming true. He was disappearing from existence.

And then a thought returned: *Nothing* was happening. He was terrified of the present repeating itself over and over for eternity. But the present was empty. Nothing was happening now, and therefore there was nothing in the future to worry about. There was no future.

His whole being focused intensely on the present moment, and as he paid closer and closer attention he began to notice something he'd completely overlooked. He was covered with millions of grains of sand, tiny crystals of quartz, and if he focused attentively enough he could feel the grains touching his skin. He felt the sand pressing against his eyelids, and by an intense effort he managed to distinguish an individual grain. He could feel its contours, its angles and sides, and with his whole awareness now centered on this single grain of sand he began to feel a movement. The crystal was vibrating. Deeper still, he focused on its lattice of molecules. They were humming, exchanging electrons in a molecular dance, binding the crystal together.

A moment later, Dara's entire body tingled with tiny movements. A million grains of sand vibrated against his skin. There was movement! Something was happening! A million, a hundred million, happenings! Although his body was immobile, imprisoned like a fly in amber, at any moment he was always free to choose. He now exercised this remaining quantum of freedom to harness the energy of the vibrating crystals. It was just enough to set himself spinning like an upward corkscrew.

"The quantum of action," he thought.

At each turn, he drew in more energy from his surroundings and stored it. An image of a spinning ice-skater flashed before him, arms outstretched, and as she pulled them in closer to her slim body the speed and energy of her spinning rapidly increased. The skater's body seemed to collapse into itself and the energy stored in her rotations approached infinity as her size shrunk closer and closer to nothingness. He felt now as if every cell in his body was spinning, a billion tiny helicopters of rotating force, borrowing energy from the molecules of sand, lifting him free.

Everything around him blurred as the once-seemingly eternal immobility gave way to an immense cauldron of activity. He could now feel his body again, pressing down on the densely packed sand beneath him, leveraging itself up, gaining purchase on something solid. He felt his entire surroundings rise like a vortex, pulling up through the layers of sub-aqua earth, through fathoms of ocean, back out into the liberty of the air.

Bright daylight.

* * *

"Congratulations. You did it. For a while there I wasn't sure you were going to make it." Arthur Young beamed over at Dara from the pilot's seat.

"You've now had first-hand experience of the descent and the Turning Point. Most important, you discovered on your own the way out. I couldn't help you there. No one can help another through the lessons of the dark night. But I was prepared to stay with you for however long it took."

The sun glinted off the glass of the cockpit, dazzling Dara. Shielding his eyes with one hand, he reached over to his companion and squeezed his shoulder in gratitude. Judging by the sun's altitude, he figured it was already nearing noon. By now, however, the passage of time seemed to hold little meaning.

Dara's head felt clearer than he could ever remember. He felt light. He felt free. "Like an acorn that has just sprouted its first leaves," he remarked to Arthur. "Ready to grow and fulfill my destiny."

"Ah, an apt metaphor. You've certainly been through the eye of a needle, and by tasting Hell you've gained an appetite for Heaven. You are a fine student." The pilot tilted the helicopter and headed for land.

Back on the beach, Young pointed out that Dara had just experienced the descent of consciousness into matter, Spirit's sacrifice of its last degree of freedom. But not quite. Deep in the heart of matter a minute pulse of purpose continues to beat. It is this quantum of choice that allows matter to reach out and capture energy.

"And *that*, my friend, is the birth of life." The old man let out a sigh of deep satisfaction. "That's what happened when a molecule first timed its vibrations with the energy of photons streaming in from the Sun, absorbing energy and storing it. *That* was the turning point, the moment when Earth began its long upward journey through evolution."

The two men sat in silence and looked out on vast expanse of ocean before them. Dara pictured the teeming varieties of oceanic life, most he had never seen, far more abundant than the forms of plants and animals living on and in the land. Life certainly was a celebration of the quantum of freedom within matter. The old visionary reached out and clasped both of Dara's hands and said that his work was done for now.

"You have penetrated the depths of Matter, and are now on the threshold of the next stage, Life. You have experienced matter's deepest secret, and tasted a power very few humans yet possess. You have opened the way to soul charge. Treat that power wisely. Use it well, and you will no longer be at the mercy of the mechanism of matter.

"Later on, when you have mastered the Shaman's Gift, you will have the power of 'shape-shifting,' to move through solid objects, even rock or steel." He hesitated. "But be careful. You are just a beginner, a novice, and if you overstep your learning, you could find yourself in serious trouble."

He tapped Dara on the thigh. "I'm taking my leave now. Hang on here for a little while to contemplate the lesson you have just learned."

The helicopter rose noiselessly into the air, without creating a wind, without disturbing a grain of sand. It climbed higher and higher like a hot-air balloon and seemed to melt into the blue haze of the sky.

32

The Shaman's Gift

Dara stretched out on the sand and looked around. "This is it," he thought. "This is my world." Above him, the blue canopy, ablaze with a fiery sun, created the illusion of a closed universe. But he knew that beyond the bright sky the infinite dark heavens, now concealed, pulsed with great mysteries of life and intelligence. In front of him, the great Pacific Ocean sparkled, receiving and holding the light from above. Behind him, the dunes with their leathery grasses; and beyond, the lush, green mountains covered with ancient rainforest. All this and more was the province of the senses, the revealed majesty of nature. He marveled at the forms of matter, living and non-living, beautiful and diverse beyond description.

"We live in a world of energy," he reflected. "We are surrounded by it, we consume it, we transform it—we are it. What a miracle, to be part of this magnificent eternal flux—*and we can know our place in it.*" A surge of gratitude swept through him, and he thanked the heavens for being alive, for each sacred moment, for the privilege of *receiving* the world.

An unusually large wave thundered ashore, throwing the sea at Dara's feet. He looked up, and felt connected—with the ocean, with the sky, and with the landscape around him.

Everything was related through a universal network of unseen currents.

By themselves, our senses would be no more than shuttered windows, he realized. To get from senses to *sensation* we need the spark of consciousness. This is what Darwin was getting at when he pointed to the gap in the evolutionary sequence between brains and minds. How could mere impulses of electromagnetic energy get transformed into the colorful, lively symphony of *experiences*? It was clear to him now that matter itself tingles with the spark of spirit all the way down, through every level of existence.

* * *

Driving back to Honolulu, Dara reviewed his experiences of the past weeks. One by one, not only had they radically altered his search for "alien" intelligence, they had transformed his life.

When he got to his hotel, he opened the package from Maya—a book about the Sea Gypsies. She had mentioned meeting them, and an old Malaysian shaman, on a trip to Asia. He flipped the pages and noticed she had written the foreword.

He sat down on a sofa in the hotel lobby next to a tall black granite waterfall, and began browsing. He tried to shut out the buzz of new tourists just arrived from the airport, swaggering under the weight of over-packed suitcases, draped in Hawaiian garlands.

On the title page, Maya had written a dedication with a traditional Ye'kuana saying: "When the people's dreams are set free, the world tilts on its axis, and the universe sings in salute."

A child ran up to the waterfall, chased by an overprotective mother. "Look Mommy, the fish are eating money." Dara looked up and saw a couple of young boys throwing pennies into the pool. A large golden koi darted away under the shade of a water lily. The concierge came over and asked the boys to leave the fish alone. He recognized Dara.

"Ah, Doctor Martin. Excuse me, the cleaning crew found a letter addressed to you in one of the other rooms." He hurried off to get it, and Dara resumed reading. The book told the history of the Mawken people, a tribe of sea-faring nomads, seen through the eyes of an old medicine man. It documented their struggles trying to maintain ancient traditions against the march of modern civilization.

The concierge returned with a small envelope. "One of the cleaning ladies found this tucked behind a cushion."

Dara recognized Maya's handwriting, and immediately opened it—a hastily scribbled note in telegraphic sentences.

I'm OK. Bechtel taking me to Malaysia. They know about N'bai. FEW now hunting him. Must warn. Go to Buddhist temple. Follow the peal-seller. Find me in Rangoon.

"Find me in Rangoon." Where the hell was that?

* * *

Making the connection in Los Angeles was the most difficult part of the trip. He had just enough time to buy a change of clothes and travelers' checks, and with Maya's book on his lap, Dara settled in on the United Airlines jet headed for Singapore. The twenty-hour flight gave him plenty of time to read and think. He pondered her cryptic message . . . warn N'bai . . . follow a peal seller. It made no sense.

He angled back his seat and opened the book. It was a new edition of an old anthropological text from the turn of the last century, *The Sea Gypsies of Malaya.* Inside the back cover he discovered a yellowed map of the Malay Archipelago. He unfolded it, and a postcard fell out—a brightly colored picture of a Buddhist pagoda. Its golden spires and fine architectural detail impressed him, rivaling the great cathedrals of Europe. He flipped it over, and could barely read a scrawled note: "To remind you of our favorite meeting place." As best he could make out, it was signed "N'bai."

Dara recalled that Maya had mentioned she had often met the old shaman at a Buddhist temple near where his cousin had a stall vending pearls and other precious gems. That's where he should try to meet her, he assumed. He slipped the card back into the book, and examined the map. It showed the coast of Burma littered with a thousand islands and atolls. A red-ink circle around the name "Kissering" singled out a medium-sized island, and a red arrow pointed to Whale Bay. He refolded the map, and began reading Maya's foreword.

"All life begins with light. In a very real sense, life on Earth is 'borrowed light,' forming the world's most fundamental living economic system. Shamanic wisdom has recognized this for thousands of years: Instead of 'food chains' and 'stock exchanges,' indigenous peoples see 'energy circulations,' and 'spirit exchanges'—economies of light."

The aircraft cabin was quiet, except for a few muffled conversations breaking through the low hum of the engines. Dara glanced out the window, thirty-seven thousand feet below the vast Pacific Ocean glinted in the sun. That's where it all began, he thought. Billions of years ago, something in the ocean responded to the magical power of light and stirred into life. It may have happened in a warm pool in coastal rocks, but the basic ingredients came from the sea. He watched the tiny shadow of a small aircraft far below skip across the surface, and he daydreamed about the watery world beneath teeming with unknown life forms.

A flight attendant interrupted his reverie, offering orange juice. He drank it and continued reading.

"Shamanic knowledge, gained from direct communication with special-hallucinogenic plants, predates by centuries if not millennia modern scientific data about the basis of life. Visions of entwined serpents, recorded throughout history and across the world, foreshadowed in remarkable detail the twentieth-century discovery of the double helix or 'twisted ladder' structure of DNA, the fundamental molecule of life."

From the footnotes, Dara saw that Maya had been inspired by another anthropological work, *The Cosmic Serpent.*

"Many shamans use plant 'guides,' such as *ayahuasca, peyote,* or psilocybin mushrooms, along with special chants, whistles, drumming, or dancing to prepare the mind for altered states of consciousness."

Dara recalled how Darwin had used whistling and a potent "magical phlegm" to induce a profound dream experience.

Maya's foreword continued: "All life comes from the same source, and uses the same codes. *All living things emit light.* DNA is actually a kind of crystal that emits photons. So we can speculate: What if spirits are photons emitted by living systems, picked up, amplified, and transmitted by shamans? This would mean that spirits are beings of pure light—as seers and mystics have always claimed."

"What if . . ."

Dara put the book down, formulating his own speculation: "What if the cosmic intelligence I've been seeking all these years is carried by photons from stars and galaxies throughout the universe?"

He sat upright, flipped his airline seat to bring him closer to the book resting on the tray table. Here was the link between science and shamanic wisdom that Maya had spoken of. Shamans may be picking up coded information not only from the plants and animals on Earth, but also from the heavens. If photons are messengers of the gods, shamans may be their emissaries on Earth.

It clicked into place: *That* is why the FEW were determined to eliminate Darwin, and are now hunting for N'bai. If shamans have knowledge of how to release the Great Dream—picked up and broadcast via photons—the rise of shamanic consciousness could spell the end of the reign of reason. The FEW maintain their power by manipulating reason and spreading misinformation through the media. That's how they control the minds of the masses. From their perspective, they simply must make sure that reason continues to dominate global consciousness.

Dara looked out the window of the 747. A fading slice of deep purple and orange glowed on the horizon. He switched off his reading light and settled in to sleep. What did Maya expect him to do when he got to Rangoon?

33

Pearls of Wisdom

A bustling modern city near the Burmese coast, Rangoon instantly penetrated his soul. As the airport taxi rolled through the humid downtown streets, Dara was struck by its distinctive sounds and the smells. He knew immediately what his guidebook meant by "every town has its own sound print." In New York, it's the incessant honking of traffic. In San Francisco, it's the clanging of the cable cars. In London, it's the rattle of diesel engines from black cabs and double-decker buses. But each town also has its own unique "smell print." In Rangoon, it was the food—a spicy aroma of peanut oil, seaweed, fish, and hot sauces common to the cuisines of Malaysia and Indonesia.

But there was another overriding smell, one Dara later came to associate with the entire archipelago: the *sea*. Whether out among the islands or in the towns and cities along the coast, the scent of the ocean always intruded. And it was different here than anywhere else he had ever been. It was neither particularly pleasant nor offensive. But it was strong and pervasive. He could smell it off the people, taste it in his food, and it invaded his dreams at night. It was tangible. It reminded him of oysters—not just their odor, but their silky texture. The air here was something you wore, something that cloaked you in its mysterious embrace. And that was the deepest impression: The islands, the sea, the people, the fields, the forests, the cities all vibrated with an air of mystery.

After he showered and ate breakfast, Dara showed the hotel concierge Maya's postcard and asked for directions to the Buddhist temple. He could take a taxi and be there in five minutes, or he could walk the back streets and do it in about twenty. Map in hand, he pushed his way through the crowded sidewalks, past fruit stalls and fish markets. The city was graced with a kaleidoscope of temples—Hindu, Buddhist, Moslem, and Christian—and he wondered if he'd recognize the one he was looking for.

Outside a particularly ornate pagoda, watched over by a magnificent gold-leafed statue of a meditating Buddha, an old street vendor approached him hawking a tray-full of what looked like semi-precious stones. "Good-luck crystals, Sir?" the seller shouted. Then whispered: "A precious pearl for your lady friend?"

Suddenly, the roar of the streets vanished as though someone had flipped a switch. *The pearl seller!* He took a second look at the temple and then at the postcard. The angle was different, but this was definitely it.

As quickly as he appeared, the street vendor slipped back into the crush of the crowd. Dara elbowed his way through and followed. Every time he might have lost him, Dara caught sight of the old man's most distinctive feature: a long, gray, plaited ponytail. When the crowd thinned out, the hawker gestured for Dara to follow, but to keep his distance. At the docks, the old man vanished down a flight of weather-eaten wooden steps. Before following, Dara looked over the side and saw about twenty sorry-looking tiny houseboats listing like drunken turtles in the tidal mudflats. Further out, in the shallows, a few gaily-colored Chinese junks stared back at the shore with wide painted eyes. No sign of the pearl seller.

Some of the houseboats were occupied, and even though they were made of what looked like nothing more than carved tree-trunks and bamboo, portions of their decks were strewn with soil. Large stones arranged in the middle served as hearths for smoldering fires. Pots of food steamed up from the decks, as mothers with infants hanging from their hips attended to cooking. Older children played around on board, sometimes vanishing below through gaps in the bamboo slats of the decks.

Dara was immediately struck by the poverty. Adults and children alike were dressed in rags, and many of the children ran about naked, skins covered in sores. The smell rising up from the houseboats was almost overpowering. Reluctantly, Dara picked his way down the wooden steps and looked around for the pearl seller.

"Pssst. Over here, Sir. This place is safe for us."

The voice came from one of the seemingly unoccupied boats. To reach it, Dara had to climb over three other dwellings, excusing himself as he rocked the tiny vessels, afraid he might upturn the cooking pots. The women immediately moved away to the back of their boats, while the children pointed, laughed, and stared at the foreigner.

"It's okay. They know you are my guest. Come on in."

"In" was inside a low-hanging roof of palm-leaves stitched together with grass, and supported by two hooped wooden posts.

"Welcome, Sir. My name is Lawong, and your good friend Maya ask-ed me to care for you while you are kindly visiting us." The old man spoke very slowly, with a thick Asian accent, and strange turns of phrase. "She ask-ed me give you news of wha' happen since she come back to our company."

He explained that Maya had arrived a couple of days ago. She was with three "big mens" when they came shopping in the market. One of N'bai's cousins, Lawong was a market trader, and an old friend of Maya's from when she stayed with his family many years ago. He recognized her and knew from her hand signals that the "big mens" were not friends. She spoke in Mawken, pretending to be haggling over the price of fruit, and alerted Lawong that many "big mens" were looking for N'bai and that he should stay away from the mainland. She said a friend of hers would soon be coming from America, and Lawong was to arrange for him to go to N'bai and "tell the story of everything that happen."

"During these times when you with N'bai." Lawong said, "Good Lady meeting big mens in Singapore to turn powerful medicine away from harming N'bai and our people."

Once again, Maya was stepping further into the lion's den, always, it seemed, one move ahead of everyone else.

"But she told me to meet her in Rangoon," Dara said. "Where is she now?"

"Kind lady with big men chiefs who live in sky houses. Those mens take away our seas and the mountains of our Orang Asli cousins."

Dara did his best to translate and piece together the information. After further questioning, he learned that Maya was probably already meeting with FEW bosses in Singapore, or was at least working her way up the chain of command. The "big mens" were corporate types—in fact, almost anyone in a suit—usually Europeans or Americans, but more commonly these days, also Chinese. The "sky houses" were the skyscraper headquarters in the city's financial district. Here, the FEW's front businesses were oil and mineral drilling, and they had invaded the fishing grounds of the Mawken to build a string of offshore platforms. The Orang Asli were an indigenous hill-tribe living in the Malaysian rainforest highlands, and much of their territory had been destroyed by strip mining. As commercial interests took over more of the sea and moved deeper into the rainforests, the aboriginal peoples retreated into progressively smaller and remoter enclaves.

"Now they want our dreams, too," Lawong said with an undisguised tremor. "I must take you to Mergui, so you can cross the water to be with N'bai. You will help protect our dreams, yes?"

"I will do everything I can," Dara said trying to sound as reassuring as he could.

Lawong beamed. "Thank you, Sir. That is very, very good. After Mergui, I must return to Rangoon to wait for new messages from the kind lady."

* * *

The train ride from Rangoon to Mergui, a sizable coastal town about four hundred miles south, passed through some of the most stunning scenery Dara had ever seen. But his mind was not in tourist mode. He was worried about Maya, hoping she knew what she was getting into and that she could handle it. Worried, too, that he was once again leaving her to deal with the goons on her own. Was Bechtel one of the "big mens" with her? Dara's mind was also on N'bai, and where their meeting would take place.

As soon as the train pulled into the station at Mergui, Lawong ushered Dara off and straight down to the busy fishing port. Again, a fleet of flimsy bamboo craft bobbed in the harbor, a familiar Mawken trademark Dara was already beginning to recognize.

"Sir, you now go with Kape in *kabang*. He take you to N'bai."

He pointed to a young man standing in the shade of a sprawling banyan tree growing between a cluster of large rocks on the dock. Lawong reached out as if to say goodbye. Dara thanked him and shook the old man's hand. He felt something small and round pressed into his palm. It was a pearl.

"This for you. It is my dream. You keep. Dream protect." And without another word, the old man turned and headed back for the station.

Kape introduced himself, a wiry youth, sun-and-sea-burned like all the Mawken. He was a little taller than the rest and walked more assured, upright, unlike most Mawken men who, from years keeping balance out at sea, lean forward as if always walking into a strong wind. Kape's *kabang* was his houseboat, now slowly approaching shore. His brothers had been out fishing while he waited on land for Lawong to arrive with the stranger from America.

Whoever was piloting Kape's boat was in no particular hurry; nor, as far as Dara could tell, going in any particular direction. The small craft zigzagged on a thoroughly inefficient course. As it drew in closer, Dara saw why it moved so erratically. Three men, using crudely carved wooden paddles as oars, hit the water completely independent of the others' strokes. They made no attempt to pull together. One moment the craft would zig to the left, only to be zagged back to the right, in the general direction of the landing strip where Kape and the stranger waited.

This was Dara's fist intimation that he was about to enter an alien world.

* * *

As the *kabang* pulled out to sea, Kape explained they were headed south for Kanmaw, but maybe they would go to Dala Island instead. They tended to blow wherever the wind favored. Once on the open sea, they hoisted a small sail made of palm leaves, picked up speed and at least were now carried in a more-or-less consistent direction. Presumably whichever island they ended up on, N'bai would get the message and come to meet them there? Or perhaps one island was just a staging post for the next?

The air was balmy and the water calm, even though a fresh breeze blowing down from the north pushed them at a fair clip along the coast. They passed countless little islands, mostly uninhabited by humans, but the beauty of the passage was marred by monstrous oil platforms, islands of steel rising up out of the sea, spewing out flames and fumes.

"My people used to go fishing here," Kape announced as they slipped by a thundering rig. The surrounding water was streaked with a patina of oil. "My father and uncles went diving here, too. In those days, before the big mens came with dragons of steel and fire, the Mawken could dive to the bottom of the sea and harvest oysters and pearls for the Chinese. These days, the oysters are gone. No more pearls. No more dreams. N'bai is our last great diver for dreams."

Dara fingered the small pearl Lawong had given him. What did he mean, "This is my dream"? The Mawken talk as though pearls and dreams are connected.

Shortly before the sun dipped below the horizon, Kape lit a fire between three large stones carefully placed in a pile of dirt on deck. Water boiled and they ate a meal of rice and coconut milk. As they sat around the fire, Dara asked about N'bai.

They said he was a great *micha-blen,* or medicine man, just like his father and grandfather before him. An old friend and teacher of Maya's, N'bai had learned to speak English in Europe, and had studied Western knowledge.

"Shaman and scholar at the same time," Dara thought, a combination that reminded him of Darwin.

"N'bai has a reputation as far away as Rangoon as a great pearl diver," Kape said. "But really, he is a healer of spirits."

Dara wasn't sure how to take what he heard next.

N'bai used shamanic powers to harness the "magic" of oysters. In their tradition, pearls are repositories of dreams.

Maya had spoken of a similar relationship between visions and quartz crystals used by shamans in the Amazon.

"Tell me about your people," Dara inquired. "How did you come to be called the Sea Gypsies?"

Kape translated the question for his companions, and they uttered a chorus of "ooohs," "ayees," and "ahhhs." They began speaking all at once, while Kape translated and embellished random sentences in no particular order. As the night wore on, Dara was able to cobble together a fairly coherent account of the Mawken.

Many generations ago, their ancestors lived on the Burma-Malaya mainland, like the Orang Asli today. In those far off times, they had been close to the land, lived in village settlements, with houses of grass and bamboo, and cultivated crops.

"Our forefathers were a peace-loving people, friendly with neighboring tribes. The children were always happy. For many long times, our ancestors lived like this."

But their days of Eden came to an end when hordes of *T'now* (Burmese) came sweeping down from the north burning and plundering, while *Batuk* (Malays) hemmed them in from the south. Defenseless, they were driven from their homelands down to the coast. Around Bokpyin, and further north at Mergui, they crossed the mudflats and mangrove swamps leading to the shallow waters of the archipelago and retreated to the islands. Their first main settlement was on Chai-an, called Kissering by the British, and today renamed Kanmaw.

On the islands, they established plantations of coconuts, bananas, pineapples, and breadfruit, and each settlement was guided by its own "great man." For a time, life was

299 Pearls of Wisdom

again peaceful. But then the fierce Batuk raided them from the south, destroying their plantations, raping their women, and carrying the men off as slaves. They moved deeper into the archipelago, colonizing smaller islands, but were constantly harassed by pirates. Only when the monsoon storms came making the seas unsafe did they get some relief from the constant attacks. When calm weather returned, the molestations began again.

During "these times" they decided to live on their boats, and built the first *kabang*. They took up a sea-roving life between the islands and became the "Sea Gypsies," as the British called them.

Hollowed out of tree trunks, with sides and decks built up from spliced bamboo, the *kabang* were designed for speedy escapes. Each boat was fitted with a sail of palm leaves, and crude gunwales for hand-carved oars. Aft, a roof of palm and grasses provided shelter from the blazing sun. One *kabang* typically housed a family of seven or more. When it was safe enough to land, they often lifted the roofs off the boats and set them up as shelters on the beaches. Here, they would prepare food, tell stories of the "old times," repair sails, build new *kabang,* and weave the ubiquitous reed mats to sit on during the day and sleep on at night.

But they were troubled not only from the T'now and Batuk on land, and pirates at sea. The Bay of Bengal is notorious for cyclones, then as now—ravaging waterspouts rip trees from their roots and smash houses into splinters. At sea, the flimsy *kabang* were frequently swamped and many Mawken ancestors drowned. Devastating *tsunamis* also took a toll over the centuries.

"In our language, *l'maw* means 'to drown' and *o'ken* means 'salt water.' Our people came to refer to themselves as *l'maw o'ken*—those who 'drown at sea.' Today, we call ourselves the Mawken, 'The Sea Drowned,' in honor of those ancestors."

Later that night, Dara read through the book Maya had given him. The account of Mawken origins in *The Sea Gypsies of Malaya* told much the same story.

* * *

They made it to Kanmaw shortly after dawn. Without any fanfare or ceremony, Dara was introduced to N'bai. Like most Mawken, the old shaman was short—about five-foot four. His skin was a deep, rich brown, and his long straight hair, formerly jet-black, was streaked with gray. Like Maya, Dara referred to him as "the old shaman," but in truth he could make no confident guess at the man's age. Many of these people looked old beyond their years, and N'bai could have been anywhere from forty-five to eighty-five.

His dark eyes sparkled with the intelligence of a wise old man, yet his beaming smile revealed a youthful vitality. His unusually high forehead gave an impression of deep wisdom. Below his flat nose, thin dull-red lips revealed discolored teeth ground down by years of habitual betel chewing. His strong jaw was softened by a few wisps of hair on his chin forming a scraggly goatee. He wore a Burmese *lungyis,* a brightly-colored skirt-like garment, tucked and folded up between his legs. His chest was bare, except for a few curled gray hairs, and around his neck he wore a leather thong holding a single, glistening black pearl. A small bag of matted grass hung beneath his left armpit on a rope of twisted vines. Dara's overall sense was of a highly intuitive and instinctively pragmatic man.

As soon as the informal introductions were over, N'bai invited his guest to accompany him to his *kabang*. They would take *chota hazri* ("little breakfast") on the sea, and N'bai would then "speak of these times." The meal consisted of a few strips of dried fish, a mouthful or two of coconut milk, and something that tasted like ripe bananas, but was the color and texture of old leather.

"The world has four zones of consciousness," N'bai began, "layers within layers of awareness." He drew a crude map in the dirt at the bottom of the boat. It looked like a giant amoeba. "This is the modern world," he said pointing at the amoeba's tentacles. "We call it the Fourth World, where reason reigns, the conqueror of dreams."

Inside, surrounded by the modern world, was the Third World, where people still lived close to the Earth, but already disturbed by the long reach of Western technology. Here, agriculture was still the main way of life, and people had not yet lost all contact with magic and myth. As best they could, they kept the old ways alive through storytelling.

Next, a narrow region within the Third World was called the "Buffer" or the "Zone of Mayhem," depending on who viewed it. N'bai drew this sector with a broken line, indicating its inhabitants lived in a kind of Limbo between worlds. From the outside, that is, from the point of view of modern eyes, it was the forgotten or discarded world of tribal people living on the fringes.

"You've seen examples of this, perhaps, in the harbors of Rangoon and Mergui?" N'bai inquired.

These were aboriginal folk whose traditional ways of life had been destroyed by encounters with conquest consciousness. They lived in a prolonged state of psychological and social confusion—unable to integrate themselves, nor welcomed, into the modern world that had overtaken them. Their most visible signs were sprawling shantytowns of mud and tin littering the outskirts of many cities in the Third World, often on the edges of forests, deserts, and marshlands.

From both sides, this was regarded as a danger zone. To the moderns, it was a lawless sector dominated by alcoholism and wild anarchy. To the indigenous peoples, from the inside, it was seen as the place of broken dreams and lost souls—a buffer between the incursions of the modern world and the remaining pockets of true indigenous ways. Very few moderns cared or dared to enter this zone, and therefore did not penetrate deeper into the last sanctuaries of the inner world—except when big business concerns got wind of untapped resources such as oil, rubber, minerals, diamonds or other precious gems. Then, of course, the bulldozers came in, leveled the shantytowns, and moved on deeper into indigenous territory.

The inner zone was the First World, the world of aboriginal peoples who had retreated, to protect their ancestral ways, further and further into the rainforests, and other remote places. These are the Original People, the

'Circulators,' and they know full well that the forces of modern civilization threaten the balance of Mother Earth.

Finally, surrounding and embracing all of this was the Great Circle, the world of the Great Spirit.

"This is not really a zone like the others," N'bai explained. "It is the source of all consciousness. Shamans and healers who communicate with the beings of light know this. Those in other zones who have lost contact with the light are unaware of the Great Circle."

N'bai took hold of the stick at the top with both hands and pummeled it into the center of the inner circle.

"I cannot draw this for you. But what you cannot see here is that my map is really shaped more like a starfish with a hole through the center." Dara imagined him to mean something like a doughnut shape, what mathematicians call a "torus."

"The inner circle of dream consciousness is really an opening," N'bai went on. "It is a receptacle for the consciousness of the world, receiving into itself all the dreams and visions of all peoples, as well as their failed dreams and poisoned consciousness. It is the zone of purification. Shamans enter the fire burning at the center of this zone to cleanse the darkened consciousness of the world."

Dara examined the diagram intently, as N'bai continued to explain:

"Through this gateway the light of the Great Spirit circulates. But the opening is getting smaller as the modern world moves further and further into the few remaining indigenous lands. If this continues, if the inner circle is ever obliterated, our entire world will be cut off from the source of Light and our planet will fall into a long darkness." His voice dropped, and Dara shared his sorrow for the loss of ancestral ways.

"That is why we must protect the Great Dream in the remotest places on the planet."

N'bai put his hand into the matted-grass bag hanging from his shoulder and took out a small, shiny black pebble. It was perfectly round, and it shimmered in the bright sunshine as though it was radiating from deep inside. He handed it to Dara, who rolled it between his fingers, feeling its smooth texture.

"It's a black pearl," N'bai announced. "This is where the Great Dream is stored."

Dara looked at the Sea Gypsy thinking he was joking, but N'bai wasn't smiling. The *micha-blen* saw his companion was perplexed and explained.

"I don't expect you to fully understand this, but I will try."

N'bai said that the Great Dream was held by a vast "fishing net" made of pearls, and each pearl itself contained the whole net. Dara translated the image of a fishing net into a more familiar metaphor. He thought of the Great Dream as a kind of hologram, stored in millions of little fragments—where each little piece contains an image of the whole.

"I like this holy-gram," N'bai enthused. "A group of *micha-blen* from different nations around the world—including tribal communities of the Amazon, Africa, the Siberian Steppes, the Arctic, Polynesia, and

Indonesia—have joined together to protect the Great Dream. The sea people, especially Maya's friend Darwin, are guiding us to create a world-wide dream-catcher."

This "dream-catcher," Dara learned, was woven by invisible tendrils of light, linking a vast network of special "stones" across the globe.

"Dreams come from the Earth and the light comes from the sky," N'bai explained, and Dara assumed he was referring to the sun. But then N'bai added:

"When the dreams of the Earth are threatened, as they are in these times, the sky spirits send balls of light to protect them. The oceans receive the light, and it is our task to use it to reconnect the fragments of our dreams."

Dara could hardly believe what he was hearing. Against his best scientific training and understanding, he himself had harbored an intuition that the fireballs over Marin and elsewhere held a deeper significance—linked to the mystery signals he had detected from deep in the cosmos. And now, half a world away, a Burmese shaman was confirming this outrageous idea. N'bai said more:

"Light is the voice of the Great Spirit, carrying messages from the gods. Together with the people of the sea, shamans learn to 'read' this ancient language."

"We need to crack the code," Dara exclaimed. "After all these years, I'm finally discovering the heavens *are* speaking to us—but not the way my science had prepared me to recognize or understand."

"Yes, the gods have been speaking to us since the beginning of time," N'bai affirmed. "But most humans no longer know how to listen."

"And Darwin's noetic code is the key to reconnecting us with Earth and the heavens?" A smile of recognition lit up Dara's face, as more pieces of the puzzle fell into place.

"The code is everyone's," N'bai corrected. "But by now I think you know that deciphering it requires a special kind of consciousness." He paused, and placed a hand on Dara's chest.

"You can see the light from the sky with your eyes, but you can understand its meaning only through the vision of the heart." He paused again, and moved to the prow of the boat.

"At this very moment, a jeweled net of pearls and other precious gems is crisscrossing the oceans and continents, connecting the Original Peoples with some of the most powerful people on the planet."

N'bai invited Dara to sit with him up front in the *kabang,* and to fix his gaze on the sea. The NASA scientist looked out over the low wooden prow at the translucent water stretching beyond a smattering of small islands to the horizon.

"It is time for you to prepare for the final part of the journey," N'bai whispered. He explained, as Darwin had on a previous occasion, that because of the scientist's highly trained intellect, Dara had to be guided back beyond the time when reason blocked out the light of his own intuition.

"You must return to your childhood dreams," N'bai told him. "These dreams are never lost, they live on in each of us, stored in the shadows of the mind as memories, visions, imagination, and stories. Shamans around the world use different techniques to coax these dreams to consciousness."

N'bai told Dara that if he had paid attention to his dreams growing up, he would have noticed a pattern weaving through his life—a story with its own cast of characters.

"Our dream characters can take on any imaginable form," N'bai explained, "shape-shifting as we grow and consciousness evolves. We must get to know all our characters, befriend them, and unite them. Only then can we know who we truly are. They dance through time so that what was past lives in us today, and today's events loop back into our past, like a dream within a dream."

N'bai pulled out an old rag from his matted grass bag and handed it to Dara, with a firm instruction to hold it over his nose and mouth and to breathe deeply. He did so, and was almost thrown to the deck by a sharp kick to the back of his nostrils. He had never smelled anything so pungent in his life. The shaman told him to keep breathing, and then stood on the prow of the little boat. He began rocking it gently to the rhythm of a low chant mixed with an eerie whistling.

Dara felt a familiar tingling in the nape of his neck, as if waves of energy were undulating up his spine. He felt a trapdoor open in his brainstem, and then, all of a sudden, his head exploded and the entire ocean and sky merged in a blinding flash.

34

Thieves of Dreams

As he drifted into a dizzy, dreamy trance, Grumbalot found himself entering an old story. According to the ancient Tales of Grummyth—the legends that tell how Grummels came to be Grummels—a long, long time ago, their ancestors were reptiles.

In distant days, two tribes vied for space to live and grow: the Cerebellums and the Neocores.

The Cerebellums, who arrived first, were borne on the backs of giant tortoises. They were placid, peaceful creatures that liked to dream a lot and would spend their days either resting in the shade, dreaming fabulous fantasies, or sometimes go wandering the plains and prairies drawing pictures on rocks and in caves, humming songs and playing games in the moonlight. They hardly ever needed to speak, because they could send each other messages silently on the wind. They lived a comfortable, carefree life.

Then one day, when the sun was high in the heavens, they heard a thundering roar on the horizon. Dazzling in shining gray armor, hordes of Neocores riding fiery lizards invaded Grummeldom and began laying down rules and regulations. Being peaceful, submissive creatures, the

Cerebellums retreated further and further into smaller encampments to avoid the onslaught.

The Neocore race prized activity and aggression, and liked everything in straight, orderly lines, including their thinking. One of the first laws they imposed on the Cerebellums was "No Dreaming." Anyone caught dreaming was ridiculed and made an outcast. Without their dreams, Cerebellums were a shadow of their former peaceful, happy-go-lucky selves. Eventually, the sleepy Cerebellums were overrun by the warlike Neocores.

Down the ages, the Neocores grew bigger and more powerful and dominated the smaller Cerebellums, almost entirely encircling them. Actually, the fierce Neocores dominated the Cerebellums so much they almost crushed and smothered them.

In his great wisdom and mercy, the Great Bore intervened and carved out the Labyrinth. It was the only place where the Cerebellums could escape. But even underground, they were not entirely safe. From time to time raiding bands of Neocores would descend into their tunnels to plunder their dreams.

In time, however, the Cerebellums came to like the darkness and even came to know its secret places where no Neocore could ever go. In fact, the Cerebellums felt so protected in their underworld they returned to dreaming as much as they liked. And if any foolhardy Neocore ever ventured into their hidden domain, they would scare him off with fiendish nightmares and other terrors of the dark. As time passed, the Neocores stopped bothering the

Cerebellums and forbade any of their clan to ever go anywhere near the Labyrinth.

Over the ages, the Neocores almost forgot all about the Labyrinth. Some of them even denied the Cerebellums ever existed. However, as a precaution, one of the strictest Neocore laws was to seal up all entrances to the Labyrinth—to keep whatever was underground, underground and whatever was above, above. "All above, no below," the Neocores inscribed these words on the portals of their academies and would chant this slogan on the Day of Logic Triumphant when celebrating their conquest.

As generations passed, eventually the tides turned and the Neocores came to fear their own stories of the Labyrinth and the strange dreams and nightmares of the Cerebellums. At night, when the moon was high, the Cerebellums would often steal their way up top, out into the open spaces, and would dance and play their dreamtime games until the first rays of dawn. They would play with all the artifacts and gadgets that the Neocores had made, mixing them up and putting them together in the strangest ways. Sometimes a Neocore might wake and see the spectacle of the dreaming Cerebellums and would cover his eyes in fear, believing he was seeing ghosts, vampires, or space aliens.

By now the Cerebellums had mastered the art of disappearing, and if ever a Neocore tried to catch one all he ever caught was his own shadow. Without a sound or a trace of what they were up to, the Cerebellums would vanish back into the Labyrinth leaving the Neocores wondering if what they saw was all in their imagination.

This, of course, troubled the Neocores no end, given their grave disdain for anything to do with the imagination.

Grumbalot like to retell this tale because it reminded him of his own ancestral lineage—an inspiration to always honor the power of dreams.

This time, deep in ancient memory, he relived the prehistoric battles of the Cerebellums and Neocores, and came face to face with the split in the cosmos that gave birth to darkness and light.

35

An Evolutionary Mistake?

"I hope that was a healing journey," N'bai announced when Dara woke. The little *kabang* drifted on the open sea, bobbing like a cork. Dara's insides felt queasy, and his head still reeled from the smell of the shaman's rag. He was glad to heave a deep breath of fresh, ocean air. A light breeze softened the burning heat from the sun, cooling him as sweat evaporated from his bare, sunburned skin. He stretched out on the bamboo deck under the shade of the flimsy sail—exhausted. Yet he felt purified.

N'bai handed him a rusty tin can, and told him to drink. The water tasted like champagne.

"When the first humans walked the Earth, there was a struggle between two types," the Mawken medicine man began to explain. "Evolution was faced with a choice: Follow the cerebellum, the path taken by the people your scientists call Neanderthals, or follow the cerebrum and the neocortex, the path taken by Cro-Magnons. As you know, the more aggressive Cro-Magnons won the struggle, and the Neanderthals were wiped out." He smiled. "At least that's how the story is told. In fact, the Neanderthals' spirit retreated into the folds of the cerebellum, where it still lives on, active in the consciousness of shamans and *micha-blen* throughout the world."

The old Mawken stopped, and rummaged in his grass bag, pulling out a small piece of paper about two inches square, and he carefully unfolded it to the size of a magazine page. It was from *The Scientific American* showing a cross-section of the human brain. He handled the picture as though it were a sacred object.

"Have you ever noticed this," he said pointing at the picture, "how the brain has three different rooms?"

Dara assumed he was referring to what modern biologists call the "triune brain"—three distinct areas reflecting the evolutionary history of animals. At the bottom is the brainstem, which controls functions such as waking up, instinctive responses, and reflexes. It is often referred to, with some justification, as the "reptilian brain." Its signature is "fight or flight."

Next, is the limbic system, including the hypothalamus that controls the flow of hormones throughout the body, and is the center responsible for emotions. It is called the "lower-mammal" brain, often typified as the "rat brain," or "horse brain," depending on your view of emotions. Its signature is the spectrum of feelings from anger and sadness to fear and joy.

Finally, at the top of the brain is the neocortex, a thin strip of cells covering the brain like the peel of an orange. It is called the "rational brain," the seat of intellect and cognition, and, not surprisingly, is almost invariably typified as the "human brain." Its signature is thought and creativity.

When Dara listed off the characteristics of the triune-brain, N'bai nodded his head.

"That is very interesting," he said, looking genuinely intrigued, and pulling the picture up closer to his squinting eyes. "Very interesting. Our heads contain three brains—snake, horse, and human." He pulled Dara closer.

"Yes, that is one story. *Micha-blen* know this very well. But I wanted you to notice something else." He handed the picture to Dara, and stood beside him, reaching up to pinpoint certain areas with his index finger.

"Here. Look. This is the cerebellum. Notice how it is overgrown by the cerebrum—almost completely surrounded by this late-arriver." Dara agreed it was hard to miss.

"Then why do your scientists never talk of this great change in the evolution of our species? The dream brain has been smothered by the thinking brain. Intuition smothered by intellect."

'I don't want to be smothered by you.' A faint echo flashed through Dara's mind from an earlier dream of Fanima in the Blue Universe. *'I want to retain my own identity. And I want you to retain yours.'* The rest of Fanima's parting words surfaced again.

"She said, 'This is a matter of grave importance'," Dara reported out loud.

N'bai looked at him uncomprehendingly.

"Oh, excuse me," he tried to explain. "I just remembered a message from a dream I had a while ago. At the time, it made no sense to me. But now it's all falling into place."

N'bai didn't inquire further. He knew that dreams speak to us across time.

"You've just told me the cerebellum is the seat of dreams, where imagination and intuition guide us." Dara sounded excited and inspired at the same time. "And now you remind me that, as evolution unfolded, this part of ourselves was smothered by the rational brain, the cerebrum."

He looked at the Sea Gypsy to see if the he'd got it right: "My dream vision, the story of the battle between the Cerebellums and the Neocores, was warning me not to let my rational mind obliterate my intuition; just as Fanima had asked that I allow both intuition and intellect to express their own identities." In his excitement he grabbed the shaman's forearms and shook them vigorously.

N'bai smiled knowingly. Then he reversed Dara's hold, grabbing the scientist by the wrist and extended his arm out straight, directing it in a curve, pointing at the horizon.

"That is very good medicine you are receiving from your dreams. But the message is even bigger. Your dream woman is very wise: Yes, you need to balance head and heart, giving each its own expression. But the message is not just about *you.* It's about the world." And he moved the NASA scientist's hand back and forth across the horizon.

"It's about overcoming an ancient clash between the two worlds—a conflict that goes back far beyond the arrival of European conquistadors on the shores of indigenous lands; back beyond the suppression of shamanic wisdom in Greece at the dawn of Western philosophy. It goes back even before the invention of agriculture and the loss of nomadic wandering. It goes back to the clash between Neanderthal and Cro-Magnon people hundreds of thousands of years ago."

Dara listened, intrigued, as the old Mawken told a sweeping tale about the origin of the human species.

"In the long unfolding of evolution, Cro-Magnons with their overgrowing cerebrums, bearing the promise of reason, overran and dominated Neanderthals who were guided by the dream wisdom of the cerebellum. Evolution had a choice: It could have taken the path of the cerebellum and offered the future of humanity to the Neanderthals. But instead, it took the other road—toward aggression and the dominance of the rational mind."

"Are you saying evolution made a mistake?" Dara asked.

"What is a mistake? If you mean that some choices lead to extinction, then perhaps you would call them errors. The path of evolution is strewn with countless dead ends." He paused, as a flying fish skipped over the surface alongside their craft.

"All evolutionary choices are designed for survival. But environments change, and once-wise choices sometimes no longer fit. When that happens, the conditions are ripe for a mutation in consciousness."

He looked at the scientist and repeated emphatically: "But to call these 'mistakes' is to take a very short-sighted view of the greater purpose of evolution."

"The journey from light to enlightenment," Dara suggested.

N'bai nodded in agreement. "Spirit works through matter by offering choices—always guiding us, speaking to us, whispering through the breath of gods, spirits, and angels."

"And we are always free to listen, or not," Dara added. He handed the picture back to N'bai, who folded it carefully into neat squares before replacing it in his bag.

N'bai then reached up and adjusted the sail to catch the wind. The boat turned, and he fell silent, nose in the air, as if sniffing for some distant message. He stood on the prow scanning the horizon, and let out a deep sigh. "Ahh, I was hoping for this." He sat down.

"Darwin is on his way to Mergui."

"He's coming *here?*" Dara yelped involuntarily at the mention of Darwin's name.

"Yes. He and I have much work to do to fine tune the net of pearls. We really don't have much time. If Maya has not been able to delay the FEW they may already be moving in."

"Can I help?" Dara raised himself up on an elbow, feeling his energy return.

"You already are—by learning to honor the gifts of reason and intuition within your own consciousness. And doing so, you are contributing to the wisdom of the world. N'bai smiled, and put an arm around Dara's shoulder, like an elder brother.

"In your medicine journey today, you dived down into the old brain, the cerebellum, where the Neanderthal dreamtime is preserved. You have learned the few first steps in shape shifting. But beware: It is a skill that requires much practice. Don't try to use it again before you are ready."

* * *

By the time the two men had completed their "talk of these times," it was mid-afternoon, and Dara was getting hungry for something other than dried fish, bananas, and tea that tasted of sweetened boiled socks. He was also feeling more anxious about Maya.

N'bai turned the tiny craft in the water as easily as a toy boat in a bathtub, and they picked up an on-shore breeze that would take them right into the calm waters of Whale Bay, on the southern end of Kanmaw.

That's when N'bai broke the news about the Visitor.

36

Nothingness

"The Visitor is a messenger from the gods," N'bai told Dara, as the *kabang* glided into a small natural harbor in Kanmaw. And when the palm sails caught no more wind, the two men leisurely rowed the lightweight vessel through the breakers onto the beach.

"You mean like an angel?" the scientist said, surprised to hear himself speak the word as though there really could be such beings.

"You may call the Visitor an angel, if you like, but you could just as well speak of an 'alien,' or an extraterrestrial. And from what Darwin tells me, 'photon' would do just fine. These are all just names we give to a reality that is beyond words. In the tradition of *micha-blen*, we know them as beings of light."

As a scientist, Dara still struggled with the notion of "light beings," but he reminded himself of what he knew from science: We are all made up of photons. At the deepest level, indeed, we *are* all beings of light.

"Who is this Visitor?" he asked.

N'bai didn't answer right away. Instead, he asked Dara to help him carry the *kabang* roof onto the sand, a little distance from a group of about ten other shelters. A small community had gathered on the island, creating an impromptu village. Young children played a Mawken version of the universal game of tag, while others shrieked with excitement as they tumbled in the surf.

N'bai set up camp, and prepared a hole in the sand to build a fire. Other Mawken, mostly men, slowly approached and sat a respectful distance away. The *micha-blen* boiled a pot of water, and dropped in some leaves and bark dust from a small skin pouch he took from his matted-grass bag. When the brew was ready, he ceremoniously passed the pot around, beginning with Dara.

"You ask many questions," N'bai finally said. "And the answers will come in good time. In my dream visions I saw a ball of fire fall from the sky and into the ocean, as the prophecies of our ancestors predicted. We will gain great knowledge from this light."

The old shaman explained that according to Mawken legends, from time to time throughout history, the world is visited by these "messengers from the gods," and their arrival is always auspicious. Dara assumed their stories referred to meteorites, and he was struck by the way they spoke of these collectively as "The Visitor." When he asked N'bai about this, the answer was both simple and cryptic:

"There is only one light, though it shines in many places. A single lamp casts many shadows."

Dara couldn't resist one more question: "Do *micha-blen* have special dreams?"

"All dreams are special," N'bai clarified, "they all carry messages. Some tell stories from our childhood. Some dreams speak with the voices of other animals. Some dreams speak for the Earth. Some bring news from the depths of time and space. All dreams come to us through the body and connect us to the world."

He paused and waved his hand to indicate the group of assembled tribes folk: "When *we* dream, we dream for the collective. And our visions have revealed that Darwin will be the first to make contact this time. The Visitor is waiting too deep, even beyond the reach of the best Mawken divers."

"What is *our* part?" Dara asked, sounding more impatient than he wanted to.

"We have to wait for Darwin before we can know that."

"But I feel so *useless* just waiting. "

As soon as he spoke the words, he heard them echoing around him, as though reverberating in a great empty hall. The sound of his own voice startled him. He glanced about to see if the rest of the group had noticed anything different. But they just looked at him, waiting. From nowhere, a loud swishing noise swooped past his left ear. He couldn't tell if it came from outside or from inside his head. He turned quickly, but saw nothing. His stomach started to churn, and his chest began heaving, expanding and contracting in waves. The brew was beginning to take effect.

"Everything has its purpose," the shaman replied, "even being useless," and his face lightened again into a broad smile. "I will tell you how I learned about the power of doing nothing." He gestured for the small group to come closer. A striking young native woman sat next to him.

"This is Nyamya," he said, introducing her to Dara. She smiled, lowered her eyes, and turned to N'bai waiting for him to speak. The shaman was silent for a few minutes, eyes closed, humming softly, rocking gently on his haunches. Everyone waited, and when finally he began speaking in English, the young woman translated for the rest of the group.

"These are strange times for the Mawken, but we are not alone. Other people are struggling to find the ways of their ancestors, too—including many people from the Fourth World in the West."

The crowd looked at Dara, and he suddenly felt as if the gaze of the whole world had turned on him. He felt exposed and vulnerable: They could see right through his skin, through the taut muscles in his face, beyond the masks he wasn't even aware he was wearing. As he looked at their faces he was drawn into their eyes, full of curiosity and compassion for this stranger among them. They held his gaze, and the longer he looked the more their faces changed, first into people he thought he vaguely recognized, then into his own relatives—parents, brothers, sisters, cousins, aunts, and uncles. Each face seemed to duplicate, then replicate into an endless series of images, and in this hall-of-mirrors he realized he was looking at his own ancestral lineage.

Finally, the faces lost all trace of individuality and became for him "the face of humanity" itself. He felt connected with the entire community of humans who had ever walked the Earth. A surge of emotion burst up from his chest, and he heaved in great sobs and gasps, releasing not just the personal pain and hurt stored in his body from childhood, but also the collective anguish of humanity.

N'bai began chanting, this time in Mawken, and Nyamya translated for Dara.

> Thank you Kanmaw for receiving us;
> thank you Life for flowing through us today;
> thank you Ancestors for giving us our life;
> thank you Earth for receiving our ancestors;
> thank you Sun and Moon for the beauty of our world;
> thank you Galaxy for carrying our solar system;
> thank you Universe for our spiraling Milky Way;
> thank you Being for creating our universe;
> And thank you . . .
>
> He paused. A moment of silence. . . .
>
> for the Light and Mystery of it all.

Dara joined in, and as he chanted the last line a completely new sensation overtook him. The silence, the space after the final "thank you," was more full of meaning and presence, more *full,* than anything he had ever known or experienced in his life. It was a vibrant nothingness, a mystery behind the mystery, the unnamable Source from which even Light and Mystery are born.

"To receive the Mystic's Gift," N'bai explained "we have to move into silence, into those spaces between words and between breaths, into the mysterious nothingness that gives birth to Being itself. It is the wordless domain beyond even the reach of intuition. Of course, I cannot tell you about it, even though I have been there myself. But I can tell you a little about some of the final steps that took me to that threshold."

The Mawken audience shuffled, and moved in closer still, forming a tight circle around the small fire, shoulder pressed against shoulder. The NASA scientist felt the whole group breathe as one organism.

"As you know," N'bai said looking at the Mawken, "many years ago I left our people to journey north to the vast land of China, to a village called Caiyuan in the mountains near the Jinsha river. I went there to study with a great Taoist sage. He had no name, or if he ever did, I never came to know it. From him, I learned the secrets of the Golden Flower, and how to walk through the Gates of Heaven."

He turned slowly to look around the circle, making contact in silence, eye-to-eye, with each person.

"When I came home to Mergui, my people often asked me what I had learned, and my reply was always the same: *'Nothing.'* Even other *micha-blen* did not understand, and I was accused of wasting my time, and being a useless shaman. All I would say was that one day I would tell you about 'nothing.' That day is here. It will soon be time for us all to move into the nothing."

Again, he fell silent, lowered his head, and breathed slowly and deeply. The silence crackled for so long, Dara was sure this was the 'nothing' he said he would speak about. A kind of shaman's joke. But N'bai did begin speaking again, more slowly. And as he spoke, Dara could see the words flying out of the shaman's mouth, each one a shining neon-colored bead threaded on rapidly dancing fibers of light. The fibers cavorted at breath-taking speeds in the space between speaker and listener. The scientist watched, fascinated, as the fibers of light wove themselves into exquisite patterns, revealing multiple layers of meaning.

He looked around at the group peering at N'bai through the curling smoke. They fixed their eyes on him, mouths open, waiting to hear about what had happened those many years ago. As the sun slipped below the horizon, the light show of words grew more intense, and Dara listened as much with his eyes as with his ears.

"Things developed very differently in China. The Taoists came from an ancient tradition with roots stretching back to the twilight days of tribal sorcerers, adept at working with nature. Often, they were solitary hermits who lived in inaccessible places on the sides of mountains and in hidden valleys—preferring to develop a feel for the 'natural way' by living close to the earth."

The storyteller fell silent once more. He opened his grass bag and picked out a small skin pouch, tied at the top by a thin piece of leather. He opened it, and carefully took a pinch of ash-colored powder and threw it into the flames. The fire gave off a burst of brilliant blue light that lit up all the faces. Dara saw that their eyes were closed, as if scanning some inner vision. The scientist closed his eyes and a vague image danced in the darkness. A trick of the light playing on his eyelids, he thought, when he saw what appeared to be the slender figure of an old Chinaman with a long flowing white beard, hands clasped in front.

"The sage returns to Tao by subtracting from his knowledge day by day, until he reaches inactivity," he heard the apparition speak.

And then the vision was gone. He opened his eyes and from the faces sitting around the fire, he was sure everyone saw and heard what he just had. He wanted to ask N'bai what had happened, when the old shaman began speaking again.

"Doing nothing, everything happens," he said. "This is the wisdom of Lao Tzu. Like water following the path of least resistance."

N'bai continued addressing the group: "Lao Tzu's advice is also good for people who wish to control or purify their minds. The more you try to silence it, the more you disturb it and the faster it buzzes like restless bees. It is best to leave it alone to follow its natural rhythms."

Dara listened spellbound. So much of what N'bai was saying made profound, yet simple, sense.

"There is a use for uselessness," N'bai reminded Dara why he was speaking about the power of letting go.

Dara saw the shaman's words twist and turn in mid-air, folding in on themselves like snakes swallowing their own tails. Now, almost as soon as a word was spoken, it evaporated leaving a pulsating gap in the tapestry of light, and each gap resonated with meaning.

* * *

The NASA scientist looked around him. He was literally a stranger in a strange land, surrounded by a group of native people who knew nothing of his life, people who were equally strangers to him. Yet he experienced a closeness with these Mawken—more, a union or *communion*—he'd never known before.

He felt a bottomless upwelling of love. It poured out beyond the group to everything in sight—the black beetles crawling over the sand, the monkeys squawking in the bamboo forests, the unseen fish going about their business in the sea, the bats flapping overhead, the air, water, and land, the Earth itself. The heavens. The stars. The Divine Light irradiating everything as much from within his heart as from the fathomless sky above. As he paid attention to this flow of limitless compassion he tried to follow it to its source but found none. All was pure emptiness, a scintillating nothingness, full of a light so bright and all consuming it consumed itself. Light and darkness were one.

"Welcome home," a familiar voice filled his head. It was Darwin.

37

Bechtel's Surprise

When Dara woke he was alone on the beach. All the *kabang* shelters had disappeared, the fires were out, and N'bai was gone.

He rubbed the sand from his eyes and sat up. The sun was already climbing toward its zenith. Strange. Last thing he remembered was hearing Darwin's voice. Everything else was blank. But he felt good. Cleaned out. If he had been a religious man, he'd have said "reborn."

The day was already hot, the air perfectly calm. The sea glinted as small translucent waves crested into shore. Everything seemed just fine, just as it should be. He was hungry, but he could take care of that later. He wasn't even concerned about being alone. He walked back toward the palm trees to be in the shade, and just to sit. There was nothing to do. Not even wait. He felt perfectly at peace. All sense of time had evaporated. He simply enjoyed *being there*.

Hours or perhaps only minutes later, his meditation was distracted by the sound of an engine. When a motor launch rounded the head, the roar filled the bay. Dara stood up. The boat pulled close to shore and dropped anchor. Two men jumped into a dingy and purred toward the beach. He immediately recognized Bechtel, who looked out of character in a Polynesian shirt and baggy shorts. The other was dressed in a white cotton suit and wore a wide-brimmed Panama hat. Dara recognized him as the tall mustachioed leader of the gunmen who shot the dolphin at Shelter Cove. They scrambled up the beach toward Dara, and he watched with a mixture of mild amusement and curiosity.

"Hoped we'd find you here," Bechtel announced, panting. "This bloody weather is a killer." Sweat poured down his face and chest. The other man looked cooler, but moved uncomfortably. He kept his distance as Bechtel stumbled up to Dara.

"Hello Graham. Where is Maya? What did you do to her?" Dara got right to the point.

"That's why I'm bloody here," Bechtel said. "The girl's got balls, I'll give her that. She persuaded the FEW in Singapore to hire her as a code breaker. Convinced them she's got the key to zero-point energy, and she's helping them crack the code. Told them that if they let her get on with it, the world would be their oyster. . . . Speaking of, where's the old pearl fisherman?"

Dara didn't know whether he meant Lawong or N'bai. So he said nothing.

"Whatever it was that fell in the ocean off California," Bechtel continued, "another one hit the sea somewhere south of here off Sumatra or Java. Reports of similar sightings off Perth, Australia, in the North Sea off Scotland, another at Tarazoute in Morocco, another in the Indian Ocean off Madagascar, one close to the Mariana Islands in the North Pacific—and god-knows-where-else. I've checked the computer data, and they're bloody full of anomalies. It's not just the quasars. Something very weird is going on. None of the sightings sound like ufos—as if anybody knows what a real ufo would look like. Eyewitness descriptions sound like meteors, 'balls of fire in the sky' and all that. But they've all fallen into deep ocean, so it's impossible to confirm. The hell of it is there's no evidence of any unusual meteor shower from radar or satellite. Bloody mystery. Seem to have materialized out of nowhere, so the FEW think the mystery lights may have something to do with ZPE—a crackling creation from the void, right in the skies above us. Maya has added fuel to that fire."

He gasped for breath, wiping his forehead with a wet handkerchief.

"But that's not why I'm here, ol' chap. Not to wonder about strange lights in the sky, or to talk about Maya. I'm here to find the old geezer Nay-bye. I'm told he's a top-notch pearl diver, or used to be before the Chinese and Japanese moved in with their cultured pearl farms. Well, the folks back in Singapore want him to do some diving for them."

"What makes you think you'd find him here?" Dara asked, taking a step back, and casually seating himself on the warm sand.

"I don't. But I was told I'd find you here, and that you might know where the old man is."

Only one person knew he had come to Kanmaw, and that was Lawong. But why would he endanger his friend and cousin? Something wasn't making sense. Give him enough time, Dara thought, and Bechtel will reveal his hand sooner or later—probably sooner, with his incessant talking.

"Do you mind if I sit down? I need some shade. Humidity here is terrible."

Bechtel spread his bulky frame on the sand under an overhanging palm, and glanced down the beach at the man in the white suit. He had turned his back and was looking out at the boat.

"See that guy? He's been sent to keep an eye on me. Nobody trusts anybody these days. Especially in the business world. Dara, I'm beginning to think we're really better off in academia. Backstabbing there, too, of course. But nothing like these guys." He turned away from the man on the beach. "Anyway, here's what I'd like us to do." He began to whisper out of earshot.

"Everybody's trying to pull a fast one on everybody else. Maya thinks she fooled the FEW into believing she was willing to help out, and they're playing along. They know she's up to something. So, when she said she needed time alone to investigate the fireballs, they agreed, and got her a boat. But they put a tail on her. They know from her papers that this old pearl diver chap is one of the key players in the NET. They want to cover all bases. So I've been assigned to find Nay-bye, or whatever his name is."

"N'bai."

"Huh? Whatever. Anyway, after Maya left they found one of those Sea Gypsies, a pearl seller, trying to leave a message at her hotel in Rangoon. They nabbed him, and with some, shall we say 'friendly persuasion,' got him to talk. He belongs to the same tribe as this Nay-bye chappie, and said he brought you halfway here to meet him. The sorry little creep is tied up back there—insurance in case he's lying." Dara's eyes widened as Bechtel pointed to the launch sitting at anchor.

"Let me see if I've got this straight," Dara said cynically. "Maya's off doing some research pretending it's about ZPE code, but she's really working on something else. The FEW desperately want to crack ZPE, but they're even more afraid this other code could undermine their global enterprise. The FEW believe they know what Maya's up to, and have sent someone to spy on her."

"That's about it, old chap."

"Meanwhile, the FEW think N'bai also knows about the other code, and they tortured an old pearl seller to reveal his whereabouts. He told you he was with me, and that you'd probably find me on this island—in fact, on this beach, in this bay."

"Not me, dear chap. He didn't tell me. He told our friend over there—the one with the 'friendly persuasion'."

"Graham, you're pretty damn twisted. Even if I knew where N'bai was, do you really think I'd tell you?"

Bechtel nodded toward the white suit.

"I'm trying to look after you, old boy. That's why I persuaded our friend here to let me talk to you first. Please cooperate. It will be much easier for everyone that way. The sooner we get hold of Nabbie, the sooner we can be on our way, and you can get back to your cozy little place in Palo Alto."

"Can't help you, *old boy*," Dara glared at Bechtel. "I really don't know where N'bai is. You're welcome to search the island, if you like. Did you happen to notice any other boats on your way in? As you can plainly see, the entire cove is empty except for your launch."

"You're telling me they left you stranded here like Robinson Crusoe? I don't buy it."

Dara smiled, and said nothing. Bechtel was visibly growing impatient. He whistled. The white suit turned around, slipped his right hand inside his jacket and started walking toward them. "I was hoping it wouldn't come to this, Dara."

"What's in it for you?" Dara asked calmly, keeping an eye on both men. Bechtel fanned himself with his handkerchief, and said it was all Dara's own bloody fault.

"Look mate, I trusted you. Got you a senior position at NASA. You were one of the best damn scientists I'd ever met, so I put you in charge of the sharpest space team in the country. You had the brains we needed to keep delivering, and that's how we kept the funding flowing. You did brilliant research. Hell, your revision of Drake's Equation and breakthrough radio-spectrum analysis changed everything. It got NASA excited about the real possibility of detecting life elsewhere, and secured funding for the SETI project. But your brilliance was also your downfall. Your crazy student theories about alien ESP should have warned me you might be a risk. My mistake. Sending you to check out the dolphin research was my biggest blunder. From there it all went to hell in a hand-basket."

He waved his arms to swat away the flies buzzing around his face. Dara simply sat and just listened.

"You went soft in the head, dear chap. I needed you to find out if Maya's breakthrough amounted to anything we could use, and you lost all sense of objectivity. You committed the capital sin of research: *You got involved!* Instead of using your fine analytical skills to realize just how subversive her work really is—undermining everything we stand for—you got into bed with her and her bloody dolphin."

Dara listened patiently as Bechtel revealed his true colors.

"You bought into that New Age crap we've been trying to keep at bay all these years. The shit hit the fan not only because you were jeopardizing NASA research, but also because the FEW got wind that something big was coming down the pike. All we had were scraps and hints from Maya's reports about a mysterious code that would unleash a powerful alien intelligence, and tap into a vast reserve of energy. In short, you got involved with the enemy. To put it bluntly Dara: You're a damn traitor to science and civilization."

He wiped the sweat off his face, and rearranged his straw hat to shade his eyes.

"Buried in Maya's footnotes I found the most puzzling snippet of all: Apparently, the big moment erupts in a couple of days during the eclipse. She calls it 'T-Day'." His tone shifted, sounding less threatening.

"Look, it's still not too late. You can save yourself a lot of trouble, and help save the world from whatever impending calamity Maya's 'Network' has in store. Just tell us where old Nabbie is, and help us stop him.

According to Maya's notes, he's the lynchpin in this whole goddamn fiasco."

The man in the white suit was now just a few feet away. Bechtel's tone stiffened again.

"I was told to rein you in before this whole thing got out of hand—which, of course, it bloody well has. You've gone way over the top. My ass was on the line. If I didn't cooperate and take care of you, we were both out of a job—or worse. We couldn't let that happen, old boy. Now could we? And yes: The rewards sure beat the pay in NASA."

"Well I guess every man has his price," Dara glanced over at the white suit, then back to Bechtel.

"You poor bastard. You think this is all about ZPE. It's far more important than a new energy source. It's about *mutations in consciousness*. You know what scared you that night at the campfire? Well it has your bosses scared, too. It's real. Believe me. It's inside you, your bosses, and everyone else. You can't escape it. And you don't need to. That's the irony and the tragedy. There's really nothing to fear."

The white suit moved closer brandishing a silver pistol.

Dara didn't move, didn't even blink. Without thinking, and without hesitation, he casually walked up to meet the man and, in one smooth, swift motion, instinctively placed one hand on the arm holding the gun, the other on the back of the man's neck. Instantly, the white suit crumpled to his knees, and Dara was left holding the gun.

"Action through non-action." Dara quipped.

He tucked the pistol into his belt. Bechtel and his henchman had no idea what had just happened. They looked stunned. Dara had even surprised himself. He realized he had instinctively expressed his soul charge, as all martial arts masters learn to do.

"Nice of you to stop by," he said to Bechtel. "Enjoy the rest of your day—*old boy.*"

He slung his backpack over his shoulder, walked down to the dingy and flung the gun into the waves.

"Hey! Don't leave me here," Bechtel screamed, running down the beach as Dara pushed the dingy into the surf.

"Now it's your turn to play Robinson Crusoe. At least you've got your Man Friday."

38

Java Trench

Lawong was alone on the launch, battered and bruised, and tied to a chair. Dara cut him loose and tended to his wounds.

"Big mens chasing good lady. She in big trouble. Very sorry him make me tell to find you on island. I very afraid."

He sounded it. Dara told him it was okay. Everything would be fine. But they should try to find Maya and warn her.

After Lawong rested a little and ate, he told Dara what he had overheard the "big mens" say. Triangulating the Mawken's jumbled report with what Bechtel had told him, along with some notes scribbled on a pad next to the ship's radio, he pieced together a plausible scenario. It seemed the FEW had agreed to let her "escape" to lead them to N'bai. Once she had found him, they would move in quickly and take care of business. They had bugged her computer with a GPS nano-beacon to guide them directly to her. Then they'd give Maya and N'bai time to work on the code. Once in their hands, the FEW's best code-crackers would do the rest.

"They bad mens steal our dreams. You stop. Yes?"

Once again Dara tried to reassure the old Mawken. He fingered the pearl in his pocket Lawong had given him the first day they met.

Bechtel was probably right about the FEW being onto Maya. But knowing her, she was still likely one step ahead—pretending to be fooled by them pretending to be fooled by her. That did not mean she was out of danger, however.

Where was she now? He tried to put himself in her shoes, to step inside her mind and think like her. He remembered that N'bai had said, "The safest place is the remotest place on Earth." Dara was certain that's where she would be. But where?

The remotest places on the planet were still deep in the world's remaining rainforests. If she were seeking refuge, the natural choice for Maya would be to be among her own people, the Ye'kuana. But her Amazonian homeland in Venezuela would be one of the first places they would look for her. Besides, that was halfway across the globe. And anyway she wasn't trying to hide, but looking for what was already hidden.

Urgently needing a clue to where Maya might have gone, Dara pulled out his backpack, and furiously scanned through the papers and books she had given him. Finally, he came across a passage in *The Sea Gypsies*, heavily highlighted in bright yellow:

> On the floor of the Indian Ocean, running from the
> Malay Peninsula in a south-westerly direction towards
> Zanzibar, is a ridge, of which the Seychelles are the

mountaintops. Between Madagascar and the mainland exists one of the deepest parts of the oceans of the world.

"That's it!" he shouted, startling Lawong. "Of course, *that's* where she is. The remotest region on Earth is not in the rainforests, not in the deserts, not in the ice fields of the poles, not even on top of the world's highest mountains. It's in the other direction: in the depths of the oceans, the safest place away from human interference. If Maya is in the remotest place, it's there. Right where the Great Dream lies waiting."

The ocean between the Malay Peninsula and the coast of Africa is vast. He looked around for an atlas, found one next to the captain's log, and tried to pinpoint the deepest trench in that stretch of ocean. It seemed to be about 250 miles north of Providence Island in the Seychelles Farquhar Group, and somewhere south of the Carlsberg Ridge, which narrowed the area down to about 130 square miles. That was still a huge body of water. He could spend days or weeks roaming it and not find anything. But he didn't have that much time. If Maya was right, and the day the world would turn, "T-Day," coincided with the solar eclipse, then they had less than forty-eight hours. It was hopeless. He'd never make it in time. Even at top speed, and assuming he had enough fuel, the Seychelles were three thousand miles away. That would take days.

But he had no choice. He fired up the engine in the high-speed launch, and set a course southwest, headed for Madagascar. Adrenaline pumped through every vein, shocking his body into high gear, yet his mind remained calm. But a clear head and a pumping heart would not be enough to get the job done.

The boat pushed ahead, cutting through the Andaman Sea on course for the Ten Degree Channel through the Nicobar islands. Desperate to try anything, he called on all his newly acquired knowledge trying to create an intention powerful enough to catapult him through time and space. He had learned from Darwin and N'bai that the mind has powers far beyond what science can even begin to imagine. Maybe "magic" is just what science has yet to discover, he thought. In any case, magic or miracle, he had no other option but to try.

Dara visualized the boat lifting out of the water and flying like a spacecraft. He pictured it dematerializing and re-materializing on the ocean just above the trench. His old scientific mind chided him for slipping into magical thinking, for being so absurdly unrealistic. But if ever there was a time and a place for magic, this was it.

He set the launch on automatic pilot, and did his best to induce an altered state of consciousness. He instructed Lawong to interrupt him in an emergency. Hour after hour, he experimented with different techniques—rapid breathing, chanting, just sitting in silence—hoping to find a warp or wrinkle in spacetime. He was hoping a change in consciousness would change reality, catapulting him beyond the usual limitations of the physical world. But nothing worked. He wanted the boat to beam itself a few thousand miles. It wasn't happening.

About to give in, Dara heard Darwin's voice again.

"Trust, my friend. Trust. Simply trust in your dreams."

He searched in his pockets for the one talisman he possessed: the pearl Lawong had given him. Holding it in the palm of his right hand, he gently stroked and rolled it with his fingers. He focused intensely, feeling its textures, watching the light wash around it and shine from within it. And in that instant his world shifted. Not the hoped-for quantum jump through space, but a shift in consciousness.

He was no longer on the boat crossing the open ocean; instead, he was riding a ball of fire shooting across the sky. And when he looked again he *was* the fireball. High above the Earth, almost in orbit, the continents and oceans spread out beneath him like a 3-D globe. He could easily make out the coastline of the Malay Peninsula behind him, with the Andaman Islands almost directly below. Beyond that lay vast stretches of the open waters of the Indian Ocean broken only by a smattering of tiny islands before the large land masses of Madagascar and the continent of Africa itself.

But instead of heading west toward the Seychelles, the fireball suddenly turned and headed due south toward the western coast of Sumatra. Something was wrong.

Then he saw it. About 200 miles off shore lay the deep, dark waters of the Java Trench. Much farther south in the middle of the Indian Ocean west of Australia, he could see the even deeper waters of the Diamantina Trench.

The next thing Dara knew, he was back in the launch with Lawong speeding toward the Equator. He double-checked the coordinates. They were on a direct course for nearby Sumatra and the Sunda Islands sprinkled above the awesome Java Trench. He was sure that's where Maya would be.

39

Communion

Maya slipped overboard into what seemed like the infinite depths of the waters above the Java Trench. Equipped with snorkel and fins, face down, eyes wide open, all she could see was translucent blue receding into blackness more than twenty thousand feet below. Floating in that azure world, in some of the deepest ocean on Earth, she sensed just how far down the sea floor lay—if Mt. Everest was submerged below her, only a small hilltop would break the surface. The immensity was so palpable she imagined it was like being suspended in the dark infinities of space.

The shaman's daughter had a rendezvous with an "alien" civilization right here at home. She was waiting for them in the ocean, where Darwin had arranged.

* * *

Persuading the FEW bosses in Singapore to let her go off on her own to research the Java fireball had been surprisingly easy. After taking the trouble to hunt her and Darwin down in Hawaii, and then flying her to Malaysia, they showed a remarkable change of heart when they met her face to face. As expected, they expressed great interest in her claim to have obtained the keys to a special code that could unlock the secrets of zero-point energy. She told them she needed more time to work on it before she would have anything to hand over. In return, all she wanted was to be left alone to continue her research into interspecies communication with dolphins. They agreed, and said she could return to Hawaii as soon as the code was in their hands.

It was all too easy. Maya knew they were playing her, and that they really wanted to stop N'bai before he released the Great Dream. She knew they would track her, so she had to find a way to meet up with the Mawken shaman without endangering him. They needed to act fast and complete Darwin's project before the FEW realized what had happened. The best way to throw them off the scent, she figured, would be to use the "plain view" tactic of not hiding anything—except her true intentions. So, she asked them to fly her to Jakarta and charter a boat.

She even told them she was headed for the Java Trench where the fireball had fallen, and that she would need state-of-the-art underwater sonar and Geiger equipment to record any signals emanating from the "meteorite." She said she would try to find N'bai and persuade him to come to Singapore. Again, they agreed without hesitation. She told them everything about where she was going, expecting they would not believe her. When they saw she had told the truth, they might be more inclined to trust her and relax their guard. Her "ace," she hoped, would be the element of surprise, keeping them in the dark about the all-important timing.

She didn't tell them that N'bai would be there, with some of his "friends" furiously working to complete the vast dream catcher before the total eclipse of the sun, now just a day away on November 11. "I hope to get what I need, and return to Singapore by the twelfth," she had told them. As long as her trackers remained at a safe distance, they would not realize that the fishing boats in the vicinity would be crewed by Mawken Sea Gypsies helping her and N'bai to beat the solar deadline.

* * *

Alone in the immense Indian Ocean, Maya dived as deep as she could searching for the pod of dolphins. At first she couldn't see anything, except a few glinting speckles of debris drifting past her like miniature stars. The water sparkled all around her, remarkably clear. As she contemplated the awesome depths below, she felt a tremor of excitement tinged with fear.

Then, the first signs of life appeared—a handful of small fish, so far down she couldn't judge their actual size. They could have been goldfish, except for their gray-white color. Gradually, they rose up closer, and she gasped, swallowing a mouthful of sea through her submerged snorkel. When she recovered, she realized they were not fish, but a pod of about a dozen dolphins. She now recognized their distinctive shapes, close enough to make out their blowholes and, when the angle was right, to look into their eyes. She never failed to appreciate their beauty and grace, mesmerized by how they moved in perfect synchrony.

Mostly, she was struck by their silence. It was tangible, broken only by the rhythmic sound of her own breathing. Then she heard a ripping noise next to her right ear, like Velcro tearing open. She reached up to adjust the strap holding her mask in place. But it was secure, just as she had fixed it before leaving the boat. The sound persisted, and when she turned her head she realized that a couple of dolphins were right there beside her, chattering.

She looked to her left, and saw more dolphins just a few feet away. A pod of about two hundred dolphins had gathered—some swimming right beside her, others going about their business far below, fading off into the distant aquamarine haze. To her left and right, two families were escorting her through their world. Eye to eye, she had no doubt they were greeting her—a visitor welcomed to their civilization.

Darwin had cautioned Maya early on to guard against projecting human mentality into other animals. Despite her success communicating with dolphins at the university, this always remained a risk in her work. "Yes, we tingle with intelligence, too—all creatures do," Darwin had said. "But our minds are very different from humans." She very quickly learned that such anthropomorphism can be the bane of interspecies research.

"There's one major difference between our two minds," Darwin had emphasized. "We have 'pod consciousness'. We do not think of ourselves as individuals, but share in the consciousness of the group. From that, we get our sense of identity."

It is the same with humans, Maya thought, but most humans have forgotten.

"*We* have not forgotten," Darwin emphasized. "We are all connected. Every sentient being is at the center of a web of relationships linking us to all other beings—not just here on Earth, in the oceans and on land. The network of sentience extends *everywhere*—throughout the entire cosmos."

Aware that Maya knew this, Darwin added: "Of course, some humans have not forgotten—especially people who still live guided by indigenous ways. But the vast majority of humanity has forgotten, and the consequences are almost beyond imagination. The moment of choice has arrived—not just for your species, but for all who share this planet. That is why we are building a vast network around the world to restore global wisdom."

Maya heard the cry of humpback whales far off in the deep. It was a mournful song, and it penetrated her heart. She was reminded of another important difference between cetaceans and humans that Darwin had pointed out:

"When humans speak, it is usually to share information about themselves or their environment. Usually, they want to *do* something, to manipulate a part of the world. When, we communicate, however, it is to create harmony and wellbeing within the pod and with the ocean."

She agreed, and added that it is the same when humans sing together.

"Singing or making music often induces a sense of unity among us. And you are right: Harmony is not about *doing*, it is about *being*. It is about *flow*. That's a very different kind of consciousness."

Darwin summed it up by saying that one kind of mind focuses on manipulation, the other aims for participation and communion.

As she floated in the deep ocean, suspended above the Java Trench, Maya was surrounded by growing numbers of dolphins. The whale chorus was closer, now, and it triggered an insight into what Darwin meant when he said that evolution sometimes makes mistakes.

Perhaps it is simply a fact of nature, that when evolution combines intelligence with an ability to manipulate the world, sooner or later the inevitable result is environmental devastation. And it's not having a *hand* that makes the crucial difference; it's having an *opposable thumb.* We might call it the difference between "thumb" consciousness and "flipper" consciousness, she thought, and smiled to herself as she imagined Darwin applauding her insight.

"Thumb consciousness" focuses on *things,* and leads to civilizations where objects are prized above all else. It produces technology and science. "Thumbless intelligence," however, focuses on inner *experiences,* and leads to a very different kind of consciousness.

For many millions of years, dolphins and whales have adapted perfectly to their aquatic environments. Humans however, are a poor environmental fit. Without big brains and opposable thumbs to help us make tools and weapons, to hunt, make clothes, grow food, build houses, and create technologies, our relatively weak and slow species would not have survived very long. *Cetaceans fit their environments; we adapt environments to fit us*—and in doing so we threaten the survival of other species.

Military technology pollutes the oceans with low-frequency sonar, drowning out the songs of the whales, and this drastically disrupts the communications they rely on for survival.

"We can learn a lot from our marine cousins," Maya had tried to convince the FEW, "provided we let them live."

The men in Singapore just laughed. But the day of reckoning had now arrived.

* * *

In just a few hours, nature will decide the future of evolution: Competition or cooperation? Reason or intuition? Darkness or light? If N'bai and his friends can complete the "net of dreams," then the forces of light will shine on.

However, if the FEW succeed in stopping them, the world will continue on the path to darkness and destruction. It is an ancient struggle, as old as the world itself. The battle began a long time ago between Neanderthals and Cro-Magnons, between the power of dreams and the force of reason. When the Neanderthals disappeared, the dream-mind was suppressed—but not eliminated. It lives on today in the consciousness of indigenous peoples and other species. *It lives in every one of us,* if only we would pay attention to our dreams.

Overhead, the sky was growing dark. A handful of small craft headed toward Maya's boat. She prayed it was N'bai. Something tugged at her legs, and she looked down. Darwin had arrived. Maya yelled in delight and dived to greet him. But he nosed her back to the surface, pointing at the sky. The eclipse had already begun.

40

Eclipse

Dara saw a handful of small boats ahead, drifting in the middle of the vast sea. They looked abandoned. As he approached, a lone woman hoisted herself out of the water onto the deck of the one seaworthy, anchored craft. When he pulled alongside, Maya was toweling herself down.

"Am I glad to see you," she shouted. "And just in time." She looked like she'd been up all night: hair straggling from a loose ponytail, streaks of grease on her face and shirt, eyes rimmed red.

"Darwin and N'bai are down below with the other divers putting the last few pieces in place." She pointed overboard. "The FEW know I'm here, they just don't know about our friends. So we have a head start. But we've got to hurry. Time is running out fast." She pointed at the sun.

He jumped aboard, and hugged her. She felt tender, almost vulnerable, and despite her exhaustion she tingled with electricity. It flowed right through him.

"We've got a job to do," she said, "and a close alignment of all our energies is crucial. We will need to communicate at the speed of light—if not faster." Maya sounded anxious.

She threw a thick rope at Dara. He caught it. The wet weight surprised him, and he struggled to keep his balance in the swaying boat. The rope was attached to a large net spread out on the deck of the yacht. Rows of tightly meshed pockets, woven into the net, glistened in the bright sun.

"Help me pull the net overboard," she urged. "This is the last one."

As they heaved on the rope, the net slowly scraped across the lacquered boards, and Dara saw that each pocket sparkled with something moist and dark.

"They're pearl oysters," Maya explained. "Darwin needs them to complete the circuit. And if we don't do it before the FEW arrive, the Great Dream is over—for a very long time."

"What circuit?" Dara asked, as he pushed the last of the net overboard.

"Down below, these nets are connected by fibers of light," she tried to explain. "The 'fibers' are high-frequency, super-aligned beams, like an invisible network of lasers crisscrossing the oceans. On land, they extend across mountains, forests, prairies, marshes, deserts, as well as villages, towns, and cities throughout the world." Her face lit up with excitement:

"Picture the Earth suspended in this vast net of light, not only spread across the surface, but interpenetrating the matter of the Earth itself, right to its molten core."

She peered through binoculars at the horizon, scanning for signs of boats or aircraft. Then turned to Dara:

"Our planet has reached a critical point where it must activate its slumbering intelligence and launch the Great

Dream." She leaned over the side looking into the blue-black deep, then slumped against the gunwale. She looked up at Dara.

"But we cannot do it alone. For some time now, shamans and sages have been in communication with the sea people, like Darwin, to build the global dream catcher. Once in place, it will act as an antenna to receive more messages from the skies—from the gods, or spirits, or light beings, whatever you like to call them, beyond the Earth. When the Great Dream is liberated, evolution will continue to unfold its deepest purpose." Her eyes beamed with optimism, even though her voice cracked, dry and hoarse.

"My people call it the 'currency of light.' Westerners know it as the noetic code. It is the silent wisdom that circulates through all of us." Maya caught her breath, and stood up. Dara held out a helping hand.

She explained that each node in the Dream Catcher is occupied by a sensitive "transceiver"—something that can both receive and emit signals at precise vibrations and frequencies. The final node must be activated during the total eclipse. Alignment of Earth, Moon, and Sun within the galaxy must be exact. Miss the moment, and the next chance wouldn't come again for thousands of years. By then, if humanity hasn't changed its ways, it will be far too late.

"We are assisting the expression of Earth's intelligence," she said, balancing herself as the boat rocked in the water. "All night and day, we've been placing special gems—pearls, quartz crystals, diamonds, and other precious stones—at critical nodes within the net."

N'bai appeared from the ocean, swam over, and clutched the side of their boat. Gasping for breath, he managed to spurt out that he and his team of veteran pearl divers had put all the pieces in place. Just a single node remained.

"We need one more crystal or precious stone to complete the global circuit."

But there was nothing left on board. Maya explained that they had been placing live oysters in the critical locations. Even if they didn't contain pearls, the coating inside their shells, made of mother-of-pearl, would be sufficient to transmit the noetic pulse.

The sky dims.

"Look! Look! I think many bad mens coming."

Lawong, perched on the prow of the launch, pointed frantically at the horizon. A flotilla of boats and aircraft were converging rapidly toward them. Darwin surfaced, and leaped and dived and splashed about in the water as if at a loss what to do next. For the first time, Dara sensed Darwin was panicking. He whistled and screeched with such an ear-piercing pitch and volume that both Dara and Maya covered their ears. The whistles were soon drowned out by the roar of approaching aircraft.

Without another sound, Darwin vanished beneath the waves, and Dara thought that might be the last time they'd see him. Maya looked at Dara, and their eyes revealed a spectrum of emotions from alarm to resignation. After all that had happened, they had been outnumbered and outwitted. It was all over.

Maya scrambled around the boat looking for the last precious stone or pearl. But they were all gone. Darwin's last whistles echoed in Dara's head, and he heard the message, "For want of a pearl, the Great Dream was lost . . ."

Then he remembered the talisman Lawong had given him for safekeeping. Without a second's hesitation, he jumped overboard and dived as deep as he could, in search of Darwin.

With the pearl tucked away in his cheek, he pushed through the clear water and felt his muscles tighten with fear as he saw the awesome black depth of the great Java Trench below.

If the incomplete node of the jeweled net lay at the bottom, he knew all was indeed lost. An experienced native diver like N'bai, even with the most modern diving technology, couldn't possibly withstand the enormous pressures of the deep. But Dara felt compelled to push on, plunging into the blackness.

Somewhere below him, he couldn't quite make out the distance, a luminous glow wavered in the darkness. Lungs beginning to ache, he kicked himself down further. Then he saw it. And it almost took his remaining breath away. Instinctively, he wanted to gasp. His eyes widened as if letting in more reality would make it easier to believe what he was seeing. He could just make out what looked like a curtain of dim light, billowing in the ocean currents, stretching as far as he could see in every direction, and receding into the blackness below. As he swam closer, he saw that the "curtain" was not a continuous sheet of light as he first thought, but a finely meshed lattice of the most exquisitely colored lines. The beams of light that now surrounded him were so fine, so thin, a million of them could fit into a tube the width of an ordinary pencil. Yet somehow he could make out each individual thread of light.

They seemed to bend and weave in the water, not through refraction, but as if guided by some internally generated motion of their own—orchestrating a ritual dance. He could feel them rippling over his skin, pulsing with purpose and intelligence, drawing him into what felt like an infinite embrace.

Then out of the darkness below, covered in a net of light, he saw the silhouette of a dolphin torpedoing up toward him. Darwin quickly grabbed the NASA scientist by the wrist and pulled him lower. The pain in Dara's lungs was unbearable now, yet he felt detached from it.

Above the surface, it's nearly dark as night.

Below, everywhere he looked, up or down, right or left, at every angle, the net-of-lights stretched out before him, enveloping him. Darwin guided the drowning diver toward a point of almost-luminous blackness, a small hole that contrasted with the rest of the iridescent net. Dara needed no instruction. He curled his tongue around the pearl in his cheek, spat it into his right hand, and immediately dropped the shining gem into the last remaining black hole.

But he fumbled and missed. The pearl fell into the darkness below. Darwin dived after it, snatched it in his beak, and with great precision placed it in the node.

The circuit powered up with a deep bass hum. Dara felt the water vibrate around him, adding to the pressure crushing his chest. As the net accumulated charge and vibrated, the pearl jiggled in its slot. Darwin indicated that Dara needed to secure the pearl, or else risk short-circuiting the entire project.

He could hardly see. His fingers felt clumsy, too chubby to work the fine tendrils of light. But this was it. He had to secure Lawong's pearl in the net. If he failed, the Great Dream was lost.

The eclipse is total. Day is now night.

All around him, the Net pulsed to the rhythms of an unseen conductor. The water suddenly erupted into life as countless torpedo-shapes swarmed from all directions. In an instant, the entire ocean exploded in a blaze of white light.

Then everything went black. Time froze like a fly in amber.

* * *

"Let me introduce myself," the Visitor says to Dara, "I am the Orchestrator of Light, an emissary from the gods bringing news from deep time. The mysterious lights your people have seen streaking across the heavens are chords in the song I came to play. *I am the echo of the Big Bang,* the intelligence that sings through you and all things. At every moment, you carry the wisdom of the ages. You only need to *listen.*"

The Visitor appears to Dara as a rapid-fire flow of surreal, cinematic characters—a million . . . a billion . . . six billion . . . countless billions of faces and forms, human and animal, plant and mineral, morphing and melting into each other—every individual expression that evolving Light has ever taken on. The images and forms change so fast it is impossible for Dara to focus on any particular one. All of life and creation are right there before him. Yet in the blur, if he doesn't try to focus, he sees every individual shape for what it is.

"You may even say I am a messenger from the dream world. Though it would be a mistake to think of me as just a dream. I am your deepest self, and also the soul of the world. I am the 'you' that is 'not-you,' the 'I' that is everywhere and nowhere in particular. I am the light that cannot be seen because I am the Light that sees."

* * *

The air filled with a cacophony of engines as boats, helicopters, and sea-jets converged on Maya's yacht. Dara came-to on deck to see a ladder dangling above him, dropped from a hovering helicopter. Two armed men were climbing down. Both the launch and the small yacht were completely surrounded, under siege. Lawong yelled excitedly across to Maya and Dara, waving wildly at the ocean.

Feeling like a drunk, Dara pulled himself, unsteady, to his feet as Maya exclaimed "Oh my! Oh my! Oh-my-God-almighty!" pointing beyond the encircling craft. He followed her outstretched hand and saw the sea was boiling. The previously calm surface churned and heaved as though stirred from the deep by a million giant paddles. The sea was teaming with life.

In every direction, as far as the eye could see, thousands, perhaps millions, of dolphins, porpoises, and whales were cutting through the water heading for the Java Trench. The air resounded with a symphony of high-pitched whistles, and Dara recognized the sound as a million-fold echo of Darwin's last call before he dived into the deep.

Maya screamed. Starboard, she spotted Darwin leading the charge. He dived and vanished.

The black disc continues to creep across the sun.

Above, in the dark night of day, the sky blazed with a billion shooting stars. An aurora, never before seen at this latitude, billowed over the ocean like a giant psychedelic curtain. Not just the Earth, but the heavens themselves joined in the moment of synchronicity.

Dara and Maya fell silent. Awestruck. The boats began to pull away, and the jets and helicopters took off again into the safety of the sky.

* * *

On the coasts of every continent, in bays and estuaries around the globe the same spectacle was happening. Millions of cetaceans, joined by a menagerie of other sea creatures great and small, filled the world with a chorus of penetrating, mind-altering whistles. In the Bay of Bengal, the Bay of Biscay, and the Bay of Fundy, in Monterey Bay, San Francisco Bay, and Hudson Bay, in Galway Bay, Delaware Bay, and Botany Bay, in the Gulf of Mexico, the Gulf of Alaska, and the Persian Gulf, in the English Channel, the Baltic Sea, the Straits of Gibraltar, and the Mediterranean . . . from California's Half Moon Bay . . . to Africa's Ungwana Bay . . . all the way to Whale Bay off Kanmaw island, the song from the sea rang out, a chant of solidarity, echoing across land and sea, a celebration of universal intelligence, of indigenous awareness and spiritual consciousness spreading throughout the world.

"It's rising!" Maya said with a calm finality.

"Now the journey really begins!" Dara heard Darwin say one more time.

Maya turned to Dara smiling, and whispered, "All is new again."

* * *

They sat on the deck, snuggled together, looking out at the ocean dotted with patches of retreating dolphins and whales. They listened to the roaring silence after the chorus of whistles had finally died down. The sun hung low on the horizon, and they talked about the different paths that had led them to this point in their lives. About the deep, intimate bond growing between them. About how they nearly lost each other almost as soon as they had met.

As the first stars came out, he pulled her closer. She looked into his eyes and promised they would be together after this. And he knew it—because *he knew they had known each other long before they met and would know each other forever.*

Epilogue

When I first met Dr. Dara Martin, he had taken time off to write up his notes, and was living in a cabin on the California coast near Point Reyes. He moved slowly and deliberately, with the ease and grace of a man comfortable in his body, someone who seemed to wear his surroundings like perfectly fitting clothes. Someone very much at home in the world.

One hot summer afternoon, after I'd finished rewriting his story, I visited him at his cabin to show what I'd done. It was a small place, clean and uncluttered, sparsely furnished with flea-market bargains: an old patched-up sofa, a dark wood table and a couple of oddly matching chairs. Dishes neatly stacked on the counter next to the sink. By the window, a telescope stared out at the ocean. Everything in its proper place, the room immediately relaxed me. It smelled of fresh lemons mixed with the scent of lavender from a bush growing just outside the front door.

Dara greeted me warmly and handed me a cool fruit juice. We talked a little about Darwin and Maya. He said she would like to meet me, but was away, visiting the university in Hawaii. Sometimes other dolphins would come by, and they'd all go swimming together in the sea off Point Reyes. I went out for a long walk on the cliffs, and returned a few hours later. He seemed pleased, but I sensed he wasn't saying something. I asked if he wanted anything changed, and he just smiled.

"You've done a fine job, but the story's unfinished."

I asked what he meant, puzzled, because I thought I had incorporated all the narrative from his own notebooks. He went over to the old wooden table by the window, overlooking the ocean, and pulled out a bundle of papers from a small drawer.

"Here. Take these. I didn't want to give them to you at first because I wasn't sure if they should make it into print. I wasn't sure if any words could capture the bewildering simplicity of it all. But now I see we have to try."

I took the manuscript, written in pencil on scraps of reused paper, and began to read.

"What's missing," he said as I scanned the first page, "is what matters most." I put the papers down, and looked up at him. He continued.

"Yes, we now know what 'intelligence seeks expression' means. Yes, we now know that contact with alien intelligence needs to take place first within our own world—in fact, within our own bodies. Yes, we know that consciousness goes all the way down to the level of the quantum, and all the way back to the Big Bang. Yes, we now know that evolution has a purpose. Yes, yes, yes, we know all this, but . . ."

He stopped, and I saw his eyes perform a remarkable thing: Simultaneously they looked deep into me and back into the depths of his own soul, as if he was remembering something and sensed I already knew it, too.

". . . but our story doesn't tell about consciousness 'all the way *up.*' It's one thing to say we know that intelligence seeks expression throughout the universe, but what does it want to express, eh?"

And then, as if the point of his entire life converged on this one moment, he asked:

"What's the message?"

He waited, looking at me, peering into me. I said nothing, half expecting him to continue, thinking his question was rhetorical, and because I didn't know what to say. But his eyes wouldn't let me go. "Well, I'm waiting," they said.

"I don't really know," I blurted out, still searching for a response. "I thought the message was that the universe is deeply intelligent. That spirit matters. Isn't that it?"

"Just as I thought," he said, releasing me from his eyes. He sat down beside me on the old tattered couch. I felt an unusual warmth radiating from his body, matched by a comforting compassion in his voice.

"There's more we have to tell them. If you've spent months studying and retelling my story and still don't know what the essential message is, how can we expect others to get it? And that's the whole point. It's not enough for them to read my story. It's not enough that Darwin and millions of dolphins and whales have activated the noetic code. It's not enough that shamans of different indigenous cultures are working within the Great Dream. It's not enough because *we all* need to enter the Dream, to experience liberation . . ." Again he fell silent for a few moments.

"And the bliss of freedom comes only with a simple, astounding, truth. *That's* what we all need to see, to hear, to feel . . . the message still echoing from the Big Bang, the message that lies at the heart of all the world's great religions, and that fires the imaginations of artists, scientists, and philosophers of all ages."

He paused again, stood up and walked to the window, flung it open, and let the salt air and the roar of the ocean flood the room.

"Listen. What do you hear? What do you *feel?*" This time it was rhetorical. Before I could respond, he went on.

"We are not who we think we are. There is something we all need to know, but it's so absurdly simple few of us have noticed it."

He beamed a broad smile, and let out a resounding laugh.

"That's the cosmic joke: *It's so simple!*" And now his face turned serious. "But the difficult thing is to put it into words in a way that really makes a difference."

He walked back over to where I was sitting, and tapped the sheaf of papers on my knees.

"After that remarkable event at the Java Trench, I came back home to sort things out at NASA while Maya took care of loose ends in Hawaii. I'd been visiting a friend in Sausalito, and driving back over the Golden Gate Bridge at sunset I had the most astounding experience of my life. The light bouncing off the water poured into me as if I was a kind of black hole. *Everything* around me—the other cars and their occupants, the bridge, the ocean, the Marin Headlands, the skyline of San Francisco, the air, space itself—seemed to be turning into liquid light, and was flowing into a hole in the center of my chest, and then out again. The entire universe was pouring into me, and *I was creating the universe.* I had to pull over into the parking lot past the toll station. You've heard of out-of-body experiences, well this was the most intense *in-body* experience I've ever had. I realized then, with full force, what Darwin had been saying all along: '*Now,* the journey begins.'

"I've tried to find the words to express that experience," he pointed at the papers in my hand. "Use them as best you can. But remember, and remind our readers, that no matter how wonderful words might be, they are never more than fingers pointing to something deeper. From there, from the page, we must find that place within ourselves where language springs to life. We must begin the journey into experience . . . a journey that begins every day, every moment."

Here, then, are Dara's final words—just as he wrote them.

* * *

One moment I was simply "me" driving home, distinct and separate from everything around me. The next moment, all boundaries began to dissolve. Not just that everything was connected to everything else, but everything flowed into and created everything else—one vast ocean of Being.

Even the distinction between matter and spirit seemed to fade away. There was just a boundless source of creativity; everything an act of pure intention. And I was at the center of it all. Not as a witness, but as an active participant. Space and time encircled me, and I sensed the presence of a vast Cosmic Intelligence.

"Welcome home," I heard it say. "I have been waiting for this moment since time began."

I was terrified, and also ecstatic to be in the presence of such a being.

"I want to show you something," the Cosmic I spoke to me. Immediately, I knew the deepest secrets of the universe were about to be revealed.

The immensity and detail of the vast cosmic panorama from the very first tick of time, generating and sustaining itself through eons, unfolded before me. Simply by focusing attention, I could be anywhere instantly and place myself in any epoch.

"That's how the Cosmos does it," I thought. "It holds itself together by creative acts of intention. And the font of creation is deep spirit."

"That's right," I heard it say.

And then I realized I was privy not only to the creation of the physical universe, but also to the archetypal forces that shape it. All of life, all existence, is an expression of this tapestry of intelligence.

As I focused on the archetypes, I felt myself drawn more and more into them, until eventually I knew I was no longer journeying through a universe "out there," but that this vast spectacle was taking place within me, actually an expression of who I was—or am.

I am the Cosmos!

It was the final truth—or so it seemed at that moment.

"Who, then, am I talking to?" I wondered.

"You can call me the Creative Ultimate—the source of all that is. I shine forth in radiance creating everything from nothing."

And then a most remarkable thing: In all the fuss and fury involved in sustaining the universe, the Cosmic Intelligence got caught up in the hypnotic dance of its own creation.

"The lure of physical existence, the sheer exhilaration of experiencing the flow of time, turned out to be far more seductive than I ever imagined.

"I forgot who I am."

For billions of years, the universe has succumbed to cosmic amnesia. The untold horrors and pains—suffered over the ages, by countless individuals, by all species, by planet Earth itself, by all the planets, stars, and galaxies—is one long immense struggle to remember.

"The universe has already lasted much longer than I originally planned," I heard the Cosmic I say, "and I'll be waiting many more billions of years before the Remembering is complete.

"My job, your job, everyone's job, is to realize this simple truth:

"We are all One."

I listened with my whole being, and was flooded with an overwhelming sense of remembering. Now it all seemed so familiar, a true spiritual homecoming. And I knew that the Creative Ultimate would stop at nothing until all life and non-life had returned to the womb of creation. Everything that had ever happened since the beginning of time was directed to that end.

And then the ultimate revelation. Deeper than infinite intelligence. Deeper than infinite creativity. Deeper, even, than infinite compassion, the essential nature of the Cosmic I revealed itself to be . . .

Unconditional Love.

I cannot find words that come anywhere near to expressing what I felt at that moment. The closest I can manage is to say that the deepest fabric of the entire universe, physical and nonphysical, is composed, utterly and without the slightest rupture or distortion, of pure, fathomless, unadulterated love. That's what shines in the heart of every sentient being. That's what radiates from the depths of matter. That's what generates the attractive forces of the elements. That's what spins the galaxies and propels the stars on their courses. That's what guides the unfolding of evolution. It's what stirs every soul, without exception, to action and transformation.

It's just that we have forgotten.

Postscript

"If we are to navigate safely through this critical moment of history, we must make a break with the past, and look at ourselves and our world with fresh eyes. This will entail a fundamental shift in thinking and perception—a shift in consciousness more profound and far-reaching than any in our history. It will mean awakening to the wisdom that lies within us all, of which the great sages have always spoken. This is our next step in evolution—not an outer step, but an inner step."

In closing this narrative, I have selected two items pasted into the last few pages of Dara Martin's notebooks. The first, above, is from author Peter Russell, who first drew attention to Earth's emerging "Global Brain," a visionary synthesizer of science and spiritual insight, as shown in his book *From Science to God*.

The second is from a letter by a very perceptive member of the Noetic Network—a man named Geoffrey Huggins. He wrote to me about his perspective on the human predicament and the "Great Initiation" our species, and our planet, is going through. The simple, and profound, wisdom in his words echoes Dara's realization after his evolutionary journey through light and matter.

"Will humanity, as we know it, survive? I don't believe that our survival is at all necessary to the universe. The dinosaurs, who inhabited this planet for about fifty times longer than we have, might have 'believed' they would never face extinction—particularly if they had had anything approaching the arrogance of humans. Their species did not survive, but the universe did. It continues to unfold in its magnificence. I am able to conceive that our species may not survive. Although this seems tragic to me, as a human, it is of but little consequence to the grander scheme of things.

"I pray that we humans do wake up in time, that we pause to grieve over what we have done, and get on with the mind shift that will bring us through this initiation. We have a huge job ahead of us. But the effort must go beyond railing against those who have created this mess. We must join together in true love and compassion. 'In the end, it will also require grace,' philosopher Richard Tarnas has suggested. We have no real concept of the power and depth of this grace. May it bless us and bring us through."

Amen.

About the Author

Christian de Quincey, Ph.D., is Professor of Philosophy and Consciousness Studies at John F. Kennedy University; Dean of Consciousness Studies at the University of Philosophical Research; and Director of the Center for Interspecies Research. He is also founder of The Wisdom Academy, offering private mentorships in consciousness. He is author of the award-winning book *Radical Nature: Rediscovering the Soul of Matter; Radical Knowing: Understanding Consciousness through Relationship,* and *Consciousness from Zombies to Angels*: *The Shadow and the Light of Knowing Who You Are.* Samples of his writings on consciousness and cosmology are available at www.deepspirit.com and www.TheWidomAcademy.org.